PORTFOLIOS OF THE POOR

Daryl Collins

Jonathan Morduch

Stuart Rutherford

Orlanda Ruthven

◆ ◆ ◆

PORTFOLIOS OF THE POOR

◆ ◆ ◆

How the World's Poor Live on $2 a Day

PRINCETON UNIVERSITY PRESS

PRINCETON AND OXFORD

Published by Princeton University Press, 41 William Street,
Princeton, New Jersey 08540
In the United Kingdom: Princeton University Press, 6 Oxford Street,
Woodstock, Oxfordshire OX20 1TW

Library of Congress Cataloging-in-Publication Data

Portfolios of the poor : how the world's poor live on two dollars a day /
Daryl Collins . . . [et al.].
p. cm.
Includes bibliographical references and index.
ISBN 978-0-691-14148-0 (hardcover : alk. paper) 1. Poor.
2. Microfinance. 3. Home economics—Accounting. I. Collins, Daryl.
HC79.P6.P67 2009
339.4′6—dc22
2008055161

British Library Cataloging-in-Publication Data is available
This book has been composed in Minion Typeface
Printed on acid-free paper. ∞
press.princeton.edu
Printed in the United States of America

7 9 10 8 6

Contents

◆ ◆ ◆

Tables

◆ ◆ ◆

Figures

◆ ◆ ◆

PORTFOLIOS OF THE POOR

Chapter One

◆ ◆ ◆

THE PORTFOLIOS OF THE POOR

PUBLIC AWARENESS of global inequality has been heightened by outraged citizens' groups, journalists, politicians, international organizations, and pop stars. Newspapers report regularly on trends in worldwide poverty rates and on global campaigns aimed at halving those rates. A daily income of less than two dollars per person has become a widely recognized benchmark for defining the world's poor. The World Bank counted 2.5 billion people in this category in 2005—two-fifths of humanity. Among these 2.5 billion, the poorest 1.1 billion were scraping by on less than one dollar a day.

For those of us who don't have to do it, it is hard to imagine what it is like to live on so small an income. We don't even try to imagine. We suppose that with incomes at these impossibly low levels, the poor can do little for themselves beyond hand-to-mouth survival. Their chances of moving out of poverty must depend, we assume, either on international charity or on their eventual incorporation into the globalized economy. The hottest public debates in world poverty, therefore, are those about aid flows and debt forgiveness, and about the virtues and vices of globalization.[1] Discussion of what the poor might do for themselves is less often heard. If it's hard to imagine how you would survive on a dollar or two a day, it's even harder to imagine how you would prosper.

Suppose that your household income indeed averaged two dollars or less a day per head. If you're like others in that situation, then you're almost surely casually or part-time or self-employed in the informal economy. One of the least remarked-on problems of living on two dollars a day is that you don't literally get that amount each day. The two dollars a day is just an average over time. You make more on some days, less on others, and often get no income at all. Moreover, the state offers limited help, and, when it does, the quality of assistance is apt to be low. Your greatest source of support is your family and community, though you'll most often have to rely on your own devices.

Most of your money is spent on the basics, above all food. But then how do you budget? How do you make sure there is something to eat and drink every day, and not just on the days you earn? If that seems hard enough, how do you deal with emergencies? How can you be sure that you can pay for the doctor and the drugs your children need when they fall sick? Even without emergencies, how do you put together the funds you need to afford the big-ticket items that lie ahead—a home and furniture, education and marriage for your children, and some income for yourself when you're too old to work? In short, how do you manage your money if there is so little of it?

These are practical questions that confront billions every day. They are also starting points for imagining new ways for businesses to build markets that serve those living on one or two or three dollars per day. They are obvious starting points as well for policymakers and governments seeking to confront persistent inequalities.

Though these questions about the financial practices of the poor are fundamental, they are surprisingly hard to answer. Existing data sources offer limited insights. Neither large, nationally representative economic surveys of the sort employed by governments and institutions like the World Bank, nor small-scale anthropological studies or specialized market surveys, are designed to get at these questions. Large surveys give snapshots of living conditions. They help analysts count the number of poor people worldwide and measure what they typically consume during a year. But they offer limited insight into how the poor actually *live* their lives week by week—how they create strategies, weigh trade-offs, and seize opportunities. Anthropological studies and market surveys examine behavior more closely, but they seldom provide quantified evidence of tightly defined economic behavior over time.

Given this gap in our knowledge and our own accumulating questions, several years ago we launched a series of detailed, yearlong studies to shed light on how families live on so little. Some of the studies followed villagers in agricultural communities; others centered on city-dwellers. The first finding was the most fundamental: no matter where we looked, we found that most of the households, even those living on less than one dollar a day per person, rarely consume every penny of income as soon as it is earned. They seek, instead, to "manage" their money by saving when they can and borrowing when they need to. They don't always succeed, but over time, even for the poorest households, a surprisingly large proportion of income gets managed in this way—diverted into savings or used to pay down loans. In the process, a host of different methods are pressed into use: storing savings at home, with others, and with banking institutions; joining savings clubs, savings-and-loan clubs, and insurance clubs; and borrowing from neighbors, relatives, employers, moneylenders, or financial institutions. At any one time, the average poor household has a fistful of financial relationships on the go.

As we watched all this unfold, we were struck by two thoughts that changed our perspective on world poverty, and on the potential for markets to respond to the needs of poor households. First, we came to see that money management is, for the poor, a fundamental and well-understood part of everyday life. It is a key factor in determining the level of success that poor households enjoy in improving their own lives. Managing money well is not necessarily more important than being healthy or well educated or wealthy, but it is often fundamental to achieving those broader aims. Second, we saw that at almost every turn poor households are frustrated by the poor quality—above all the low reliability—of the instruments that they use to manage their meager incomes. This made us realize that if poor households enjoyed assured access to a handful of better financial tools, their chances of improving their lives would surely be much higher.

The tools we are talking about are those used for managing money—financial tools. They are the tools needed to make two dollars a day per person not only put food on the dinner table, but cover all the other spending needs that life puts in our way. The importance of reliable financial tools runs against common assumptions about the lives and priorities of poor families. It requires that we rethink our ideas about banks and banking. Some of that rethinking has already started through the global "microfinance" movement, but there is further to travel. The findings revealed in this book point to new opportunities for philanthropists and governments seeking to create social and economic change, and for businesses seeking to expand markets.

The poor are as diverse a group of citizens as any other, but the one thing they have in common, the thing that defines them as poor, is that they don't have much money. If you're poor, managing your money well is absolutely central to your life—perhaps more so than for any other group.

Financial Diaries

To discover the crucial importance of financial tools for poor people, we had to spend time with them, learning about their money-management methods in minute detail. We did so by devising a research technique we call "financial diaries." In three countries, first in Bangladesh and India and a little later in South Africa, we interviewed poor households, at least twice a month for a full year, and used the data to construct "diaries" of what they did with their money. Altogether we collected more than 250 completed diaries.[2] Over time the answers to our questions about how poor households manage money started to add up and reinforce each other—and, importantly, they meshed with what we had seen and heard over the years in our work in other contexts: in Latin America and elsewhere in Africa and Asia.[3]

We learned how and when income flowed in and how and when it was spent. Looking at poor households almost as one might look at a small business, we created household-level balance sheets and cash-flow statements, focusing our lens most sharply on their *financial* behavior—on the money they borrowed and repaid, lent and recovered, and saved and withdrew, along with the costs of so doing. Our understanding of these choices was enriched by the real-time commentary of the householders themselves. We listened to what they had to say about their financial lives: why they did what they did, what was hard and what was easy, and how successful they felt they had been. It was, surprisingly, the tools of corporate finance—balance sheets and cash-flow statements—that offered the structure with which we could begin to understand what it takes, day by day, for poor households to live on so little.[4]

Purchasing Power and the Finances of the Poor

So far we have discussed the challenges of living on one or two dollars per day, in keeping with the well-known poverty benchmarks set by the Millennium Development Goals of the United Nations.[5] These dollars-per-day-per-person figures are specially calculated and take some explaining.

They are adjusted to capture the fact that the cost of living varies between countries; that is, a dollar goes farther in Delhi, Dhaka, or Johannesburg than it does in New York. The standard "market" exchange rates used at the bank or airport to convert between dollars and rupees, takas, or rand do not always adequately capture that fact. So adjustments are made by the UN using a set of conversion factors known as "purchasing power parity" (PPP) exchange rates. The PPP-adjusted dollars attempt to account for the greater purchasing power in the countries we study than market rates would imply.

Calculating the PPP conversion factors has been a major research project in itself, housed at the World Bank International Comparison Program, and the numbers continue to be refined.[6]

In our context, one limitation of the PPP factors is that they are based on lists of goods and services meant to reflect the consumption patterns of the entire population of each country, rich and poor. The lists include purchases of cars, computers, restaurant meals, and the like. Here, though, we are interested in the purchasing power of the poor specifically. This is of particular concern given the high degree of inequality between rich and poor in South Africa.

Fortunately, a new set of "Poverty PPP" conversion factors, focused on the goods and services typically purchased by lower-income households, is being calculated, though it is not yet available. Because we lack Poverty PPP numbers, we chose to stick with market exchange rates for the remainder of this book. The average market exchange rates at the time of the Bangladesh, India, and South Africa financial diaries were 50 Bangladeshi takas per US dollar, 47 Indian rupees per US dollar, and 6.5 South African rand per US dollar.

To give a sense of how PPP-adjusted dollars would differ from the market rate dollars used in the book, table 1.1 provides two sets of conversion factors.

Table 1.1 Purchasing Power Parity Comparisons

	Comparison year	
Sample (and study year)	*1993*	*2005*
Bangladesh (1999–2000)	2.67	2.88
India (2000–2001)	3.69	3.75
South Africa (2004–5)	1.96	1.72

Note: The ratio of the value of $1 in PPP terms relative to the value of $1 exchanged at market exchange rates.

The top right cell of the table shows, for example, that when in the text we discuss $1 held by our Bangladeshi households, that $1 could actually buy what it would take $2.88 to buy in the United States (in the 2005 reference year). This ratio is helpful to keep in mind—even though we have reservations about the appropriateness of applying these specific national-level conversions to our samples.

Using market exchange rates avoids two other complications. First, the Millennium Development Goals were set based on dollars as valued in 1993. When UN documents discuss one-dollar-a-day poverty, they usually mean a dollar in terms of what it could buy in 1993. And, to add a second wrinkle, the international poverty line was set using the median poverty line of the 10 poorest countries in the world, which was not *exactly* one dollar per day, but $1.08 (in 1993 PPP dollars). So in order to assess whether households are above or below the one-dollar-a-day line, we need to compare their inflation-adjusted PPP earnings to $1.08. Likewise, the two-dollars-a-day line is actually $2.15.

To provide a concrete example what it would be like to convert the earnings of the financial diaries households to dollar-a-day equivalents, consider Hamid and Khadeja's household (discussed below). They earn $70 a month between the three members, calculated from takas using market exchange rates—that is, 50 takas equals US$1 in 2000. Dividing by 30 yields $2.33 per day, or $0.78 per person per day. Multiplying by the number in the top left cell of table 1.1 (2.67) yields that $0.78 is equivalent to $2.08 when converted into 1993 $PPP. Hamid and Khadeja thus fall just below the internationally recognized two-dollars-a-day poverty line.

Although we use market exchange rates to convert from local currency to dollars throughout this book, in appendix 1 we give further examples of how the financial diaries incomes match up against Millennium Development Goal benchmarks.

To get a first sense of what the financial diaries reveal, consider Hamid and Khadeja. The couple married in a poor coastal village of Bangladesh where there was very little work for a poorly educated and unskilled young man like Hamid. Soon after their first child was born they gave up rural life and moved, as so many hundreds of thousands had done before them, to the capital city, Dhaka, where they settled in a slum. After spells as a cycle-rickshaw driver and construction laborer and many days of unemployment, Hamid, whose health was not good, finally got taken on as a reserve driver of a motorized rickshaw. That's what he was doing when we first met Hamid and Khadeja in late 1999, while Khadeja stayed home to run the household, raise their child, and earn a little from taking in sewing work. Home was one of a strip of small rooms with cement block walls and a tin roof, built by their landlord on illegally occupied land, with a toilet and kitchen space shared by the eight families that lived there.

In an average month they lived on the equivalent of $70, almost all of it earned by Hamid, whose income arrived in unpredictable daily amounts that varied according to whether he got work that day (he was only the reserve driver) and, if he did get work, how much business he attracted, how many hours he was allowed to keep his vehicle, and how often it broke down. A fifth of the $70 was spent on rent (not always paid on time), and much of the rest went toward the most basic necessities of life—food and the means to prepare it. By the couple's own reckoning, which our evidence agrees with, their income put them among the poor of Bangladesh, though not among the very poorest. By global standards they would fall into the bottom two-fifths of the world's income distribution tables.

An unremarkable poor household: a partly educated couple trying to stay alive, bring up a child, run a one-room home, and keep Hamid's health in shape—on an uncertain $0.78 per person per day. You wouldn't expect them to have much of a financial life. Yet the diversity of instruments in their year-end household balance sheet (table 1.2) shows that Hamid and Khadeja, as part of their struggle to survive within their slim means, were active money managers.

Far from living hand-to-mouth, consuming every taka as soon as it arrived, Hamid and Khadeja had built up reserves in six different instruments, ranging from $2 kept at home for minor day-to-day shortfalls to $30 sent for safe-keeping to his parents, $40 lent out to a relative, and $76 in a life insurance savings policy. In addition, Hamid always made sure he had $2 in his pocket to deal with anything that might befall him on the road.

Table 1.2 Hamid and Khadeja's Closing Balance Sheet, November 2000

Financial assets	*$174.80*	*Financial liabilities*	*$223.34*
Microfinance savings account	16.80	Microfinance loan account	153.34
Savings with a moneyguard	8.00	Private interest-free loan	14.00
Home savings	2.00	Wage advance	10.00
Life insurance	76.00	Savings held for others	20.00
Remittances to the home village[a]	>30.00	Shopkeeper credit	16.00
Loans out	40.00	Rent arrears	10.00
Cash in hand	2.00		
		Financial net worth	−$48.54

Note: US$ converted from Bangladeshi takas at $1 = 50 takas, market rate.

[a] In the Bangladesh and Indian diaries remittances to the home village are treated as assets, given that for the most part the remittances entail debt obligations on the part of the recipients or are used to create assets for use by the giving households. In South Africa, remittances are treated as expenses given that they were mostly used to support the daily needs of family members living at a distance.

Their active engagement in financial intermediation also shows up clearly on the liabilities side of their balance sheet. They are borrowers, with a debt of $153 to a microfinance institution and interest-free private debts from family, neighbors, and employer totaling $24. They also owed money to the local grocery store and to their landlord. Khadeja was even acting as an informal banker, or "moneyguard," holding $20 at home that belonged to two neighbors seeking a way to keep their money safe from their more spendthrift husbands and sons. This does not mean that men are necessarily less responsible with money than women. Hamid himself also used a moneyguard, storing $8 with his employer while waiting for an opportunity to send it down to the family home.[7]

Hamid and Khadeja's involvement in finance did *not* mean that they ended up with debts that they found impossible to manage. Although their "net worth" (the balance of their financial assets and liabilities) was negative, the amount was small relative to their total annual income, and their "debt service" ratio—the proportion of their monthly income that they had to spend on servicing their debts—was manageable. Negative net worth was in fact quite rare in our sample: among the 152 households we studied in South Africa, only 3 percent were in this position. We should not assume, then, that poor households are always deeply in debt and always have negative net worth. The reasons for this phenomenon, and for many other aspects of balance sheets like Hamid and Khadeja's, are explored in more detail in later chapters, and are on show in the portfolios found in appendix 2.

Balance sheets like this one, however revealing, don't tell the story of how Hamid and Khadeja managed their money on a day-to-day basis. That story comes from studying cash flow rather than balances—from tracing the ebb and flow of cash into and out of savings and loan and insurance instruments. In the year that led up to the balance sheet, Hamid and Khadeja "pushed" $451 of their income into savings or insurance or into loan repayments, and "pulled" $514 out of savings or by taking loans or agreeing to guard money for others. That total turnover—$965—is more than their total income for the year, which, at an average of $70 a month, came to about $840. So each dollar of income earned was subjected to $1.15 of intermediation—of being pushed and pulled through financial instruments of one sort or another. This book reviews the recorded behavior and commentary of our 250 diarists to show how and why they intermediated as they did, and how and why better, more reliable instruments would help them do it more successfully.

◆ ◆ ◆

In addition to saving, borrowing, and repaying *money*, Hamid and Khadeja, like nearly all poor and some not-so-poor households, also saved, borrowed, and repaid in kind. Khadeja, sharing a crude kitchen with seven other wives, would often swap small amounts of rice or lentils or salt with her neighbors. She would keep a note of the quantities in her head, and so would her partners in these exchanges, to ensure that their transactions were fair over the long haul. Virtually all of the rural Bangladeshi households followed the well-established tradition of *musti chaul*—of keeping back one fistful of dry rice each time a meal was cooked, to hold against lean times, to have ready when a beggar called, or to donate to the mosque or temple when called on to do so. For rural respondents in India and Bangladesh, the intermediation of goods and services rather than cash was common, and included borrowing grain to be repaid after the harvest, repaying a loan with one's labor, or using labor to buy farm inputs. We recorded much of this activity. But because our story is focused on how poor households manage *money*, we have focused our discussion only on those transactions where cash was involved.

We also tracked changes in physical assets, like livestock and land, and found them to be important in the portfolios of the poor. However, we noticed that most of the wealth changes over the year were in *financial* rather than physical wealth. For most of the households in the sample, we were able to track a "net worth profile," including physical as well as financial assets, over time. We calculated the breakdown of net worth between financial net worth and physical assets for the median South African financial diaries household at the beginning of the study, in February 2004 and then at the end of the study, in November 2004. Physical assets certainly made up the larger proportion of net worth,[8] thanks to the substantial stock of wealth most households hold in their homes and livestock.

However, we found that physical assets *changed* very little over the year. Livestock may have been bought or born, but they also died or were sold or eaten, and housing stock changed very little, leaving the overall physical wealth value essentially unchanged. The action was instead in financial assets.[9] Taking a snapshot of household portfolios would have missed the dramatic change in financial assets and led us to mistakenly focus on physical assets as the more important part of net worth to understand. The data suggest that although households certainly can and do save in physical assets, financial management is the stepping-stone to understanding how households build net worth.

Following Hamid and Khadeja's financial activity every two weeks allowed us to discover other types of behaviors, constraints, and opportunities that are not revealed in large, nationally representative surveys. Partly this is because the diaries yield data of unusual quality on particularly hard-to-measure quantities. We uncovered activities that Hamid and Khadeja might not have thought to mention to a team completing a one-time survey—that they had credit with a shopkeeper, for example, took loans from neighbors, lent out a little to others, and stashed money in a hiding place at home for themselves and for others. Because these activities are "informal" and not written down, they are easy to overlook or hide, but Hamid and Khadeja's diary data shows that these practices form a large part of their financial lives.

It was sobering, then, to find that we would have missed much of the action had we undertaken only single, one-time interviews of each household. Using the South African data, we did a "flow of funds" analysis—comparing all inflows to all outflows of money in each time period for each household—and found that, in the earliest interviews, we were often missing more than half of a household's financial activity in a given week. It took roughly six rounds of interviews and visits before we felt confident we had something close to the full story.[10] It took time for our respondents to trust us, and it took time for us to fully comprehend information that came piecemeal and was expressed in language colored by assumptions that we didn't at first understand.

But those fragments of data eventually resolved into yearlong movie reels that changed our understanding. The frame-after-frame views revealed much greater levels of financial activity than large surveys usually show, and much more active management of finances. Without the pieces, it would have been easy to imagine that Hamid and Khadeja would be unsophisticated about their finances because they are only partially literate, or would be unable to save in a disciplined way because they are so poor. We might have blindly accepted arguments that they are especially eager for loans to run a small business, or that, if offered loans, they would fall rapidly into deep debt. Or we might have assumed that because money is tight, they would always demand rock-bottom prices.

All of those assumptions are right some of the time. But they are wrong much of the time. Uncorrected, they can mislead businesses that plan strategies to work with households like Hamid and Khadeja's, and misdirect policymakers who design interventions to hasten their escape from poverty.

Portfolios

What explains Hamid and Khadeja's unexpectedly intense financial life? The best answer to that question came from the couple themselves, and from the many other poor householders who worked with us on the diaries. Khadeja told us, "I don't really like having to deal with other people over money, but if you're poor, there's no alternative. We have to do it to survive." When you live on a small, irregular, and uncertain income, we learned, just getting food on the table is hard to manage out of current income. Managing all of life's other expenditures out of current income is next to impossible. Whenever you need to make such an expenditure—repairing or rebuilding the family home, doctors' fees, a fan for the hot season, a new set of clothes for a festival or wedding—there are three common courses:

First, in the worst case, you may be forced to go without. This happens only too often, with consequences that threaten lives and wreck opportunities.

Second, you may be able to raise the money by selling assets, providing you have assets to sell and a buyer willing to pay an acceptable price.

Third, in the best case, you can use past income or future income to fund today's expenses.

The third course entails the decision to intermediate—the decision to save (to store past income that can be spent at a later date) or to borrow (to take an advance, now, against future income). More simply, it is the choice to set aside something out of current income that can be used to build up savings or pay down debt. Small incomes mean that poor people are more often than others placed in the position of needing to intermediate. The uncertainty and irregularity of their income compounds the problem by ratcheting up the need to hold reserves, or to borrow when the income fails to arrive. For these reasons, we would argue that poor people need financial services more than any other group. Poor households with a pressing need to intermediate have to manage a collection of relationships and transactions with others—family, neighbors, moneylenders, and savings clubs, constituting a set of formal, semiformal, and informal financial providers—that can fairly be described as a portfolio.[11]

Economists and anthropologists have built rich and independent literatures on the constituent parts of these portfolios. We now know quite a bit about how moneylenders set prices and how local savings clubs operate.[12] Economists have further contributed to understanding how well the pieces come together to smooth the ups and downs of household consumption.[13] But what has been missing is a close look at how portfolios function: not just how well the pieces work but how they work together. Focusing on *how* gives new insight into the day-to-day nature of poverty and yields concrete ideas for creating better solutions for it.

So far, we have looked, briefly, at only one such portfolio—Hamid and Khadeja's. In all we worked with more than 250 poor and very poor households in both urban and rural locations in three countries. They lived in three slum locations in the Bangladeshi capital, Dhaka, and in three Bangladeshi villages; in three more slums in India's capital city Delhi and two villages in a poor north Indian state; and in two township sites, one outside Johannesburg and the other outside Cape Town, as well as in a remote village in the Eastern Cape of South Africa. The initial work in Bangladesh was done in 1999–2000 and involved a total sample of 42 households. This was quickly followed by a slightly bigger sample of 48 households in India in 2000–2001, and then by a much larger sample of 152 households in South Africa in 2003–4.[14] In addition, we returned to Bangladesh in 2003–5 for a set of 43 diaries, using a slightly different format in order to investigate the financial lives of microfinance clients.

Appendix 1 shows that some of the financial diaries households in South Asia and in rural South Africa were poor by the one-dollar-a-day definition used in the Millennium Development Goals, and many others by the two-dollars-per-day definition, although we also took a number of households who fell above this line but lived close by and shared the lifestyle and culture of their poorer neighbors. The South African sample allows insight into the financial lives of better-off households in low-income communities, in the urban sample especially. In the South African urban samples, few live on average incomes of less than $2 a day, and about 40 percent of them live on more than $10 a day. These urban households, however, remain on the fringes of the urban economy and are poor or very poor by local standards.[15] In appendix 1 we describe the design and execution of the financial diary work, and give data on the study sites and the range of occupations, incomes, and demographics of the households we worked with. The portfolios in appendix 2 provide a further sense of the kinds of people, environments, and livelihoods that we encountered.[16]

Small, Irregular, Unpredictable

It would be wrong to claim that Hamid and Khadeja's is a "typical" portfolio of the poor. This is not just because we selected our households from 14 locations in three countries on two continents, but also because we encountered a very wide range of behaviors involving many financial devices and services that don't appear in Hamid and Khadeja's case. These financial devices were used in a myriad of combinations with varying degrees of intensity and a wide range of values and prices serving an endless list of needs and objectives. Therefore, we cannot claim that the behavior of our 250 households is typical of poor households throughout the world. Nevertheless, it is striking how many commonalities we found among our households, despite the differences in their environments.

Every household in our 250-strong sample, even the very poorest, held both savings and debt of some sort. No household used fewer than four types of instrument during the year: in Bangladesh the average number of different types of instruments used was just under 10, in India just over eight, and in South Africa, 10. These numbers refer to the *type* of instruments used: the number of times these instruments were used in the year was of course much greater. In Bangladesh, for example, the 42 households between them used just one instrument—the interest-free loan—almost 300 times in the year. In all three countries total cash turnover through instruments was large relative to total net income: in Bangladesh and India it ranged between 75 percent and 330 percent of annual income, and in South Africa reached as high as 500 percent for some households. Some instruments seem universal: almost every household borrowed informally from family and friends, and many, including the very poor, reciprocated by offering such loans to others. Certain kinds of savings clubs and savings-and-loan clubs were found in all locations in all three countries, though with local variations. We heard the same themes over and over again when we asked our households to comment on what they were doing: many of the diarists told us they found informal transactions unpleasant but unavoidable; many, like Khadeja, also said they wished they had better ways to save.

Of all the commonalities, the most fundamental is that the households are coping with incomes that are not just low, but also irregular and unpredictable, and that too few financial instruments are available to effectively manage these uneven flows. It is a "triple whammy": low incomes; irregularity and unpredictability; and a lack of tools. In the villages, farmers earn the bulk of their income during two or three peak harvest months, earning nothing during troughs. Farm laborers get a daily wage when there's work to do; at other times they sit around idle, migrate to towns, or scratch a living from other sources. In the cities and urban townships, self-employed folk like Hamid have good and bad days. Women's paid work in the town, such as maidserving, is often part-time, occasional, or temporary. Unless they are very fortunate, even full-time, permanently employed poor people suffer at the hands of employers who pay irregularly. Grant recipients, of whom there are a large number in the South African sample, suffer when the grants arrive late—as they did twice in one year in one township because of rioting. Payment once a month may also be an inconvenient interval at which to receive money: we discovered devices used by grant recipients to package two month's worth of grants into a single sum or, conversely, to break a month's grant into smaller, more frequent installments. As we noted at the outset, the reality of living on two dollars a day is that you don't literally earn that sum each day; instead, your income fluctuates up and down. If you did earn a steady two dollars per day per person, you could plan more easily and enter into more fruitful relationships with financial partners. Lenders, for example, tend to be much more willing to advance loans against a regular flow of income.

These facts made us see how policy perspectives on poverty can hamper understanding. The "dollar-a-day" view of global poverty powerfully focuses attention on the fact that so much of the planet lives on so little. But it highlights only one slice of what it is to be poor. It captures the fact that incomes are small, but sidelines the equally important reality that incomes are often highly irregular and unpredictable. Dealing with unpredictability is an intellectual and practical challenge, one that must be well managed if welfare and futures are to be safeguarded.

Hamid and Khadeja kept track of their transactions in their heads, like many of the poorly educated or illiterate diarists, but their records were accurate. When we asked how they managed to do this when so many transactions were ongoing, Khadeja said, "We talk about it all the time, and that fixes it in our memories." One of their neighbors remarked, "These things are important—they keep you awake at night."

For all the households we came to know through the diaries, living on under two dollars a day requires unrelenting vigilance in cash-flow management—strategies to cope with the irregularities of income. Short-term cash-flow management is vital to ensure that the family doesn't go hungry, and chapter 2 takes a closer look at how the diary households manage this basic task.

Coping with Risk and Raising Lump Sums

Longer-term money management in poor households, we found, is associated in particular with two other concerns. The first is how to cope with risk. The households we met live lives that are far more uncertain than those in better-off circumstances. The diarists are, as a group, less healthy, live in neighborhoods with weaker security, and face income volatility tied to the swings of local supply and demand, no matter whether they are employed or self-employed or are small-scale entrepreneurs. Those sources of uncertainty pile on top of others: in urban Bangladesh, slums can be cleared without warning; in India, crops fail when the rainy season is late or short; in South Africa, the spread of AIDS makes mortality a concern even for the young and able-bodied. While some seem able to shrug it off, most adults in poor households, we found, experience occasional or chronic anxiety about these risks, and seek to mitigate them in every way they can, including managing their money. We explore this behavior in chapter 3.

The second concern around which longer-term money management revolves in poor households is the need to build or borrow usefully large sums of money, the subject of chapter 4. Hamid and Khadeja's rent had to be paid in a fixed total; Hamid's medicines meant bills owed to pharmacists; Khadeja needed to make up-front investments in thread and cloth to run her sewing business. Beyond that, the couple wanted better furniture for their room, and had ambitions eventually to own their own home. They had one child and were planning more, and they wanted their children to be well educated and healthy and to secure good jobs and marriages. Each of these events requires chunks of cash at a single moment.

We have just identified three needs that drive much of the financial activity of the poor households we met through the financial diaries:

1. *Managing basics*: cash-flow management to transform irregular income flows into a dependable resource to meet daily needs.
2. *Coping with risk*: dealing with the emergencies that can derail families with little in reserve.
3. *Raising lump sums*: seizing opportunities and paying for big-ticket expenses by accumulating usefully large sums of money.

These needs are so fundamental that they become the themes of the next three chapters of this book.

The Portfolio Perspective

The main categories of personal financial behavior—borrowing, insurance, and saving—are associated in our minds with the typical needs that they serve. Borrowing is associated with the financing of current opportunities and needs—to start or expand a business, perhaps, or to buy consumer durables. Insurance is linked with protection against risk, and saving with building large sums for the future. It would be tempting to imagine that the three topics described at the end of the last section would be principally about borrowing, then insurance, then saving.

In reality, life doesn't always allow us to match instruments with uses quite so neatly. We all know of cases where an insurance policy or a pension had to be unexpectedly cashed in to serve some unexpected need, for example. The poor households we met in the diaries were especially likely to combine many different kinds of instruments to achieve their needs, and this is one of the main reasons their portfolios turned out to be surprisingly complex.

For example, there are so many risks, resulting in so many emergencies, that it is unrealistic to expect poor households to contain them by means of the single financial strategy of insurance. Dealing with emergencies is so crucial that even where insurance is available to them, poor households often have to draw down savings and seek loans to make up the losses in full. Similarly, both saving and borrowing need to be deployed, often simultaneously for the same purpose, to manage cash flow on a day-to-day basis and to create usefully large lump sums.

However, within the broad categories of "saving" and "borrowing" there are important distinctions, and it is possible to associate certain kinds of saving and borrowing with specific needs. The kind of saving needed to manage day-to-day basics, for example, is different from the kind of saving needed to raise usefully large sums. For the first kind, poor households seek to keep money in places that they can access freely and frequently, both to maximize the amount they save and to ensure that they can retrieve the savings at short notice. Security is important, but so is convenience. Reward (in the form of interest receivable) is of less importance: thus they may hide savings at home or entrust cash to their next-door neighbor.

When households try to build savings into large sums, the mix of characteristics shifts. Now security is very important, since the money may have to be stored for some time as it builds, and reward is valued more highly. But a new characteristic enters the mix—structure. The poor, like all of us, tend to want to have their savings cake and eat it, but when you're more hungry than average, the temptation to eat it is all the stronger. Structure—in the form of curbs on the liquidity of the savings, and rules defining the term, timing, and value of deposits—helps self-discipline, as the poor often know. Hamid and Khadeja are not unusual in holding their tiny total savings in a range of instruments with different mixes of characteristics, including an insurance savings plan that requires fixed monthly premiums.

Similarly, the three drivers of need may cause the poor to approach different kinds of lenders who offer loans that vary in value, term, price, repayment structure, and availability. Sometimes local informal lending, which tends to be interest-free, will be best for day-to-day management, but on the other hand it may also make sense to take a larger loan from a more formal lender in order, say, to buy a stock of food if it can be stored safely at home. The diaries show that in Bangladesh, for example, bigger loans often come from microfinance institutions, but sometimes diarists deliberately choose a more expensive moneylender because the looser repayment schedule fits their needs better, or because the money *must* be found quickly after an emergency has struck or a not-to-be-missed opportunity has arisen.

This is not to suggest that poor households are blessed with an abundance of choice when they are deciding where to place savings or where to seek a loan: unfortunately, that is almost never the case.[17] But to the extent that they have choice, they exercise it.

Perplexing Prices

These insights come from considering the financial activities of poor households as *portfolios* composed of a mix of instruments, and then tracking those mixes over time to discover how they were deployed. We would not have spotted them if we had just looked at how households use individual instruments, or looked at their mix of instruments at just one moment in time. We would have missed the way in which sums are "patched" together from an array of instruments, and we could not have fully appreciated the hopes and stresses that accompany this process, nor the play of intrahousehold relationships. For example, we wouldn't have discovered that while Khadeja stores money for others, her husband chooses to keep some of his reserves out of her hands, storing it instead with his employer: Hamid confided to us that his wife disapproves of his habit of sending so much money to his parents' village home, and might have sought to stop the cash going that way. The financial diary methodology forced us to confront our assumptions and take a fresh look at the financial lives of poor people.

This is especially so when it comes to understanding prices. Prices reflect both the demand for and supply of financial services, and economists have tried to understand prices by looking at both sides.[18] Using our portfolios, we have been able to look closely at deals as they played out over *time* and at the social environment in which deals are struck, and we find that the pricing story is complex at an even more basic level than understanding supply and demand.

Some poor households pay fees for good ways to save—an idea that may be puzzling to those of us used to being paid interest on bank deposits, rather than having to pay for the service. Our surprise is amplified when the fees, interpreted as interest rates and expressed on an annualized basis, seem very high. Savers who use roving deposit collectors—the *susus* of West Africa are the best-known examples—generally save daily for a month and then get back, at the month's end, all their deposits less one day's worth. That's a monthly rate of minus 3.3 percent, or minus 40 percent at an annualized rate. *Minus*

40 percent a year on savings? Can that be rational? But to a mother in a poor household saving 10 cents a day to ensure she can buy three dollars' worth of schoolbooks for her daughter before the school term starts next month, 10 cents is an eminently affordable fee. Where else can she be sure of getting the money out of temptation's way, and enjoy the discipline of having a collector call on her each day to make sure she saves?

As with savings, so with loans. Households pay finance companies and moneylenders amply for the chance to borrow. Top interest rates, expressed on an annualized basis, are the equivalent of 200 percent or more—astronomical relative to the kinds of charges levied by US or UK banks. According to the diaries, however, few of these "high cost" loans are actually held for a full year. In South Africa, for example, most are held for less than a month; some for just a week. The conversion into annualized interest rates allows us to compare interest charges on loans of different durations, and the year is a convenient standard. But the diaries show that the attempt to gain clarity by annualizing may distort the nature of the costs and choices.

For example, a 25-cent fee charged for a moneylender loan of $10 for a week may sound quite reasonable even to Hamid the motor-rickshaw driver, who earns just $2.33 per day and for whom a $10 loan may mean the difference between being able to buy his son new clothes for the Eid festival and having him go to the mosque in last year's rags. But on an annualized basis (assuming compounding of the interest) such a loan costs 261 percent per year. That doesn't sound at all reasonable. One of the lessons from the diaries is that interest paid on veryshort-duration loans is more sensibly understood as a fee than as annualized interest. When researchers annualize all interest rates, they may be following standard accounting practices but distorting the real picture.

The adjustment works in reverse, too. For example, when policymakers say, as they sometimes do, that microcredit providers offer a good price *as long as it beats the annualized interest rate charged by moneylenders*, there is something amiss. The diaries show that few borrowers would expect to pay the high moneylender rates for a relatively large, long-term loan. Annualized rates may not be the most appropriate way to compare a large, yearlong microcredit loan with a small, short-term loan from a moneylender, and poor households may not be behaving irrationally if they sometimes choose the moneylender over the microcredit provider.

Other pricing conundrums are there to be looked at, as we do in chapter 5. Poor households may choose portfolio combinations that rich-country financial advisers would regard as odd. For example, they may be quite happy to take a loan—paying a high price for doing so—even when they could instead draw on their own savings accounts. That may sound odd when opportunities for secure saving are plentiful, but when it's hard to find a safe place to save, the perceived value of savings already made is that much higher. To give themselves security, the poor may even borrow in order to have something to save. Khadeja did just that. She spent part of a loan she took from a microlender (at about 36 percent interest for a yearlong term) to buy gold. The microcredit loan represented a rare opportunity to get her hands on a sum large enough to buy a substantial lifelong asset offering security against the disruptions in family life so common and so painful for women like her—divorce, desertion, or death of her husband. She wasn't often given the chance to borrow in this way, so she thought it best to grab the opportunity at once. The fact that the loan could be repaid in a series of small weekly payments made it manageable: it allowed her to use a year's worth of small weekly savings to achieve a single big lump of savings. Price was only one aspect of the loan, less important than the repayment schedule that matched installments to the household's cash flow.

Reimagining Microfinance

The world is paying attention to the connections between poverty and finance as never before, and over the past decade the idea that poor households are "bankable" has been widely embraced. This transformation in thinking provides great hope for the households we came to know. Part of the credit goes to Muhammad Yunus, the Bangladeshi economics professor who, in December 2006, received the Nobel Peace Prize for the work that he and the Grameen Bank have done over the last 30 years. The Grameen Bank proves that households like those in the diaries can save and borrow—and repay their loans promptly and with interest. By 2006, Grameen was serving over six million poor customers in villages throughout Bangladesh. Two competitors, ASA (Association for Social Advancement) and BRAC (a name, not an acronym), operate at similar scales and fully cover their costs by charging interest and fees. Early pioneers in Latin America and elsewhere in Asia have independently helped to lead this movement.

We weren't surprised to find that many households in the Bangladesh diaries were microfinance customers, and the diaries described in chapter 6 focus exclusively on them. By contrast, most of India's and South Africa's poor remain unserved by microfinance. However, in both countries there are efforts to bring microfinance and other financial services to low-income households. Grameen Bank "replicas" in India collectively reached 10 million customers in 2007, an increase of 3.1 million from the previous year. From the 1990s, India's social banking sector joined the movement, lending to groups of women organized in jointly liable "self-help groups," allowing India's banks to reach an additional 11 million families by 2005. More recently the Indian government has ordered banks to offer "no frills" accounts as part of its "financial inclusion" policy. These accounts reduce the paperwork needed to open an account and eliminate the minimum balance requirements that had previously kept poorer customers away. In South Africa, the pro-poor microfinance sector remains relatively small, although some groups are growing steadily.[19] More importantly, the banking sector has an agreement with the government under the Financial Sector Charter to increase access for the poorest. The Mzansi account, a low-cost savings account offered by formal banks, is one result of this effort and was being launched just as we were wrapping up our financial diaries in South Africa

One of our goals in launching the financial diaries was to revisit some of the main issues in the debate about providing financial access to the poor. Is credit the main need for financial services felt by poor households? Should the credit go exclusively to small enterprises, or can other ways of fighting hardship and lack of opportunity be identified? Should most of it be disbursed to women, organized into groups who share responsibility for each other's loans? Is making sure that everyone has a bank account enough to achieve that broader purpose?

When Yunus started Grameen, his focus was not on microfinance but on micro*credit*. Moving to microfinance from the narrower goal of microcredit begins with the recognition that poor households want to save and insure as well as borrow. Lately, Grameen itself, as we discuss in chapter 6, has taken up the cause of saving with energy and innovation. The financial diaries show in daily detail why the shift from an exclusive focus on microcredit to the broader microfinance is an important and welcome advance. But the diaries also show the need to push further.

The idea of microcredit has long been associated with the promotion of enterprise: to enable people to purchase productive assets and working stock to set up in business. Microcredit has thus come to be closely associated with the customers' "microenterprises" (the name signals their small scale; often such enterprises employ just the owner and no other workers.) When the turn toward microfinance opened possibilities, it did not entail a reassessment of the uses for microcredit. A fundamental but easily overlooked lesson from the diaries is that the demand for microcredit extends well beyond the need for just *microenterprise* credit. The poor households in the study seek loans for a multitude of uses besides business investment: to cope with emergencies, acquire household assets, pay schooling and health fees, and, in general, to better manage complicated lives. In chapter 6 we show that microcredit is often diverted from its intended uses (of running businesses) to other uses ranked more important by households. This lesson has not yet been well recognized by promoters of microcredit and microfinance.

Organizing borrowers into groups who pledge joint liability for each other's loans (also known as "social collateral") has been the chief mechanism to ensure repayment on unsecured loans to the poor. But microfinance institutions and banks are experimenting increasingly with small loans to individuals, disbursed against smaller land parcels, deposits or liquid assets, or even against strong credit records already established. In this endeavor, they can learn from the cash flows of borrowers and the individual lending arrangements of the informal sector, reported in detail in these financial diaries.

Pledges to ensure that each individual has a bank account might be the first step toward an inclusive financial services sector. Promoting bank account outreach—even if it didn't help the poor to borrow, would surely enhance their access to a safe place to save and a simpler and cheaper way to move money around. But the Indian experience shows that developing the physical (branch) infrastructure of banks, and even pushing accounts and subsidized loans toward the poor, will not address issues of access unless products are *priced* to allow banks a good return, and *designed* to suit the lifestyle, income levels, and cash flows of the poor.

Reliability—on a Global Scale for the Poor

Whether or not the microfinance movement was right to stress loans for microenterprises, or has been too slow to embrace savings and other services, its greatest contribution is, to us, beyond dispute. It represents a huge step in the process of bringing reliability to the financial lives of poor households. For many poor people, having to deal with unreliable financial partners is just part of a general environment of unreliability that they must live with every day. Institutions that they interact with in other aspects of their lives are unreliable as well: the police and the courts, for example, or the health and education services.[20]

Through their financial behavior, poor households show that they are impatient for better-quality services, inventive in bending such services to suit their own purposes, willing to pay for them, and longing for more reliable financial partners. Microfinance providers have made a determined start in responding to these demands, and now many others are joining in, urged on by an increasingly well-informed public.

It is hard to exaggerate the importance of these developments, which we saw clearly when we looked at microfinance through the eyes of Bangladesh diarists. Irrespective of how microcredit loans were used, borrowers appreciated the fact that, relative to almost all their other financial partners, microfinance providers were *reliable*. That is, the loan officers came to the weekly meetings on time, in all kinds of weather; they disbursed loans in the amount they promised at the time they promised and at the price they promised; they didn't demand bribes; they tried hard to keep passbooks accurate and up-to-date; and they showed their clients that they took their transactions seriously.

In return, we noticed that these Bangladeshi microfinance clients often prioritized the repayment of microcredit loans above those of other providers. That didn't surprise us. For poor households, as we have seen, financial lives are often uncertain. The income that provides the stuff of their financial transactions is small and often irregular and unpredictable, and most of their financial partners are not as reliable as they would like. When you need money, moneylenders may not have the funds to lend, and moneyguards may not be able to return your savings. Savings clubs may break up because of poor management, misunderstandings, or accidents that befall members. Money stored at home can be lost, stolen, or wasted on trivial expenditure. The poor deserve something better.

Could it be, then, that financial services will become the first globally reliable service that the world's poor enjoy? We hope the insights described in this book will help achieve that end.

Chapter Two

◆ ◆ ◆

THE DAILY GRIND

Subir was 37 when we met him, and his wife Mumtaz only 29, though their oldest son Iqbal was by then at least 14. They had come to Dhaka, Bangladesh, when Iqbal was a baby, soon after their scrap of land in central Bangladesh was washed away by the great Ganges River. They had three more children, all sons, and Mumtaz was pregnant again and delivered her fifth son midway through the research year ("No more!" she told us). Day by day, Subir and Mumtaz focused on managing life on a dollar a day per head—and sometimes less. Their strategies, and those of other diarists, are the subject of this chapter. We will see how their money management responds to the challenges of living on income that is both low and uncertain, and how doing so determines much of their financial lives.

Subir and Mumtaz had arrived in Dhaka almost penniless, and like many others in that situation had chosen to set up home on government-owned land, settling in an area known as the "fire slum" (*pora bosti*) because it had burned down so often. They built a hut of rough timber clad in woven bamboo with a few sheets of corrugated tin as a roof. At least they had no rent to pay, and utilities cost them little: their bathroom was the local water pump, and their toilet a public one set up by an NGO. They paid a few pennies a month for electricity for their one lightbulb.

Our opening chapter asserted that it is not just the *low value*, but also the *uncertain timing* of their incomes that makes money management so important for poor households, and so it was for Subir and Mumtaz. Institutions such as the United Nations and the World Bank usually focus on explaining why incomes, totaled over the year, are so low, and what can be done to raise them. But the unpredictable ups and downs of income are also an important part of what it is to be poor, and they cause many of the specific challenges faced by the households we came to know.

The low returns and uncertain availability of work opportunities lead households like Subir's to patch livelihoods together from different sources, each irregular and unpredictable. For a while, Subir, who generally pedaled a hired rickshaw, enjoyed a spell driving a motorized rickshaw. On good days, he earned $2.50. Most of the time, though, he pedaled a rickshaw—extremely demanding work that only the very fittest can do day after day. Subir, like most men of his age, found it too exhausting to do for more than four days a week. Even when he was working, his earnings fluctuated with weather conditions, political strife, harassment by the police, and simple good and bad luck.

Toward the end of the year, their teenage son, Iqbal, got a job in a garment factory at $27 a month. Iqbal, who had never attended school regularly, then gave up scavenging for scrap materials for a dealer in their slum. His younger brother Salauddin, 10, continued to rag-pick, and earned $6 in a good month. After the new baby was born, Mumtaz returned to a job working as a maid, earning some $10 a month. A boarder earlier had been contributing another $7 a month, but he left when the baby arrived. Taken together, total household income peaked at an average of $3.15 a day for the seven of them. In bad times, it fell as low as $1.90 a day. They fell into the poorer half of the Bangladesh sample.

Making these uncertain income flows deliver a stable home life was a constant preoccupation for Subir and Mumtaz. Most of the time they succeeded. They never had to beg, but they did skip meals, and the quality of their food varied. Sometimes we found them eating hot meals three times a day—mostly rice and lentils, sometimes a bit of fish, or, as a rare treat, even beef. Usually, though, they ate twice, and in really bad times just once a day. But at least they ate something every day, and it is a tribute to their resourcefulness that they managed that.

Subir and Mumtaz and their family survived thanks in part to financial tools. The most intensively used tools, however, were not those celebrated by advocates of microfinance for the poor. In the year we spent with them, Subir and Mumtaz did not, for example, seek a "microcredit" loan to fund the expansion of a small business. True, Subir could have earned more if he owned his own rickshaw rather than renting, and a loan would have hastened the purchase. But, as we show below, he had good reasons not to do so. Others looking at the couple's situation might instead stress the importance of helping people like them to save to build up meaningfully large assets. Borrowing and saving for the long term are indeed important to poor households, as later chapters show, but long-term goals were not the *primary* financial concern of most households we met. Instead households like that of Subir and Mumtaz borrowed and saved mostly to meet pressing short-term needs: their main objective was cash-flow management. Being able to manage immediate needs is a precondition for considering long-term ambitions—but the way that poor people achieve it has received scant attention from policymakers and others arguing for financial access for the poor.

The most basic objective for households like that of Subir and Mumtaz is to make sure that there's food on the table every day, and not just on days when income flows in. As we argued in chapter 1, the poor households we met actively employ financial tools not *despite* being poor but *because* they are poor. When it came to managing money, Subir and Mumtaz put a premium on the flexibility and convenience of their financial tools, even though those tools were not always reliable. Their juggling reminds us that money is fungible—it can be split and combined in a number of ways. We argue in the concluding section that embracing this flexibility of money can open vistas for financial providers looking for better ways to serve poor households.

Diary households in both the urban and rural areas of all three countries employ strategies and have portfolios that, no matter how they vary in detail, are similar in important ways. Most important, they are characterized by frequent small-scale transactions. Both saving and borrowing are involved, often with multiple partners and using several different kinds of instruments simultaneously. The result is portfolios with large flows of cash: large relative to the level of outstanding debt or of savings held at any one time. The primary goal is managing cash flow. Richer people's objectives, like maximizing the returns on assets or minimizing the cost of debt, are, of necessity, secondary. Even policy initiatives designed to help poor households build stronger balance sheets through accruing major assets, such as Individual Development Accounts (IDAs, a subsidized long-term saving mechanism for low-income households in the United States), work best if the households can first manage cash flows. Asset building is an important objective of poor people's portfolios, and chapter 4 discusses this process further, but in this chapter we suggest that understanding the financial lives of poor households starts with a focus on cash flows rather than balance sheets.

The next section of this chapter describes the importance of frequent and small transactions used for basic money management. The sections that follow show why this pattern holds: multiple occupations leading to low incomes—often patched together from uncertain parts—result in a "triple whammy" of incomes that are not just small but also irregular, and that have to be managed with financial instruments that do not always fit the household's cash-flow patterns. The balance of the chapter describes how households cope with the triple whammy—and where hidden costs lie. The concluding section brings together ideas on ways to help poor households cope with their most basic, daily challenges.

Small Balances, Large Cash Flows

Though the households we worked with included some that were very poor, none lived hand to mouth, if we take that phrase to mean that all income is consumed directly and immediately. It is a remarkable finding, and not what might be expected in communities where some scrape by on less than one dollar per day per person. But the finding remains hidden if we look only at asset accumulation. Not surprisingly, the diary households have relatively few financial assets. Year-end asset values tend to be small: a median value of $68 in Bangladesh, $115 in India, and $472 in South Africa.[1] Even adjusting for differences in purchasing power in different countries,[2] these assets are not large, and might lead us to assume that they could sustain little financial activity. But what we learned is that data on balances told us little about what happened during the year. The financial diaries were designed specifically to lift the veil on a wide array of financial activities that take place day to day and week to week.

The story is revealed when we look at cash flows rather than balance sheets. During the year, all of the financial diary households pushed and pulled through financial instruments amounts far greater than their year-end net worth.[3] By "push" we mean deposit, lend, or repay. By "pull" we mean withdraw, borrow, or accept deposits. If cash flowing into the household is not immediately consumed or invested, it is pushed or pulled through a financial instrument in one way or another. We use the expression "turnover" to mean the total sum of money being "pushed" into instruments plus the money being "pulled" out of them. Table 2.1 shows the households' high turnover in financial instruments. As we describe later, most of the activity runs through informal devices, below the radar screen of regulators and bankers.

The high level of financial cash flow is particularly surprising when considered in relation to income. We might call this ratio the "cash flow intensity of income": the sum of funds borrowed, paid out, recovered, deposited and withdrawn, divided by income of all sorts. In India, households shifted, on average, between 0.75 and 1.75 times their incomes, with high-velocity money movers like rural small traders shifting more than three times their earnings in an average month. In South Africa, the monthly turnover in cash flows was slightly more intense, at about 1.85 times the monthly income.

Table 2.1 Year-End Financial Asset Values and Annual Cash Flows through Financial Instruments for Median Households

	Bangladesh		*India*		*South Africa*	
	Year-end asset value	*Annual financial turnover*	*Year-end asset value*	*Annual financial turnover*	*Year-end asset value*	*Annual financial turnover*
Rural	57	568	18	590	220	3,447
Urban	74	547	169	810	792	6,264

Note: US$ converted from local currencies at market rates.

In general we found that the flows moving through financial instruments are large relative to income even in households with low incomes and small balances. In Bangladesh, where rural incomes are lower than urban ones, median turnover in the countryside is nevertheless higher than in the town. In South Africa, the poorer half of the households turned over a bigger multiple of their income than the richer half. This is despite the fact that many of the richer households were wage employees and had their wages paid into bank accounts from which they would then withdraw cash, inflating the value of turnovers. The lowest annual turnover of the entire financial diaries sample was $133, that of a rural Indian household living from the income generated by a tiny farm and wage labor. Nevertheless this small turnover was still more than three-quarters of their very small income. Most households have turnover in excess of $1,000 over the year, and many have much higher. This attests to our general notion that lower incomes require *more* rather than *less* active financial management.

◆ ◆ ◆

Subir and Mumtaz's portfolio for the Bangladesh research year 1999–2000 is given in greater detail in table 2.2. For each of the categories of instruments they used, we show the closing balances, as we did for

Table 2.2 Portfolio Summary for Subir and Mumtaz over the Research Year

	Closing balance	*Turnover*
Financial assets		
Semiformal Informal		
Microfinance savings	10.20	49.40
Private loans out	30.00	117.00
Home savings	5.00	18.00
Subtotal	$45.20	$184.40
Financial liabilities		
Semiformal Informal		
Microfinance loan	30.00	47.00
Interest-free loan	14.00	84.00
Private loan	15.00	105.00
Pawn loan	0	10.00
Moneyguarding	2.00	66.00
Shop credit	4.00	50.00
Subtotal	$65.00	$362.00
Financial net worth	−$19.80	
Total turnover		$546.40

Note: US$ converted from Bangladesh takas at $ = 50 takas, market rate.

Hamid and Khadeja in chapter 1. We also show the total turnover during the year (the flows in and out of each class of instrument). By placing the balances and the flows alongside each other, we highlight one of the big points made above: balances are small relative to flows.

Balances are sometimes so small that one might conclude this is not a "portfolio" at all, in the sense in which a modern financial adviser would use the term. Nevertheless, the fact that there are many different instruments and that the flows are relatively large shows, clearly, that Subir and Mumtaz, and households like them, are financially active. We need to pause for a moment and adjust our perspective if we are to understand the real importance of these poor-owned portfolios.

Multiple and Uncertain Occupations . . .

Understanding the reasons for high turnovers is the starting point for understanding the financial lives of these households. We move to that task by showing how, despite a wide variety of occupations, the income characteristics of our diary households led them to the predicament that we call the "triple whammy."

Some of our diary households are headed by someone with a long-term permanent waged or salaried job. But these are the exceptions. In the Bangladesh diary set, for example, there are only two households out of 42 that obtain most of their income from a single permanent job: both are private car drivers living in the capital. There are other waged jobs—quite a few urban households are like Subir and Mumtaz and have one or more members working in the garment factories—but, as with that couple, these jobs provide only part of the total household income, the rest coming from self-employment, casual employment, or petty businesses. Jobs that appear permanent may turn out not to be. While just over half our Delhi households received regular wages from a single source, half of this group lost their jobs during the year and had to search for new work (sometimes several times), while most of the others were hired on contract and thus had no rights to regular work or benefits. In the countryside, in both Bangladesh and India, there are farming households who depend for the large part on their crops, but even in their case at least a part of their income comes from other sources. The wealthiest farmers will also have secondary jobs such as teaching or own some form of transportation, and the poorer ones will also labor on other people's land or on public works, or seek casual jobs in retail, transport, or construction, or in casual self-employment like the cigarette-rollers of India.

In South Africa, social welfare pays out monthly grants to the elderly, children, and the disabled.[4] The system reaches down to many poor households: in our South African sample of 152 households, 27 percent had grant support as their main source of income. Within our sample, these government grants made up 48 percent of the average household income in the rural areas and 10 percent in the townships. These monthly payments certainly make income more regular, and we later show that this regularity does make it easier to engage in higher levels of financial intermediation. But these incomes are small: in the rural areas, a grant meant to support one person supports, on average, a family of four. As a result, grants are rarely enough to cover costs, and most households supplement them with small business, casual work, and remittances from working relatives. Moreover, having come to rely on regular monthly payments, grant-dependent households are left particularly vulnerable when they don't arrive on time. During the study year, we observed several occasions where grants were not paid out. Sometimes households, such as Sabelo's (whose situation is summarized in table A1.2 in appendix 1), were the victims of bureaucratic glitches, and twice during the study year grants were not paid out in the urban township of Diepsloot because of riots.

Figure 2.1 illustrates the kinds of employment we encountered and reveals some differences between the three countries, especially between South Asia (Bangladesh and India) on the one hand and South Africa on the other. In the figure we offer three definitions of employment and show what proportion of adults in diary households are engaged in them. We see, at the left of the figure, that more than 40 percent in South Africa enjoy regular wages, a rate two or three times higher than in South Asia, where earning steady wages is far from the norm.

In the center of the figure we have widened the definition of earning activity to include casual work, such as minding someone's store or doing farmwork on an irregular basis. Under this definition, the percentage of adults employed increases sharply for Bangladesh and India, to about 40 percent, and moderately for South Africa, where it captures about 55 percent of all adults. The third definition casts the net as wide as possible, to include adults who undertake any type of income-earning activity. India easily surpasses South Africa in employment when it is defined this broadly: in India, many adults are self-employed at least part-time in subsistence farming, trading, tiny service industries like rickshaw pulling or maidserving, or in home-

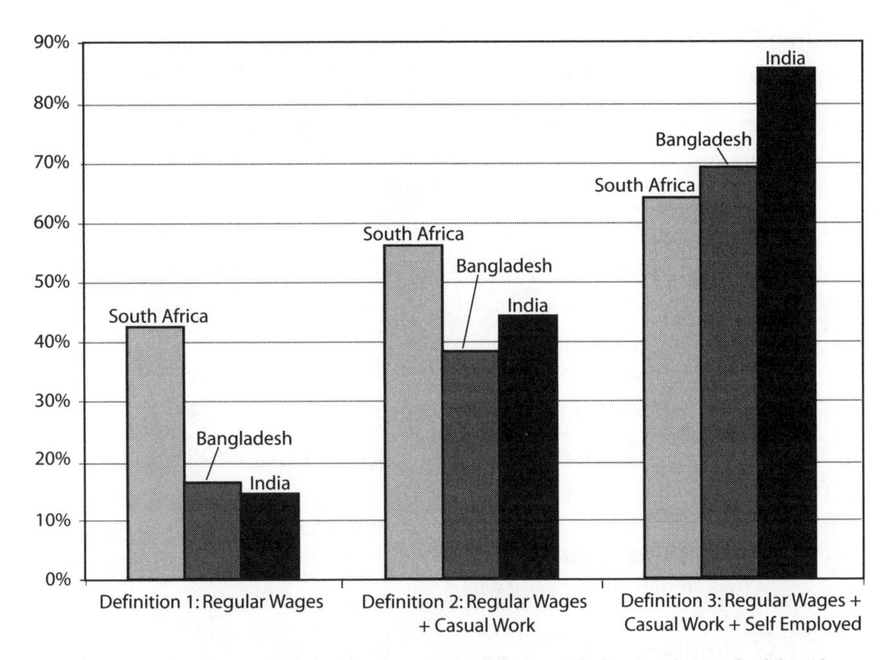

FIGURE 2.1. Income-earning categories of financial diaries households. Share of financial diaries adult individuals within each category (percent).

based production such as rolling cigarettes, or sewing, or rearing poultry and selling eggs.

Notice that in South Africa fewer than 70 percent of the adults who could be earning income in some way are managing to do so, whereas in India more than 85 percent of adults bring in some income through work of some sort. This figure does not include the South African social welfare grants discussed earlier, and these grants may explain the difference in income-earning patterns between South Africa and South Asia.

One other difference between South Asia and South Africa is the number of children at work. If we judge by the evidence of the financial diaries households, South Africa has managed to do away with child labor for the most part. But in Bangladesh, two of Subir and Mumtaz's boys had been working since they were about eight years old. In the Bangladesh sample as a whole, eight out of 42 households, and in the Indian sample, 10 out of 48 households (19 percent in each

Table 2.3 Annual Income of the Median Diary Households

	Annual household income (US$ [market])	
	Median	*Range*[a]
Bangladesh urban[b]	720	420–1,700
Bangladesh rural[b]	740	380–2,100
India urban	637	241–2,611
India rural	497	171–2,404
South Africa urban	3,919	504–23,337
South Africa rural	2,090	238–49,982

Note: US$ converted from local currencies at market rates for the research year.

[a] Some extreme outliers have been eliminated from the range.

[b] Bangladesh estimated from periodic surveys; India and South Africa from regular diary data.

case) had children under the age of 15 who worked for at least some of the time during the research year.

. . . and Low Incomes

When occupations are intermittent, part-time, casual, or multiple, and where children may also work, it is not easy to measure total household income. For Bangladesh, where we focused on financial transactions and didn't systematically collect income and expenditure flows, we have estimates of income based on periodic enquiries. Our researchers in India and South Africa, on the other hand, aimed to record *all* income and expenditure flowing in and out of their sample households. Based on these data, table 2.3 shows both the median household income and the range of incomes for the urban and rural parts of our sample for all three countries.

To give some meaning to these statistics, we include an extensive table in appendix 1 that shows daily per capita income data for a selection of households chosen to illustrate their varying sizes, locations, and occupational patterns, with notes about ways in which the value and nature of the income intersects with their financial behavior as noted in the diaries.

Unpredictability

The first element of the triple whammy that poor households face, then, is low incomes. The second element, the uncertain timing of cash flows, is well brought out by the diary methodology.

Seasonal variations in income affected many households. Figure 2.2, based on diary data from the north Indian rural sample, shows the income of two middle-ranking groups: farmers with average holdings of 3.5 acres, who are directly affected by seasonality, and traders, who are indirectly affected by the spending patterns of the farmers.

The two groups experience a small peak in November (the main harvest and the time of the Hindu festival of Dewali and, in the research year,[5] the Muslim month of Ramadan). But the much larger peak is from February through May, the local marriage season. All farmers who can do so hold back their grain from the November harvest, to sell and spend after February. Traders, on the other hand, mostly without farmland, earn the bulk of their annual income during these two festival seasons, so their peaks and troughs are different from those of farmers. Even small farmers, like Sita (featured in chapter 4), whose income derives mostly from farm labor, face sharp fluctuations in income since available work is concentrated around the months of August, November, and December. The annual income of her three-person household, at $353, is far from the lowest in our sample. But it is extremely uneven, with 60 percent falling in four farming months between June and September, leaving a long trough when monthly income went as low as $9.50 and averaged $13.50 for three consecutive months.

For small farmers, income is also highly unreliable, far more so than for larger farmers. While rural Indian respondents agreed that the research year was generally a bad year for farming, larger farmers mostly met their expectations of harvest, while small and marginal

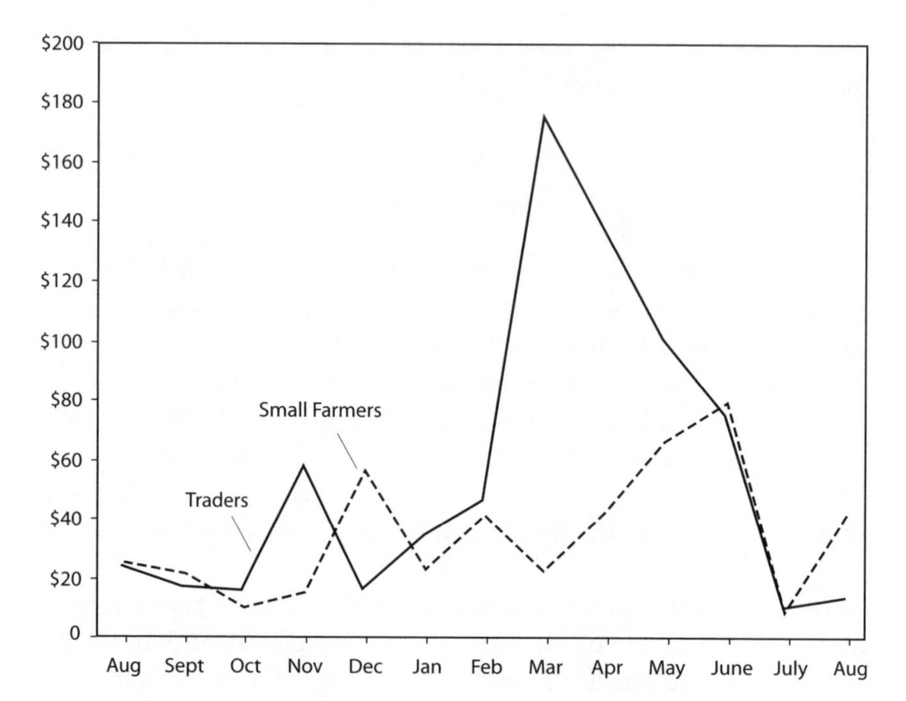

FIGURE 2.2. Incomes of two Indian occupational groups, aggregated monthly. US$ converted from Indian rupees at $ = 47 rupees, market rate.

farmers recovered only 25–30 percent of what they'd expected. One cause was the disadvantaged position of their land on the tail end of canal irrigation, but an equally important problem was their inability to raise timely finance for farm inputs when required, in unpredictable weather conditions.

So both small regular monthly incomes and modest seasonal incomes produce a need for intermediation, explaining why poor households that experience these patterns in income tend to hold portfolios of transactions and relationships.

But there is no doubt that *irregularity*, and above all *unpredictability*, of income causes even more serious challenges in cash-flow management, resulting in ever more innovation in trying to address them. Figure 2.3 illustrates this effect with a case from South Africa. Pumza is a sheep intestine seller living in the crowded urban hostels of Cape Town. She supports herself and four children with her business. Every

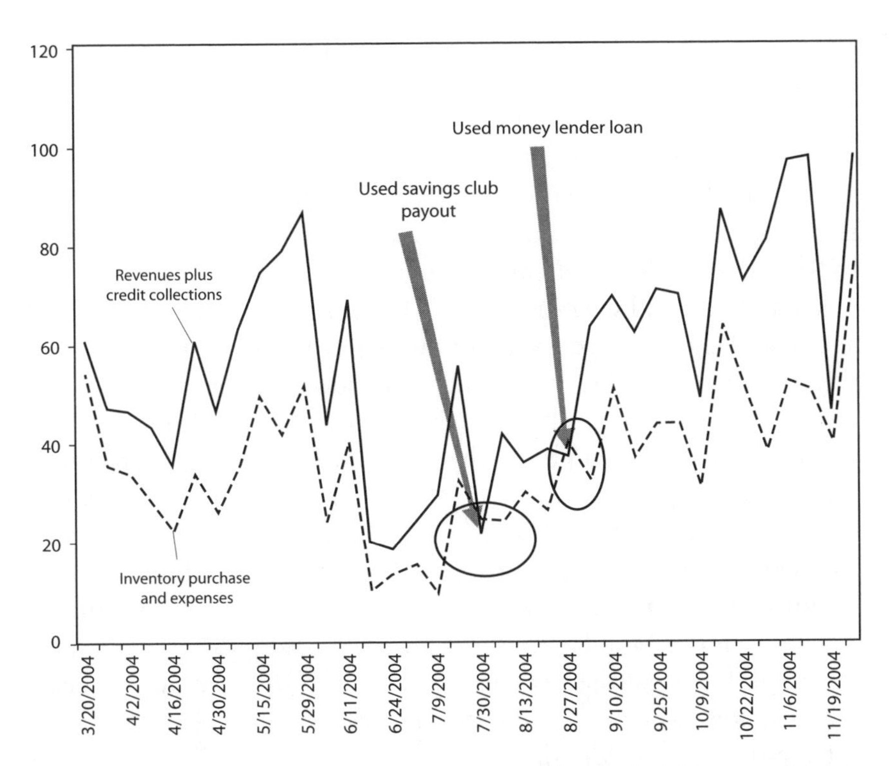

FIGURE 2.3. Revenues and inventory expenses of a South African small businesswoman. Daily cash flows aggregated fortnightly. US$ converted from South African rand at $ = 6.5 rand, market rate.

day she buys intestines, cooks them on an outside fire between the hostel buildings, and sells them to passersby. On average she earns revenues of about $6–$15 a day from this business from which she needs to pay for her stock and expenses, as well as support her family.

She tries not to give credit to customers, knowing that it will hurt her cash flow, but she broke this rule five times during the year for special customers. She needs to spend about $5 every day buying the raw sheep intestines, and about once a month she travels to buy wood for the fire, an expense of between $1 and $5, depending on how much wood she buys. On the whole, then, this can be a fairly profitable business, and indeed Pumza tends to make a profit of about

$95 per month. A government-provided child support grant of $25 a month supplements this income. So this family of five lives on a monthly income of about $120.

These figures show that Pumza isn't in the poorest of households, but they don't reveal the fluctuations in cash flow that Pumza experiences as a result of her business. Sometimes business does not go well, so Pumza does not earn enough revenue to buy stock for the next day. She could sell her old stock, but customers prefer fresh meat and would choose to go to one of the other sheep intestine sellers in the area. If she's lucky, these times coincide with the receipt of her child grant, which helps tide her over. Otherwise, she borrows from a moneylender. She had to do this several times during the research year even though, with interest rates at 30 percent per month, she knows that such loans are not an ideal solution to her cash-flow problem. During May, she and a group of three other sheep intestine sellers formed a savings club, a financial device we'll talk more about in chapter 4. From Monday to Thursday, each paid in $7.50 a day, and they took turns getting the entire pot of $30. That way they evened out cash flow to help tide them through the lean days. Pumza's day to get the pot was on Monday. However, despite this plan, when one partner failed to pay, she ended up going to the moneylender once again. After four weeks of trying to make the club work, it fell apart. Later in the year, Pumza took on a temporary government-sponsored job cleaning streets for four weeks while her daughter kept the sheep intestine business running. She started another savings club with three other coworkers in this job. Contributions were $30 every week, so every month, Pumza would receive a payout of $120. During July, when the weather was cold and rainy and potential customers for sheep intestines stayed indoors, a payout from this club helped Pumza bridge her business cash flow.

Of course, small incomes can be difficult to manage even if they come regularly. Siraz, for example, is a car driver in Dhaka, Bangladesh, who earns about $77 per month. He received his wage every month on time, but the wage was so small that any hiccup during the month—a child's illness, an unexpected visitor to entertain—would require him to dig into savings or to borrow. Still, in Siraz's case the fact that people knew he was paid regularly made it easier for him to borrow. In the South Africa sample many households survive primarily on the basis of the government grants we have already referred to. The grants arrive monthly, with no payouts in between. They are regular and relatively predictable, but arrive at intervals that are too long for some recipients and too short for others. Those who find the monthly interval too long may pair with another recipient or join a group of recipients to share the grants as they come in. Those who find the interval too short may pool their grants to give to just one recipient each period. We give examples later in the chapter.

Does a Formal Sector Job Bring Security?

Thus far, we've discussed the insecurities of farm and informal income, but similar insecurities exist in formal labor. A case from Delhi provides an illustration.

Somnath and Jainath are two brothers who left their wives and children in the village and shared a hut in Delhi's Indira Camp, a semiauthorized squatter settlement that provides labor to the factories of Okhla Industrial Area, Delhi's foremost industrial zone. The brothers worked in the finishing sections of export garment factories and received wages at daily or piece rates. As peripheral workers hired by a broker, they faced excessive work at some times and no work at others. They got work through "emergency orders" rather than as core workers in the factory. Variations in their workload were reflected in their income flows. Their combined monthly wage fluctuated between \$85 and \$53 and stopped completely for four months in the middle of the research year. For two of these months they were in their village, but it took them two months to find work after they came back to Indira Camp. Jainath returned to the garment factory, but was told he could earn his earlier wage only if he worked 12 hours day, seven days a week.

Before they left Delhi, the brothers had managed, between them, to remit an average of \$26 per month to their village, but after returning to Delhi they sent nothing, and this neglect made them very anxious.

They had also borrowed money, first to get home, then to cover their stay, and then to get back to Delhi, a debt of over $100, most of it with interest. Only by the goodwill of their landlord and a grocery store manager, both acknowledging their good payment record in the past, were the brothers able to sustain themselves into a fifth month, when work finally came their way. By that time they had accumulated debts of $120. Somnath paid a bribe of $4 to get his job back, but only three months later, lost it again. When he received his final salary, Somnath managed a small remittance of $11 to his wife and child, the first since he had left Delhi for the village seven months earlier.

To compound their difficulties, the brothers' hut was robbed the following month and $64 was stolen. Somnath found factory work and managed to arrange a small wage advance to keep the grocer happy as their shop bill rose. But within a fortnight he was once again out of work, told that there were no orders for the factory. As the long dry summer loomed, Somnath worried that he would be out of work for several months. His fears were realized. When we finished our research and left Indira Camp in July 2001, Jainath had left for the village, also dismissed by his employer, though with a promise to take him back in September. Somnath was holding out in Delhi as the stakes, and his debt, continued to rise: loath to borrow from relatives and ashamed to go home and admit defeat, Somnath couldn't leave until he'd paid the accumulated debt of nearly $90 to the grocer and landlord, on whose goodwill he had depended so heavily.

A formal sector job, then, doesn't necessarily translate to more reliable income in South Asia. In South Africa, however, labor laws are much more rigorously enforced, and when households do manage to find a waged job, they tend to have a fairly reliable source of income. Even grant recipient households could depend on regular monthly grant income. In our study, these households were able to "leverage" their more regular sources of income to engage in larger-scale financial intermediation: with a regular income, they were more comfortable taking on higher levels of debt and lenders were more willing to provide loans. As table 2.4 shows, regular wage earners in South Africa are usually better off in terms of both absolute income and income per capita than those earning irregularly (those whose income

Table 2.4 Regular versus Irregular Income Households, South Africa

	Wage-earning households	*Grant-receiving households*	*Irregular income households*
Share of sample in profile	49%	27%	21%
Financial statistics			
Average monthly income	$635	$188	$235
Average monthly income per capita	$219	$61	$87
Debt/service ratio	13%	17%	7%
Debt/equity ratio	22%	23%	19%

Note: US$ converted from South African rand at $ = 6.5 rand, market rate.

comes from a small business piecemeal work, or remittances from relatives). But grant recipients, who are *poorer* than irregular earners, still have debt service and debt-to-equity ratios that are nearly the same as regular wage earners.

Like a small start-up business, a poor household may indicate financial health by carrying a certain level of debt. A start-up business needs to take on debt in order to invest and grow. Likewise, poor households need to access debt so they can weather interruptions that may threaten their investments in the long term. Accessing debt can prevent a family from lowering its nutritional intake or pulling children from school in an emergency.

Policymakers in South Africa worry about debt levels growing too high. In our sample some households did take on more debt than their incomes could handle, or borrowed with terms of credit that were not transparent. The South African National Credit Act, introduced in 2007, is intended to improve transparency and curb overzealous commercial consumption lending.[6] However, many of the high debt situations in the South African financial diaries developed through borrowing outside of the formal financial sector, beyond the scope of regulatory policy. Many grant recipients did not increase debt through formal lenders, who would require a payslip, but through informal debt at a local store or with a local trader.[7] Moreover, in many instances debt did not arise from reckless consumption, but from stretching too small an income over too many mouths to feed, a matter of meeting basic needs between payments. Regular income in the form of a grant eliminated one part of the triple whammy and allowed these households access to more financial opportunities to manage their small incomes.

Partners in Money Management

In the portfolios of our diary households, common patterns emerge. One is that most transactions are carried out with "informal" partners rather than with formal institutions like banks and insurance companies. The partners are often neighbors, who seldom keep documentation of agreements, and certainly nothing that would hold up in court.

This doesn't mean that poor households are simply at the mercy of grasping moneylenders. Far from it: the most frequent partners are friends or relatives offering interest-free loans. Turning back to the financial portfolio of Subir and Mumtaz, we note a number of kinds of loans in table 2.2. Subir, an affable man with lots of charm, managed to borrow often and without owing interest. In just two months—November and December 1999—he borrowed five times, all from neighbors and colleagues, and Mumtaz borrowed once, from her sister. The sums were tiny: none of them exceeded four dollars, and all were quickly paid back from rickshaw income. Small as they are, interest-free loans like these, which featured in many of our diaries, did the job they were intended to do—they ensured that the household members ate something each day. They constitute one of the two core elements of managing money for everyday survival, and as such they deserve more of our attention when we are thinking about how to improve financial services for the poor.

The other core element is small-scale savings. Every household we met made some attempt to save. All the older members of Subir and Mumtaz's household, for example, saved at home in some way:

Mumtaz in a locked box in a drawer in the cupboard, Subir in a cloth bag tied into the roof timbers, and son Iqbal, who set himself an ambitious target of saving $20 in a clay bank bought from the market (he failed: he broke it open when he thought he had about $5 and found only $2). Often they had small savings at home even as they took loans, and this behavior offers us another insight. Poor households less often *choose between* alternative instruments (say, loans and saving) than they maximize access to *both* in a world where nothing fits perfectly and access is constrained. Spending money is patched together from various sources—a bit from savings, another bit from a moneylender loan, another from an interest-free loan, and so forth.

The tools used for informal saving and borrowing are generally close at hand (savings hidden in the hut, loans from nearby neighbors) and flexible (that is, without strictly fixed terms or payment schedules), two hallmarks of desirable cash management tools. Convenience has also been taken to heart by the microfinance providers operating in our Bangladesh study areas. When we first met them, Subir and Mumtaz told us that they had decided not to join a microfinance institution (an "NGO" to them) because their main need was to save, not borrow. If they borrowed, they might not be able to make the regular weekly repayments. But then they heard about an NGO where borrowing wasn't compulsory, and joined it, at first just to save. They used the savings account primarily to patch gaps in their cash flow, saving small sums when they could, and drawing down the balance when they needed to for food, travel costs, medicine, and the like. This account provided them with useful liquidity in times of need: they withdrew sums of $10, $5, and $4.60.

When, later in the year, they grew comfortable with Mumtaz's NGO, they began to borrow from it. They might have put their NGO loan toward the purchase of a rickshaw for Subir, freeing him from the cost of renting one. Such microlending to support microenterprise or self-employment has been a leading premise of the microcredit movement. But the couple decided that buying a rickshaw was too risky because they had nowhere safe to park it at night.[8]

Instead, they used the loan to stock up with rice, bought a wooden cupboard (their only piece of furniture apart from an old bedstead), and lent $20 to a fellow rickshaw driver at a nominal 17.5 percent interest per month, a loan that was repaid three months later with about half the interest honored and the rest forgiven. In short, they used the funds mainly for basic consumption needs for themselves and others. The couple's behavior with their NGO loan should make us think carefully before we conclude that loans for poor people are of little value, or may even be a dangerous temptation to fall into deep debt, unless they are used for working assets. Rightly or wrongly, Subir and Mumtaz believed that there were other constraints, besides the lack of capital, to their buying a productive asset—in this case the risk of loss. They may have been too timid, but they also saw other good uses for the loan: a stock of food, a piece of furniture, and the chance to strengthen a financial relationship with a colleague and make some money at the same time.

Against the backdrop of small-scale do-it-yourself saving and frequent interest-free borrowing, the couple engaged in a wide range of other deals to bridge gaps between income and expenses. They took goods on credit from two grocery shops and a restaurant. They raised $10 once in the year, when things were especially tough, by pawning Mumtaz's only necklace (happily Subir redeemed it from rickshaw income a few weeks later).

Through vigilance and energy, Subir and Mumtaz managed to keep their family fed. The process was never easy and required tools that were flexible and easy to access. The informal sector has proved to be the best provider of those tools so far, and the challenge for the formal sector is whether it can do better, with services that are just as flexible and convenient, but also more reliable and more liquid. It might be tempting to learn "tools of the trade" by watching the local moneylender, but as the next section describes, the most important providers of loans are not moneylenders but friends and neighbors.

Small-scale Lending and Borrowing

To manage day to day, the diary households patched and stretched their savings and their loans, a strategy that was called into play whenever an employer failed to pay on time, a spell of unemployment hit, or a visitor suddenly arrived, to name just a handful of reasons. Perhaps because saving is something that an individual or a household can do without involving others, virtually every diary household saved. In Bangladesh, for example, not a single one of the 42 households, even the very poorest, was without some form of do-it-yourself saving. And yet for none of these households was saving-at-home a sufficient strategy: all of them had to turn to others in their community to bolster their capacity to manage their money. So while saving was the most ubiquitous instrument, much more cash flowed through loans. In Bangladesh, when we looked at all withdrawals from saving and all loans taken by the households, including the very smallest transactions of each type, loans outnumbered savings withdrawals by four to one.

Overwhelmingly, the loans were taken locally, in the "informal market." In Bangladesh, 88 percent of all borrowing deals were informal, a figure that climbs to 92 percent for the poorest part of the sample. In India, 94 percent of all borrowing was informal, which, again, climbs to 97 percent among the poorest respondents. Of all respondents in the poorest category in India, only one household had borrowed from anything but an informal source, and that was from a microfinance institution. But the term informal "market" is misleading here, because in all three countries most of these loans were interest-free. While moneylenders loom large as lenders of last resort, charging fees that can stretch the capacities of borrowers, informal-sector borrowing usually means paying zero interest, and in general the smaller the sum the more likely that is to be the case.

After home savings, interest-free borrowing was by far the most frequently used financial instrument in all three countries. It complements rather than contrasts with the households' attempts to save at home, because interest-free borrowing and lending is in essence a way of harnessing the savings power of a neighborhood or family network to address the cash-flow problems of its individual members. To tap into this network the diary households needed to be part of it: the portfolios of the poor are thus portfolios of transactions and relationships. Better-off people might manage money on an everyday

Table 2.5 One-on-One Interest-Free Borrowing and Lending

	Borrowing		*Lending*	
	Average number of loans per household	*Average amount*	*Average number of loans per household*	*Average amount*
Bangladesh	6.9	$14	2.8	$14
India	4.9	$28	1.4	$54
South Africa	2.8	$190	3.0	$132

Note: US$ converted from local currencies at market rates.

basis with a credit card. For the poor households in our study, the main strategy was to turn to each other, using one-on-one lending and borrowing between friends, family, and neighbors.

Table 2.5 shows the incidence of interest-free lending and borrowing over the course of the financial diaries study. The "average number of loans per household" is the total number of times that borrowing or lending happened in the country samples, divided by the total number of households in the samples. Both urban and rural areas are included. Lending and borrowing were constantly observed among the households, and in rather small amounts. Most loans were short term—repaid in days or weeks rather than years. In South Africa, for example, it usually took about two months for a borrower to repay a loan. In Bangladesh, most of the very smallest loans were returned within a month.

These interest-free borrowings and lendings were ubiquitous among the households in all three samples. In Bangladesh, for example, 41 of the 42 diary households took one or more such loans in the research year, and 24 households gave such loans. In India, 44 of the 48 households took one or more such loans in the year, and 22 out of 48 gave such loans.

Interest-free borrowing and interest-free lending relate to each other in interesting ways. Often there is an understanding that the borrower will return the favor and lend when the need arises: we call this "reciprocal" lending and borrowing. In other cases, the borrowing flows one way and the creditor in one deal is unlikely to become the debtor in the next: this might be called "obligatory" lending since it depends on the lender's sense that he or she is obliged to help out the borrower with a loan. "Obligatory" lending appears to be common in Bangladesh and India, where there are many fewer reports of interest-free lending by the diary households themselves than of interest-free borrowing. This suggests that many poor people go to wealthier people (people outside the range of our enquiry) for such loans—better-off family members or employers, for example, who feel some sense of responsibility to help out.

To smooth their consumption, then, poor people often lean on those around them with marginally more resources, and this is true not only in purely cash transactions, but also in groceries taken on credit, in rent payments delayed, and in advances taken against wages. All these transactions have in common that the advance (whether in goods, services, or payment for labor) is given within an existing relationship that reduces the risk to both borrower and lender.

Interest-free transactions between households in the informal network are not confined to borrowing and lending. In all three countries, there is a well-established tradition of "moneyguarding"—storing cash for others seeking a safe haven for savings or for cash that needs to be kept aside for some later purpose. Subir and Mumtaz, whose story started this chapter, did so. They sometimes looked after money for neighbors: they accepted $18 from a group of young workers who were planning to carry the money back to their village a few weeks later. Banks may not have regarded Subir and Mumtaz as potential clients, but the young men who had come to Dhaka from Subir and Mumtaz's rural district saw them as their temporary personal bankers.[9]

Certain arrangements defy pigeonholing as saving or borrowing. For example, people may agree to share their wages or salaries, if their money arrives at different times. In South Africa, some women have money-sharing arrangements built around the receipt of their monthly grants from the government. Nomthunzi and her neighbor Noquezi each receive an old age grant of $115 a month, but they receive their payment at different times of the month, Noquezi on the third and Nomthunzi on the twenty-first. They always exchange $31 out of the $115 grant, so they are able to receive a boost of income before their next grant is paid out. In this way, just as their cash is running low, the other comes along with a fresh $31 to tide the recipient over until the next grant. A contrasting arrangement was used by Nomveliso and her sister. Nomveliso is bringing up three grandchildren using government grants for old age and child-care totaling $141 a month. She once opened a bank account to save money, but it is now inactive: the time and cost to visit the bank aren't worth the bother. Instead, she has an arrangement with her sister to pool their child grant of $26 so that each gets $52 each second month—a more substantial and in their view more useful sum. The difference between these two examples is that Nomveliso and her sister get a double-sized grant every other month, so they are building a lump sum. Noquezi and Nomthunzi are tiding each other over in the middle of each month, so they are dividing up their cash flows to make them stretch further. This "grant timing" is an elegant informal instrument in which the timing of transactions is defined by the grant recipients themselves, thus adding reliability and lessening the unpredictability of much that goes on in the informal sector. It combines lending and mutual insurance, but stops short of creating dependence. As such, it shares the virtues of some kinds of savings clubs, especially the RoSCAs, that we look at in chapter 4. Both hold lessons for the design of commercial loan products.

The Full Triple Whammy

We have looked at the first two parts of the triple whammy—incomes are low, and cash flows are irregular. The third part of the triple whammy is that existing financial instruments are not well suited to address either of these problems. In the previous section, we saw that the diary households rely almost exclusively on the informal sector when they need to intermediate these low and irregular cash flows on a day-to-day basis. A few statistics from diary records will show just how much the informal sector dominates. Two of our countries—

Bangladesh and South Africa—have well-developed formal or semiformal financial sectors that do reach down to poor households like those of our diarists. In Bangladesh, microfinance institutions (which we count as semiformal) reached no less than 30 of our 42 diary households (21 households held loans and savings during the research year and another nine held savings only). Despite this role, their share of turnover and of balances in the Bangladesh portfolios was small: just 15 percent of all turnover, 13 percent of all household financial assets, and 21 percent of debt. Since these numbers include *all* dealings that our households had with microfinance institutions—including the relatively large loans for small businesses and capital purchases that we will look at in chapter 4—the microfinance institutions were responsible for an even smaller share of transactions aimed at day-to-day money management.

In South Africa a number of formal providers, including formal lenders, provident fund providers, and insurers feature in the portfolios of our wealthier diary households. Nevertheless, if we ignore the monthly direct deposit transactions through banks that are more common in South Africa than in South Asia because more people get paid wages or grants, the formal share of transactions in our diarists' portfolios was as small as it was in Bangladesh.

Informal transactions have many virtues. First, they are conveniently close at hand. Using your own home as your savings bank is the ultimate in convenience, and doesn't require dealing with others. In transactions with neighbors, friends, and relatives, paperwork is rarely required—especially important in places like Bangladesh and India, where many household heads are illiterate. Your partners are people whose culture is your own and whose behavior can be predicted. Second, as we have just seen, there is often no financial price to be paid, and even when there is—as we shall see in chapter 5—the terms can be flexible and the price can sometimes be negotiated down. There are rarely difficult deadlines to meet.

But the dominance of the informal sector in the lives of our diary households should not be interpreted to mean that poor households are happy with the instruments available and have no need of anything else. Far from it. In the next section, we outline the limitations of informal finance, to help us imagine how we might improve financial services for the poor.

UNRELIABILITY

Many of the shortcomings of informal finance are aspects of its general *unreliability*. Its lack of capacity—its financial shallowness—is perhaps the most important. Your partners—be they reciprocal lenders, moneylenders who charge interest, or moneyguards to whom you have entrusted some savings—may simply not have the cash on hand when you need it. Or they may behave unreliably—promising you a certain sum at a certain time but failing to follow through. This is one of the greatest tensions in the financial lives of the poor: the people best placed to help—neighbors and family members—are typically poor themselves. They are trying to manage their own tenuous financial lives and are not always able to help others. Diary households often complained that they had to approach several lenders to put together even a small sum. Insecurity is another aspect of unreliability: savings stored at home can be lost, stolen, washed away in storms, captured by relatives, or eroded by trivial expenditure; savings stored with moneyguards or clubs can be poorly recorded and stored, or even misappropriated.

LACK OF PRIVACY

We have seen that the world of informal finance is accessed through networks based on kin, community, and workplace. That is not always good news. Reciprocity, for example, has costs as well as benefits: one diarist told us, "I don't like borrowing interest-free loans because then I'll be obliged to reciprocate." Informal deals are rarely private, and exposure to the public gaze can cause much social discomfort, a nonfinancial cost of informality. This can also be the case with borrowing from informal lenders who charge interest. Sultan, a carpenter in Delhi, told us that he prefers borrowing on interest from intermittent lenders in his squatter settlement, but dislikes it when they use one's debt as a basis for intimidation and rude behavior.

Approaching several people for loans before getting one is not merely an inconvenient outcome of the financial shallowness of the informal sector, but a source of stress and shame.

For migrants who have left poor families in the village to make good in the city, this embarrassment is acute. Somnath from Delhi, whom we met earlier in the chapter, avoided recourse to relatives at all costs, because he was ashamed and anxious that, if he couldn't repay on time, he would strain the relationship. Similar feelings were voiced by as many as half the Delhi respondents: they would go to several informal sources (colleagues, neighbors, the grocer, one's employer) before they would resort to relatives. Sultan the carpenter explained this reluctance, telling us that, although he has many relatives living close by who are in a better financial position than he, he avoids taking money from them. These relatives provide support out of love and duty, he told us, a kind of social security. If he took a loan from them and wasn't able to repay it, he might lose the social relationship with them, which he valued greatly.

The time, energy, and emotional toll of borrowing informally appear to be global phenomena. Rekha, from Bangladesh says, "I feel proud when I give loans and shameful when I have to take them. Still sometimes I have to take them, there's no other way of managing." Lungiswa from Lugangeni, South Africa, told us, "I would take groceries on credit from one place in town. The owner gives it to you easily, but then he also embarrasses you when he asks you in front of everyone when you are going to pay. So I'm going to take credit from another place, even though I'm charged interest." Ranju from Delhi's Okhla Industrial Area explained that she avoids immediate neighbors for reciprocal borrowing and lending since such people could hold it against her when they talk. Instead, she relies on two families from her village residing in the same slum but several lanes away.

LACK OF TRANSPARENCY

One might hope that being so open among neighbors and friends about your financial trials would at least reduce your chances of being duped. Unfortunately this is not always so: informal deals can lack transparency. Delhi respondents, for example, reported several cases of informal deals between individuals which went bad because of cheating. One moneyguard made off with two months' worth of a respondent's income. A "friend" of another respondent had given her fake gold as collateral for a secured loan. Two respondents had passed on their savings club receipts to friends in greater need who never paid up, and several respondents reported that wages kept back with employers were never fully paid.

In South Africa, *spaza* shops are local stores in townships and villages that cater to those without enough time or money to travel to larger stores in commercial centers. Because *spaza* shops' costs include transporting goods over bad roads and long distances, and because they have few competitors, prices are usually higher than in larger stores. One would therefore think that poor rural households would avoid these shops and put up with the inconvenience of travel to buy their goods elsewhere. But in our rural sample *spaza* shops were often used because one could take goods on credit and pay later in the month. Nearly 80 percent of the rural sample in the South African financial diaries used credit at these shops to bridge cash flows each month. But the terms of this arrangement were not transparent. The interest charged was not typically discussed, and borrowers often found that they owed money after they believed their debt to be paid.

An example is Mamawethu, a middle-aged woman living in rural Lugangeni, South Africa, with her two daughters and two grandchildren. Disabled by arthritis and asthma, she received a government grant of $115 a month. Two sons lived in Cape Town and sent remittances now and then, but for several months they were unable to do so. During that time, Mamawethu took credit worth $15 at one of the local *spaza* shops, and repaid several months later. However, the *spaza* shop owner told her that she still owed $54 because of the accumulated interest. In frustration, she used $54 from her savings club payout of $62 to pay back the *spaza* shop. During the next month, when she had no cash to buy groceries, she borrowed $15 from a moneylender. Even though she would pay 20 percent per month interest, at least, she said, she knew the rate was fixed.

Households in all three countries conducted an overwhelming proportion of their saving and borrowing on their own or with informal partners. Both the strengths and the weaknesses of these informal devices offer lessons for the design of financial services for the poor. We have noted that informal arrangements offer flexibility and convenience but may lack reliability, privacy, and transparency, and rely too heavily on kindness, goodwill, and norms of mutual obligation. An important element of reliability rests with rule-bound agreements, clear expectations on both sides of transactions, and professional relationships—elements essential to formal transactions but mostly absent in informal ones.

Enter the Formal Institutions?

If the formal sector is to meet the financial needs of the poor, more attention will have to be given to the cash flows of poor households. Two features of cash-flow-friendly finance have emerged strongly from this chapter: bite-size payments that can be extracted from normal household cash flows, and flexibility in payment schedules. Happily, both features have been taken up—separately—by formal providers seeking to do more business with the poor, and examples can be found in our diary work in South Asia.

The first of these features—small, frequent payments—has already been embraced by "semiformal" microcredit providers. Muhammad Yunus and his Grameen Bank—joined by others in Latin America, Africa, and Asia—offer loans that can be paid back in small weekly or monthly installments. Much of their success in showing that the poor are bankable has depended on this feature, which acknowledges and respects the small cash flows of poor households.

Bangladesh was the only one of our three countries where microfinance institutions had a large presence. Microcredit loans there were ostensibly restricted to business uses, but as Subir and Mumtaz's case shows, they can be diverted to other, sometimes multiple, uses—including short-term consumption needs. The loans were repaid in weekly installments starting the week after disbursement, and in almost every case where a microfinance loan was taken by a diary household, a fraction of the loan capital was retained at home to ensure that the first weeks of repayment would be covered. We take another look at how microfinance services were used in chapter 6.

When Subir and Mumtaz took a loan from the local microfinance NGO, they on-lent some of it, as we have seen, to their boarder Hanif, the young lad who slept in a corner of their hut. This worked well: Hanif got a capital sum he wanted, and repaid the loan by giving 10¢ of his wage each day to Mumtaz, which she deposited into her savings account at her NGO's weekly meetings. Both deals—that between Mumtaz and her NGO and that between Mumtaz and her boarder—worked well because the tiny-but-frequent repayment schedule matched their cash flows.

Informal devices often feature small, frequent payments (we will analyze them in more detail in chapter 4). But just as often they feature flexible payments, our second key feature. While there may be a general understanding of how and when a loan between neighbors, relatives, and colleagues is repaid, there is rarely a fixed date or schedule. While it may be difficult to raise an informal loan, there is a certain give and take in the modalities of repayment, because relations between borrower and lender are so often tied by kin, village, or workplace. This flexibility is mimicked by modern credit cards and overdraft facilities, and India's commercial banks have, in the last eight years, likewise tried to reproduce it by refashioning their seasonal crop loans as the "Kishan Credit Card."[10]

The seasonality and unpredictability of farm income, we have shown, leaves small and marginal farmers in dire need of products to help with cash-flow management. Those who can produce land documents have long accessed bank finance in India. But the loan products on offer were rigid, disbursed at particular times twice a year before each of the two agricultural seasons, to be repaid all at once after six months. Kishan Credit Cards disburse at any time, in whole or in parts, up to an agreed credit limit, to be repaid as preferred by the client, provided the whole balance is cleared once a year (after which a new draw can be made). Three households within the Indian sample were making use of this innovation, and as the following case of Tulsidas illustrates, the product's flexibility is highly appreciated, although further creative ingenuity and informal contacts are still required for a farmer to overcome seasonal and low income.

Tulsidas farmed 10 acres of fertile land and reared sheep, producing an annual income of about $700, supplemented by spending a few months each year in Bombay working as a security guard for $37 a month. Tulsidas's main challenge was to retain his harvest to avoid low prices for small amounts. Of a total produce of 6,300 kilos of grain, he sold 2,000 kilos for $164 in November 2000, soon after harvest, to finance the winter crop and buy warm clothes. Then from December right through August 2001 he lived on a bare minimum by selling 200 to 400 kilos a month. That August he sold sheep to finance the next crop. Out of his 6,300 kilos, he was left with 3,000 to be sold as prices climbed during the growing season.

December 2000 through July 2001 was thus a "strategic" lean period for Tulsidas, with spending kept to a minimum (an average of $37 a month for a family of 12) to realize the benefit of higher grain prices after August. Although he had a high credit limit on his Kishan Credit Card, he had spent it the previous year, to pay off debts and rebuild his house, and still owed the full balance of $575. However flexible its product, the bank couldn't be tapped at that moment.

Instead, Tulsidas managed to avoid selling more grain over these months thanks to a friend who ran a grocery store in the village. First, the grocer forwarded him groceries worth $72 to supplement the meager grain income. Second, in March 2001 when the bank asked Tulsidas to clear his loan with interest in full a year after he took it, he turned again to his grocer friend for help. Rather than selling off grain, Tulsidas persuaded him to put up the full sum of $575 for a few days, to allow Tulsidas to clear his balance and then draw down the full amount again. This he did, and with his fresh loan in hand, Tulsidas repaid his friend—and held on to his ever more valuable stock of grain.

Both Mumtaz and Tulsidas showed creativity in devising arrangements to fit their circumstances, taking a standard product—the NGO loan or the new-and-improved "crop loan"—but bending it to make it work for other ends. Such behavior is not unusual in the diaries. Being poor does not disqualify you from being inventive in your finances.

Both of the innovations we have described here—breaking loan repayments into small pieces, and flexible lines of credit for small and marginal farmers—help households manage loan installments despite the ups and downs of their incomes. They are good examples of designing products to fit real cash flows.

Conclusions

In developed countries, the aim of personal financial management is generally wealth accumulation and asset-building, acquisition of property, a retirement plan, and investment in children's futures. The view that aspirations like these should be achievable for the poor has taken root most firmly in the United States, where there has been a movement to create publicly subsidized savings plans for poor households, known as Individual Development Accounts (IDAs). The policy has been tested in studies dubbed the "American Dream Demonstration."[11]

Having more assets would certainly help the households in our study, adding a cushion in difficult times and creating resources for major investments. In chapter 4 we discuss the difficulties faced by our diary households when they try to create sums large enough to buy tangible assets like property and intangible ones like pension coverage. But we should beware of looking through *only* the asset-building lens when planning improvements in financial services for the poor: the diaries show that the challenges and priorities of the households are, in many ways, more fundamental.

Even when financial growth is low or absent year on year, just having access to basic financial services can have a fundamental impact, one that may be as important as asset-building. This is because when incomes are low, financial strategies need to focus in large part on coping with the irregularity and unpredictability of income in order to get food on the table and address other basics. If that focus is not in place, hunger and other forms of deprivation loom, and the household can slip quickly into destitution. The diaries reveal what one-off surveys tend to miss: poor-household incomes are not merely low but awkwardly timed, and the financial services used to address this irregularity in incomes are imperfect. This chapter has been devoted to the consequences of this triple whammy.

Not surprisingly, poor households put a great deal of effort into "cash-flow management"—making sure that money's on hand when needed to meet basic expenses. In the rich world, a household's portfolio of financial instruments is usually managed on the basis of risk and return. The portfolios of poor households are instead managed to ensure that money can be obtained in the desired amounts at the desired times. Money is scarce and its supply erratic, so dealing with cash flow is usually more urgent than calculating the best mix of return and risk. If wealthy households can indulge in a slow and steady style of financial management not unlike that of an established company, poor households tend to look more like start-up companies, judiciously allocating cash on hand and constantly looking out for new funds. Cash-flow analysis, rather than balance-sheet analysis, is the way to begin understanding their financial lives. These financial efforts, though, would have been hidden had we only looked at the accumulation of household assets from one year to the next. Year-opening and year-end balances may scarcely differ, but in the months between all manner of financial tools are used intensively.

Richer people manage their basic cash flow using a wide range of reliable devices: credit cards, debit cards, checks, automatic teller machines, and the like. But even they can run into cash-flow problems, so it is not surprising that poor households, who lack the luxury of such services, have to work even harder to manage their money. Patching cash-flow mismatches between income and expenditure is ideally done through saving and dissaving, but, because appropriate vehicles are hard to find, poor households more often turn to small-scale borrowing and lending with friends, relatives, neighbors, and employers. It is often hard work, and it can carry high costs—some of which are social and psychological and not just economic.

For poor households, then, having alternative sources of reliable, convenient, reasonably priced financial tools would make a big difference. In this context, it is notable, and even surprising, that helping them with cash-flow management has received limited attention in microfinance strategies.

◆ ◆ ◆

In recent years, business experts have made the case that the world's poor constitute an enormous and largely untapped market for goods and services, a next frontier for retail business. Marketers eye billions of dollars' worth of soaps, radios, mobile phones, and financial services to be sold to customers like our diary households if only retailers can develop the right products and marketing strategies.

If you take the view that the poor constitute a viable market—that there is a "fortune at the bottom of the pyramid," as C. K. Prahalad has put it—product development starts with a recognition of households' financial ups and downs. Seeing that the poor could not afford many of their existing products, multinationals like Proctor and Gamble and Unilever found a solution by selling single-serve packets of shampoo to poor households in India. The single-serve packages, costing a few cents each, turned out to be a popular option for people lacking the daily cash flow to easily purchase large bottles of shampoo, regular-sized tins of tea, 200-count bottles of aspirin, and the like.[12]

The innovation did not reside in the nature of the products. There is nothing special about the shampoo itself. Rather, it came from discovering a way to suit payments to patterns of household cash flows. The insight arose from understanding the financial lives of the poor and responding effectively to their needs.

What features are needed for a mass market in tools for cash-flow management for the poor? Our priority list would start with basic reliability and flexibility: services that are rule-bound, transparent, and simple to understand. Loans that are disbursed on the date promised, in the amount agreed upon, and at a standard price. Savings accounts that allow ready access and convenient withdrawals, with deposits and withdrawals made in any value. Insurance contracts that pay out quickly and with little haggling when needs arise. These qualities are demanded (and often taken for granted) by the world's richer households, but they are no less important for the world's poor.

The diaries show that informal financial mechanisms tend to be quite flexible, but not always reliable. Microfinance services, on the other hand, tend to be reliable, but not always flexible. One element of inflexibility in microfinance is the insistence by some lenders that all loans be invested in businesses. They do so partly because they believe that an important part of their mission is to foster economic development through business growth, and partly because they fear that loans cannot be repaid without revenue from business. The diaries show, however, that poor households need to borrow for a wide range of needs, not just business, and that they are prepared to find ways of repaying loans from ordinary household cash flow.[13] For the diary households, today's reality is that so-called business loans are already being used for many nonbusiness purposes, as chapter 6 will show. Embracing the notion that households seek loans for general purposes will open up possibilities for innovation and expansion for microfinance providers.

There are other simple ways to make loans more flexible. One idea common in informal lending (and sometimes in microfinance lending) is allowing penalty-free grace periods when cash-flow problems hit. Another idea, introduced by Grameen Bank in the past few years, is to allow borrowers to "top up" their loans (by borrowing again what they have repaid) part way through the repayment schedule, to increase liquidity. We return to this example in chapter 6. Another important path is the development of loans with a range of terms, including short-term "emergency loans."

Yet another innovation is to offer loans secured against liquid assets commonly held by the poor, since the security allows for more flexibility in repayment schedules. Here, the experience of India's banks is again instructive. Indian banks have fulfilled their obligation to lend to "priority sectors" (the poor) mainly by lending to jointly liable groups of poor customers (building on the pioneering work of the Grameen Bank). But the banks are also lending against deposits and gold, to individuals, at rates slightly higher than to joint liability groups but on more flexible terms. A 2003 study of five rural banks showed that such loans, while small in terms of dollars disbursed, account for 25–35 percent of all accounts. The study pointed out that it is the less well-off customers who pledge either their old fixed deposits or jewelry as security to tide over cash-flow constraints and concludes that—despite their non-priority sector classification, indeed perhaps because of it—these loans could become the principal banking product for low-income individuals.[14] Moreover, because poor households strive to enlarge their access to both savings and loan services, they are often happy to take loans secured against their own savings: indeed this is regarded by some of them as an ideal situation in which they enjoy liquidity even while they preserve their precious savings.

These features—small frequent payments, flexible schedules, and loans against small-scale physical and financial assets—are the ones we highlight for the specific task discussed in this chapter: managing money on a day-to-day basis. We do not dwell here on features important for the other key money-management tasks we have identified—risk management and building lump sums: these will be discussed in the next two chapters.

Improved money-management tools will not solve all the problems faced by poor households. But they will help them do better. In human affairs, incremental improvements can provide the basis for broader changes. Because, as the diaries show us, money management is a matter to which poor households themselves already devote much time and energy, the potential impact of improved tools is exceptionally promising.

Chapter Three

◆ ◆ ◆

DEALING WITH RISK

IN 1974, Jaleela and her baby fell seriously ill with dysentery. Jaleela, one of our Bangladeshi respondents, recalled the acute difficulty she then faced. The family had no savings to speak of, and her husband was unable to raise loans quickly enough to pay for treatment. He resorted to mortgaging her marriage jewelry to a pawnbroker. Happily, mother and child survived, though the jewelry was lost. Years later, her husband, a rickshaw driver, fell ill and couldn't work, and the family went hungry for three days until a neighbor supplied them with food. Then in 1992, Jaleela again fell seriously ill. She used a microfinance loan for treatment, but that wasn't enough: she had to draw down all her savings before she was cured.

To be poor in Bangladesh, India, or South Africa is to live not only with the difficulties of managing life on a day-to-day basis, but, like Jaleela's family, to live with the risk of large-scale disruption to lives and livelihoods. Jaleela's story shows that the disruption caused by health problems often requires solutions far beyond the medical cure. Even though Jaleela and her family eventually received medical treatment, their health problems also became financial problems. In each instance, financial solutions became part of the full equation they needed to solve.

In the previous chapter, we saw how the diary households went about stretching small, awkwardly timed incomes to ensure that they were able to put food on the table every day and fulfill other needs that arose. To achieve these basic objectives, they were driven to frequent small-scale intermediation, resulting in portfolios characterized by turnovers that were large relative to incomes, and which passed through many different kinds of financial instruments, most of them informal. The diaries revealed poor households to be active money managers, in search of flexible and reliable financial tools suited to their cash flows.

The financial diaries are also full of tales about the anxiety that comes from anticipating emergencies and dealing with them when they occur. Risk is omnipresent, despite the overall economic and political stability in the three countries we study. This chapter looks at the financial impact of these risks. We show how poor households cope, and describe the financial tools and strategies they have developed to shelter themselves. Self-help, of course, is no substitute for access to public safety nets and commercially based insurance. Neither typically exists in sufficient quality or quantity in poor communities, however, and we show how the diary households seize the tools at hand. Those tools offer protections that are too often fragile and incomplete, and we describe the improvements that can come from better access to insurance and, importantly, flexible ways to save and borrow.

If one did not know better, it might be tempting to assume that Jaleela and others we met through the financial diaries would be financially unsophisticated, and unable to use insurance products when offered. In fact, many of the households did use financial tools of one sort or another to protect themselves from risk. Some households purchased formal insurance contracts: they understood the terms, at least in broad outline, knew the costs, and tried hard to keep up with premium payments. All the same, much "insurance" was obtained through the same informal relationships with neighbors and relatives that, as we saw in the previous chapter, are used to deal with day-to-day money management needs.

Jaleela's story shows that when specialized instruments—formal or informal—are unavailable or insufficient, emergencies are addressed by selling assets, drawing down savings, and borrowing. Loans are a critical part of this mix, reminding us once again that borrowing for poor people is not only, or even mostly, for funding businesses but also for managing the many exigencies of a life of poverty.

The portfolio approach offers a further perspective. It shows how households work to meet their needs by patching together sums of money from different sources. Single solutions are rarely comprehensive, but they don't need to be so in order to be useful. While desirable in principle, comprehensive solutions can be complicated and expensive, raising the risk that they may never get off the ground or be sustainable. The portfolio approach shows the power of well thought-out partial solutions. Nowhere is this clearer than in examples of how South African households patch together resources for funerals.

Living with Risk

Poor communities live with risk as a matter of course. In 2000, national-level statistics show that in India and Bangladesh, for example, about 9 percent of children under age five died. In South Africa, about 6 percent died.[1] The child mortality rate reflects conditions—notably, weak health care infrastructures, poor sanitation, and the spread of infectious diseases—that intensify health risks for adults and the elderly as well. Coping with health risks can quickly become a major focus in the financial lives of the diary households.

During the research year, a total of 167 financial emergencies were experienced by our diary households. Table 3.1 shows the most frequently occurring kinds of emergencies for the three countries. Serious injury and illness, as well as death itself, predominate, followed by major losses to income and property.

Several contrasts between South Asia and South Africa are apparent. In South Africa one event—the funeral of a family member—dominates, and yet it doesn't feature in the top five or six events in either Bangladesh or India. This is because, as we shall detail in this chapter, funerals are expensive in South Africa. Social conventions

Table 3.1 Most Frequent Events Causing a Financial Emergency, by Country, with the Percentage of Country Sample Affected at Least Once during the Study Year

Bangladesh 42 households		*India* 48 households		*South Africa* 152 households	
Event	*%*	*Event*	*%*	*Event*	*%*
Serious injury or illness	50	Serious injury or illness	42	Funeral of family outside the household	81
Did not receive expected income	24	Loss of crop or livestock	38	Serious injury or illness	10
Fire/loss of home or property	19	Loss of regular job	10	Funeral of member of the household	7
Loss of crop or livestock	7	Theft	4	Theft	7
Business failure	7	Abandonment or divorce	4	Violent crime	4
Cheated/cash loss	7	Serious harassment by officials	4	Fire/loss of home or property	3

require funding elaborate gatherings before, during, and after funerals, and the rising rate of AIDS-related deaths means that these expensive events are becoming more frequent.

On the other hand the incidence of other shocks, such as illness and injury, income loss, and loss of property, is much higher for the diary households of Bangladesh and India than for the households of South Africa. A reason is that in Bangladesh and India, far fewer of our diary households enjoyed the social services that are available in South Africa. With regular government grants, emergencies are easier to deal with. And with free, state-run health clinics, serious illness, though it may mean time off work, is less likely to have a financial impact sharp enough to rate as an emergency, as it so often does in the other two countries.

Many of the property losses in Bangladesh were caused when slum environments were cleared by police or by contractors doing infrastructure work. Because Dhaka's urban slum dwellers are aware of these risks, they tend to invest less in housing that has an insecure tenure. Homes may be huts that are quickly packed up and shifted on a handcart to another location. When we revisited our Bangladeshi households in 2005, all three of our urban research sites had been wholly or partly destroyed since we were there in 1999–2000. Knowledge of the potential risks allowed the Bangladeshi households to take precautions and not overinvest in their homes.[2] So although one in five Bangladeshi diary households experienced the destruction of property, these losses were not necessarily the most severe that those households suffered in the year.

The high figure of 38 percent for loss of crop or livestock in India in table 3.1 is partly explained by a poor harvest during the research year, with losses stacked toward small and marginal farmers (those holding four acres or less) who, as discussed in chapter 2, lacked the resources to mitigate the effects of untimely rains and whose land was poorly positioned in relation to irrigation networks. The figure is further swelled by the risks associated with using livestock as a store of wealth—an imperfect strategy even in good times and one that, in bad times, leads to severe losses when animals become sick or are stolen.

The table shows events that happened to our households during the research year. But Jaleela's story above reminds us that a lifetime can be filled with many unexpected events, repeatedly setting poor households back and diminishing their chances of moving out of poverty.

Getting Protection

Individuals in rich countries prefer—and in some cases are legally obliged—to take out insurance to cover those things they stand to lose: their homes, their cars, their health, their lives. Had she lived in such a country Jaleela might have had health insurance to deal with her own illnesses and job security or unemployment benefits to deal with her husband's. Few of the financial diaries households were insured against emergencies or loss of assets, yet they faced a longer list of potential risks than a family living in a rich country, and for them the consequences of loss could be more dire. Low incomes and difficult living conditions leave poor households exposed to illness and crime. Their homes are not sturdy against weather and fire, and their livelihoods are not secure.[3]

Our diary households are not alone among poor people in being inadequately protected by insurance. Although many national surveys don't even ask about insurance, those that do ask find that few respondents have it. One study reports that fewer than 6 percent of the extremely poor in a wide range of countries are covered by health insurance, for example.[4]

Family and neighbors play important roles in the absence of such formal insurance arrangements, and economists have started to quantify the degree to which the informal mechanisms fill in gaps. One line of research focuses on "village insurance," where households in the same village "insure" each other against household-level shocks.[5] In the diaries, we do find many cases of neighbors helping each other out, not only with cash-flow management, as we saw in the last chapter, but also in risk management, as we'll see in this one. Much of that help is given in the form of reciprocal gifts or flexible loans between relatives. But less often do we see an entire community combining resources to help one particular family in need. Many households do participate in informal financial groups, like savings clubs. Rarely, however, are these groups based on the notion of the whole village coming together to help out those of its members who get into trouble—they are, rather, based on a structure of *self*-insurance.

Even in an example of informal insurance groups that we'll introduce in this chapter, the burial societies of South Africa, membership is not given automatically to everyone in the village. Each household has to contribute payments, and payouts are rule-bound and contingent on the amount paid in. This is not the "risk sharing" embedded in the concept of "village insurance." Households actively seek ways to individually self-manage their own risks through a variety of financial instruments, including reaching out to relatives. This suggests, as does the literature on village insurance, that simply relying on one's neighbors to help you out in an emergency is not enough—households (and extended kin networks) must and do try to self-insure.

Some of our diary households *were* investing in financial tools specifically designed to protect against emergencies. The tools fall into a small number of distinct categories: life insurance in India, life insurance and credit-life insurance in Bangladesh, and funeral coverage in South Africa. Each offers lessons for creating better financial tools.

INDIA: STATE-SPONSORED INSURANCE FOR THE POOR

India has long had a commitment to maintaining public safety nets.[6] The employment guarantee scheme started in Maharashtra state, for example, promises a low-wage job to any able-bodied worker who needs one. The scheme has been particularly good in helping poor workers patch together incomes during seasons when work is unavailable and during other times of difficulty. The government has also run public-backed social insurance in the form of subsidized group insurance schemes.

Until the opening of the sector to private providers in 2001, insurance in India was the monopoly of the state-run Life Insurance Corporation (LIC) and General Insurance Corporation (GIC). The legislation that opened the sector to private companies included a requirement that a proportion of policies must be issued to the "rural sector." At the time of our work (2000–2001), however, the only insurer that provided services to our respondents was the LIC. It offered a choice of endowment policies varying in values, terms, and payout arrangements. Clients pay life insurance premiums based on their age, making payments quarterly or biannually and taking back their savings with profits if they complete the term. If they face an accident or die during the term, they or their heirs take the full value of the matured policy.

LIC policies are marketed by freelance agents whose outreach is far greater than that achieved by any other insurance product. Eight (a sixth) of our Indian respondents were contributing insurance premiums during the research—all of them, bar one, in the rural site. None of the eight were from the poorest group but two were middle-ranking traders, with no or very little farmland.

One is Ismael, a cloth seller with elderly parents, a wife, and a growing family of four young children to support. He was already paying $6.50 a month toward two contractual savings schemes in a Post Office account when we first met him. Then an old friend who was an LIC agent persuaded him to buy an LIC endowment policy that required a premium of $39 every six months. After making the first premium payment Ismael realized that it would be a significant strain for him to raise that amount of money at a time, twice each year. He renegotiated with his friend to change to a policy that required a more manageable $10 every three months for an insured payout of $1,064 due after 20 years.[7]

For our poorest respondents, even premiums as low as $10 quarterly might have proved hard to manage. The problem is less the annual total of the payment, than the fact that respondents needed to pay a big lump sum quarter after quarter. One respondent told us he took his LIC policy from an agent who was related to him, even though he lived far away, because he knew his relative would advance the money if he couldn't pay the quarterly premium by the due date. Several other respondents revealed that they borrowed from elsewhere in order to meet the quarterly premium payments.

For households like Ismael's the policy would have been easier to manage if the premium was collected weekly or biweekly in smaller amounts.[8] Such policies do exist, but agents are reluctant to offer them because they entail more visits to the client. The unintended consequence is to screen out customers who are willing and able to pay but who require a payment plan more sensitive to cash flow. One solution, which is increasingly being seized on by insurers in India and elsewhere, is to partner with a microfinance institution (or similar entity) that regularly meets with customers—and engage it as the agent for premium collection. We describe another reason to create such partnerships in the next section.

BANGLADESH: "PRO-POOR" PRIVATE LIFE INSURERS AND CREDIT-LIFE COVERAGE

Bangladesh is famous for its microfinance institutions, and the hands-off approach that government has applied to them has also seeped into the insurance industry. The Bangladeshi government permitted private insurance companies before India did, and the country began experimenting with life insurance run by private, formal, regulated insurance companies designed with poor people in mind. Eight of the 42 Bangladesh portfolios held balances with these "pro-poor" insurers. Of these households, six were in the urban sample and two in the rural. This rather high level of penetration by the pro-poor insurers indicates, accurately, the speed with which they expanded soon after their start in the early 1990s.

As in India, the schemes took the form of life endowment policies. Most had 10-year terms. Clients paid a small weekly or monthly premium and took back savings with profits if they completed the term, or their heirs took the full value of a matured policy if they died. To keep things cheap and simple, the companies went against some of the established principles of insurance. Most strikingly, clients faced almost no selection criteria—no health check or other personal details were collected, for example, and people of almost any age could qualify to open a policy.

The insurers were deliberately trying to bring to life insurance what the microfinance institutions had done with credit, an ambition reflected in the weekly or monthly frequency of the premium (to keep it small), in the informal and decentralized operation in the slums and villages, and also in the decision to hold premium flows in the communities rather than bring them to the head office, and to lend them back to clients using microcredit methods (that is, in a group setting with frequent repayments made on loans with a one-year term). This combination—simplified life coverage attached to a 10-year savings plan with the added promise of borrowing rights—proved very attractive to many poor and middle-income households.

Alas, the schemes ran into trouble when they broke another established principle of insurance: they failed to provide a reliable service. The diaries have shown us that the first rule for any formal provider starting to serve the poor is that services should at least be more reliable than those available in the informal market. The Bangladeshi pro-poor insurers suffered multiple problems: administration was so loose that fraud became commonplace; nepotism was rife in the awarding of jobs; cash flows were not tracked, so that for many clients the promised loans never materialized; and many agents were incompetent or became lazy and failed to visit their clients regularly.[9]

Unfortunately for our diarists the research year (1999–2000) came just at the time when these problems peaked, with existing clients becoming anxious and would-be clients becoming cautious. This largely explains the ineffective performance that pro-poor insurance has in the Bangladesh portfolios. The two rural households—among the wealthiest and most aware—had already cancelled their policies and were trying to get their savings back. Neither made premium payments during the year: one of them managed to get back the full $5.50 he had contributed, but the other had mentally written off the $67 he had already invested. Much the same was true in the urban sample: three clients had lost touch with their agent. Sadly for her, Khadeja, whom we met in chapter 1, was one of them. By the end of the research year, her agent had simply stopped coming, and she was unable to trace him, losing $76 in the process. That left three urban clients who had paid in during the research year. But of these three, only one had paid in full each month to an agent who was calling regularly. No one got the promised loans.

Since the research year, the insurance companies running these schemes, especially the well-known one that had devised it, have tried again. We didn't find evidence of improvement when we revisited our diary households in 2005—none of the households mentioned in the previous paragraph got their money back—but we are aware that the schemes have been relaunched with many modifications. Their failure in the first round illustrates the difficulties of offering such services *en masse* without a firm foundation in the villages and slums. The microfinance institutions, of course, have such a foundation: they run weekly meetings with batches of clients with whom they have many transactions, so it is much easier for them to bring on new products. This situation has led some observers to recommend partnerships—say between microfinance institutions and formal insurance companies—as a promising way to offer good-quality insurance products to poor people, and a number of trials of this method are now running.[10]

That brings us to the second kind of insurance used by our Bangladesh households. Nearly all microfinance providers were offering debt forgiveness on death, or "credit-life" insurance, as one of the features of their lending. Payment for these schemes was built into the price of the loan, so they don't appear separately in the portfolios. Still, some 21 households, one-half of our sample, held a microfinance loan at some time in the year, and most of them would have been covered by such schemes, which are generally liked by clients. Some providers have gone beyond this form of insurance, offering payouts on the death of any current client irrespective of her loan or savings status. The Grameen Bank diaries (described in chapter 6) show that several microfinance institutions currently offer such a product both to their predominately female clientele and to their husbands.

SOUTH AFRICA: FUNERAL COVERAGE

By far the most interesting country in respect to insurance and risk-coping offerings for poor households is South Africa, and we will examine it in some detail.[11] South Africa has a strong, rich-world-style insurance industry supplying a broad range of products. However, these instruments were not much used by our diary households, and, where they were found, they were mostly held by the better off in the sample.

A notable exception to this rule is funeral insurance. Funerals are extremely important events in South Africa, requiring enormous time, energy, and money. The severe impact of HIV/AIDS has led to a dramatic increase in the probability of death before the age of 60 in South Africa's population.[12] Although medical and care-taking costs

Table 3.2 Stages in Holding a Funeral, South Africa

Immediately following the death	The funeral parlor is contacted and burial arrangements made
Then, for 1–2 weeks	Prayer meetings are held until the funeral takes place; refreshments are provided for 20–70 people.
2–3 days before the funeral	Relatives from other areas arrive; the household of deceased must feed, and often host, them. Food is bought for the funeral.
Funeral	The funeral starts with a prayer meeting at the deceased's home for 200–600 people; mourners then travel to the cemetery in rented taxis or buses (paid for by household of the deceased); mourners return to the house for the feast (4–6 sheep or a cow slaughtered, and vegetables, rice, potatoes, and salads served).
Umkhululo: the ceremony that accompanies the shedding of funeral clothes	Takes place several months after the funeral. There is a feast and African beer is served.

Source: Roth 1999 and Collins 2005.

during illness are also burdensome,[13] our financial diaries show that these costs are dwarfed by the overwhelming cost of funerals. Table 3.1 shows that deaths affected more than four-fifths of the South African diary households during the study year, and funerals were by far the most common financial emergency they had to face.

The complexity of South African funerals, set out in table 3.2, begins to explain why they are such financial and emotional burdens. One broad study of funerals in South Africa showed that, for households with incomes in the range of $155-$300 a month, funerals typically cost in the order of $1,500.[14] The South African financial diaries suggest that households need to spend about seven months' income on a single funeral. Such costs cannot be met out of cash flow, and if they are to be met at all a financial instrument, or combination of financial instruments, must be brought into play. In response to this situation, South African households do not only rely on whatever savings they have and whatever loans they can get: almost all of them invest in special financial instruments that we will refer to generally as "funeral insurance".

About 80 percent of the South African diary sample had at least one funeral insurance scheme of some kind in place during the research year, and most respondents had more than one. There are several types of funeral insurance in use, formal and informal, which we place in three general categories. Regulated financial companies[15] offer formal "funeral plans." In these, a monthly premium is collected either by cash or through a debit order on a bank account. When the death occurs and a death certificate is produced, the company pays out, usually in the form of a cash lump sum. During the study year 26 percent of our diary households held at least one plan of this sort.

A second category is informal policies administered through groups, usually in the village or local neighborhood, called burial societies; 57 percent of our diary households were members of such groups during the research year.[16] Though they are all community-based, they run along differing lines. In one common variant, the members pay regular premiums in cash at a monthly meeting, and the fund is accumulated in a bank account in the society's name. Normally it is not lent out, though exceptions occur. Everyone pays the same amount, so when a death occurs the relatives receive a set payout that may be in cash, kind, or both.

Both of these devices work by collecting premiums in regular increments and in small amounts. The practice reinforces an idea discussed earlier in the context of the Indian insurance providers: price is not the only determining factor of demand. It also matters very much how and how often collections are made.

Other kinds of burial societies use a very different practice and are less structured. In this kind of society, members do not pay monthly premiums or hold regular meetings, and no transactions take place except when a death occurs. Instead, they rely on reciprocity—members promise to give a set amount of cash or to contribute food in kind when a funeral affecting any other member takes place.

Another form of coverage is offered by funeral parlors. These businesses collect contributions, usually in cash at monthly intervals. Subscribers may drop in at the parlor to pay, or the parlor may send someone round to the home. When a death happens, they provide a fixed set of goods and services, and sometimes a lump sum of cash to the bereaved. During the study year 24 percent of our diary households held policies of this sort with funeral parlors. In practice, funerals are paid for by combining resources from a variety of sources—and we give examples of that below.

Between them our South African diary households invested heavily in funeral coverage. Of the 80 percent who held funeral insurance of some kind, many were multiply covered, using more than one kind of plan or having more than one account in any one type of plan. Out of an overall portfolio of 17 financial instruments, households would usually have at least one informal funeral instrument (a burial society) and one formal funeral instrument (a company or funeral parlor plan). Funeral coverage made up at least 10 percent of the instruments that composed the household portfolios, with households spending an average of 3 percent of gross monthly income in total for all of their funeral coverage instruments.

In a later section we will be looking carefully at how well these schemes worked in the event of an actual funeral. But before doing so we can consider, first from a theoretical position, and then colored by our intimate knowledge of the households, whether they were getting their money's worth, and which plans offered the best value.

A rough way to compare policies is to assess the coverage per rand contributed. This is the payout that the insured would receive for each member covered, divided by the monthly premium paid. We put together data for the 132 financial diaries households with any type of funeral plan, burial society, or funeral parlor plan and did a basic coverage-per-dollar-contributed calculation, taking into account differences in the number of people covered under each plan. In most cases the number of people covered ranged between four and six.

Higher coverage per dollar contributed means better value. We calculated the coverage per dollar contributed for the three main types of coverage. The value of burial societies seems to run neck-and-neck with formal funeral plans. Burial societies offer an average of just over $105 of coverage per dollar contributed, compared with an average of just under $105 of coverage per dollar contributed for formal funeral plans. In comparison, funeral parlor plans run a distant third, offering only $84 of coverage per dollar contributed.

It is particularly striking that the informal instruments—the burial societies—provide such good value on financial terms alone, even before taking into account other social benefits. Members of a burial society usually receive a great deal of practical assistance and moral and psychological support around the time of the funeral. Not only do fellow members provide comfort during the mourning period, they also take up much of the work of preparing and serving the feast during the burial, often providing the cookware and eating utensils. If one were to take the social benefits of burial societies into account, they would look even more attractive than formal funeral plans.

The downside is that burial societies are not always reliable. They offer attractively high payouts for low premiums, but do not always have the financial strength to deliver them. In the year that we ran our diaries, none of our sample households suffered from failure by a burial society, but we know from other sources that many burial societies experience cash-flow problems, risking insolvency. FinScope, a survey of financial behavior in South Africa, shows that close to 10 percent of burial societies run out of money and fail to honor their obligations.[17] If we take this institutional risk into account, burial societies look less attractive.

And although burial societies on the whole may seem to offer better value than formal funeral plans, a few formal funeral plans were very competitively priced. Indeed, we can use diary data to examine the pricing of formal and informal funeral insurance products in the context of a specific household.

Thembeka is a 44-year-old woman living in Lugangeni with her two teen-age children. Her husband works in the mines in Johannesburg and sends home money every month. Among households in Lugangeni, Thembeka's enjoys slightly above average income. Moreover,

Thembeka works hard to manage the income well, and she prides herself on being very involved in several savings clubs (which we'll discuss in the next chapter).

Thembeka has three funeral instruments—two burial societies and one funeral plan. The funeral plan is with a well-known funeral insurance company in the area, and Thembeka pays her monthly fee straight into their account at the Post Office.[18] The two burial societies are not as regular. For one of them, she pays every month, plus an additional fee whenever someone dies. For the other, she pays in kind whenever someone dies, with no monthly fee. All the plans cover Thembeka and her husband, plus the two children who live with them and two older children who live outside the household. In total, if they had to pay for funerals for the entire family, they would need about $7,700. However, the plans will pay out just under $4,500, so they, like most of the financial diaries respondents, are underinsured.

In terms of financial value, Thembeka's funeral portfolio is fairly typical of others in her village. Table 3.3 details the coverage she held. The overall coverage per dollar contributed was $60 compared to an average household portfolio coverage per dollar contributed of $68 in the village. It would appear that the first burial society offers the best value. However, this plan is one where all the members need to contribute every month, and if the rate of funerals increases, the value will erode quickly. Thembeka had only belonged to this burial society for two years when we met her, so it still had a little time to prove itself. On the other hand, she had belonged to the funeral plan since 1985, and she had been able to observe its reliability over time.

This information suggests that formal banks can offer a product that competes effectively with burial societies and be welcomed by consumers. One well-known retail bank in South Africa provides a funeral plan for $5.88 a month with a payout of $2,322, enough to pay for most of the funeral costs.[19] These plans are aimed at the kind of low-income households in our financial diaries sample—several of them had subscribed to this plan and others were considering doing so. One concern, however, is that these plans often have layers of

Table 3.3 Thembeka's Portfolio of Funeral Coverage

Type of funeral insurance	*Coverage*	*Monthly premium*	*Expected payout*	*Coverage per dollar contributed*
Burial society	Covers 2 adults and 4 children	Pay in kind when someone dies; usually costs $3.08 each time	$2,154	$108
Burial society	Covers 2 adults and 4 children	Pay a monthly premium of $3.10 plus contribute whenever someone dies	$1,538	$38
Funeral plan	Covers 2 adults and 4 children	$3.28	$769	$35
Overall portfolio average				$60

Note: US$ converted from South African rand at $ = 6.5 rand, market rate.

administration that make it difficult to get the payout in time to purchase all the things needed for the funeral. Speed and ease of payout matter a great deal to households, and improving these systems would help make these types of plans attractive and beneficial to more poor households.

These formal funeral plans will more likely complement rather than displace traditional burial societies. Several diary households with formal plans continue with their burial societies because they provide social benefits as well as financial ones. Members are likely to continue to value that solidarity even if they purchase an additional formal funeral plan.

As we mentioned above, Thembeka is underinsured for her expected funeral costs, and this is typical for our South African diary households. For two-thirds of them, the funeral policies they hold would not cover the total expense of the funeral, and in most cases would pay for less than half. As a result, as we show in the next section, funds for funeral expenses are pieced together from a variety of sources, even though funeral policies do take care of a large chunk of those costs.

Patching from Here and There

So far we have looked at the take-up of specialist instruments that are available to some of our diary households for dealing with risk: life and some other forms of insurance in India, life endowments and credit-life coverage in Bangladesh, and funeral coverage in South Africa. We turn now to what happens when an emergency actually occurs.

In South Africa, where many of our diary households suffered deaths, diary data provide us with reliable accounts of how the funerals were financed. The data in table 3.4 come from the rural funeral held when the mother of one of our diarists passed away. Xoliswa's mother, Busisiwe, died in April 2004. Until then, Busisiwe's old-age grant of $115 per month was used to feed all five members of the household—Busisiwe, Xoliswa, and three children. Added to the expense of the funeral was a debt of $108 owed to the owner of the local *spaza*—a village general store—from a loan taken during Busisiwe's illness to pay doctor's fees. This loan had to be settled, and was repaid at the time of the *umkhululo* (the ceremony that accompanies the shedding of funeral clothes), as the sources-and-funds analysis in table 3.4 shows.

For the funeral, Xoliswa spent just over $2,400. The funeral plan with the funeral parlor provided the coffin, undertaker's fee, and cost of collecting the body, worth about $465. In addition, the funeral plan paid out $464 in cash to help pay for the funeral feast. A burial society paid out an additional sum, in cash, of $155. Xoliswa also received payouts from two savings clubs that Busisiwe belonged to, worth a total of $155. The relatives gave her 13 goats, 10 of which were slaughtered for the funeral. They saved the other three goats for the *umkhululo* that followed a month later. The relatives also gave about $279 in cash. About $449 was spent on other food, and the balance saved for the *umkhululo*. As in other funerals we analyzed, a

Table 3.4 Sources and Uses of Funds for Xoliswa's Mother's Funeral

Sources of funds		*Uses of funds*	
		The funeral	
13 goats from relative	906	Slaughtered 10 goats for funeral	697
Cash contributions from relatives	279	Bought and slaughtered 1 cow for funeral	310
Cash payout from burial society	155	Food for funeral	449
Cash payout from funeral parlor	464	Coffin and funeral fees, provided by funeral parlor	465
Funeral parlor provision of coffin and funeral fees	465	Saved 3 goats for *umkhululo*	209
Savings club payouts	155	Save for *umkhululo*	279
Total	$2,424	Total	$2,409
		The *umkhululo*	
3 goats saved from funeral	209	Repaid store owner	108
Additional cash contributions from relatives	280	Slaughter cow (exchanged for 5 goats)	348
Saved money from relatives' funeral contributions	279	Bought 2 goats (for exchange for cow)	139
		Bought food for *umkhululo*	170
Total	$768	Total	$765

Note: US$ converted from South African rand at $ = 6.5 rand, market rate.

large portion of the cost of the funeral—in this case 60 percent—was for food.

The table itemizes the sources and uses of funds for both the funeral and the *umkhululo*. Of the total cost of the funeral, the burial society payout was 6 percent and the funeral parlor plan payout (including both the cash and the in-kind provision of the coffin and services) was 39 percent, so that, in all, insurance paid 45 percent. But cash and in-kind contributions from relatives also took a large portion of the cost (49 percent). The savings club payments made up the rest.

In addition to the funeral, Xoliwsa's family needed to give the *umkhululo*. They had this feast a month later, in May, and it required another complicated set of transactions and expenses. At this stage they were also under pressure from the store owner to repay the $108 loan they took from him during Busisiwe's illness. To fund the expenses of the *umkhululo*, they took the three remaining goats that relatives had donated for the funeral and used $139, saved from the relatives' cash contribution to the funeral, to buy two more goats. They then exchanged the five goats for one cow, which they slaughtered for the feast. The relatives also contributed another $280. The event required them to spend about $170 for food. None of these expenses were covered by insurance.

Xoliswa's case, then, shows that her two investments in insurance—the funeral parlor plan and the burial society—provided her with a sizable portion of her funeral costs when her mother died. For the remainder of the costs, she had to turn to relatives for support, and to draw down savings from her mother's saving club (more on these sources in the next chapter), but her two funeral plans certainly helped her manage these heavy costs on a very meager income.

◆ ◆ ◆

Despite Xoliswa's forethought in buying funeral coverage, in the end she found herself in the situation that typifies our diary households from all three countries: for the most part, the financial consequences of emergencies have to be anticipated, and then dealt with, using general-purpose financial tools mainly of an informal kind. Because Xoliswa had generous relatives and a store of savings she could access, she didn't have to borrow. But that isn't always the case, as our second example of a South African funeral shows.

Thembi was a 50-year-old woman in a low-income township, living in a house that she had inherited from her parents. She was a member of an informal burial society and of a savings club, but hadn't

Table 3.5 Sources and Uses of Funds for Thembi's Brother's Funeral

Sources of funds		*Uses of funds*	
Payout from burial society	154	Undertaker	538
Contribution from relative	231	Tent	91
Contribution from relative	154	Pots	35
Contribution from relative	154	Food	649
Rental of tent by relative	91	Sheep	100
Rental of cooking pots by relative	35		
Purchase of sheep by relatives	100		
Borrow from aunt's burial society (no interest)	154		
Borrow from cousin's savings club (30 percent per month)	92		
Borrow from cousin (no interest)	108		
Thembi's grant money	92		
Brother's grant money	49		
Total	$1,414	Total	$1,413

Note: US$ converted from South African rand at $ = 6.5 rand, market rate.

managed to accumulate much savings. She struggled with depression and several other chronic illnesses and spent heavily on medication. Her brother, who lived with her, died from tuberculosis in June 2004.

Because her brother lived under her roof, Thembi was responsible, by local custom, for paying for the funeral. She knew that her burial society would pay out $154, but didn't know where the remainder of the money would come from. Table 3.5 shows a consolidated set of accounts for the funeral.

Of the sources of funds for the funeral, only 11 percent came from the burial society. The lion's share (76 percent) was paid for by relatives. Even then, Thembi needed to find an additional $495, and for someone living on a disability grant of $114 per month, plus a part-time job paying about $55 per month, this was a huge burden. She had no savings she could draw on—the money was locked up in a club that she couldn't access for some months. She spent $92 from her grant income, and she found $49 of her brother's own disability grant among his clothes, but that still left her needing to borrow. Happily, a cousin offered an interest-free loan of $108, and she was able to borrow a further $154 from a burial society of which her aunt was the treasurer.[20]

For the final $92 Thembi went to a cousin's saving club and took a loan at 30 percent a month, hoping that she would be able to repay it quickly. Her choice of lenders was very restricted. She had no regular job and no payslip, so none of the formal lenders would advance her the money. Moreover, most would not lend such a small amount. Thembi knew this and, under stress to produce enough money for the funeral, didn't want to undertake an expensive bus ride and an intimidating visit to a formal bank, just to be told that she couldn't have a loan. She knew that her cousin belonged to a savings club that earned money for its members by lending the fund out (more on these practices in the next chapter). It was convenient and friendly, if potentially expensive, to use their service. The remainder of the year was spent trying to pay back the loans from these various sources. She managed to pay back the burial society loan within two months, but had paid back neither her cousin nor her savings club by the end of the year.

Health Problems Are Financial Problems

When emergencies happen, households reach for whatever resources they can. Often these coping mechanisms are expensive. Worse, they may seriously damage the household and its future prospects, devouring assets or destroying livelihoods or imposing intolerable debt. The stories below show how poor health affects people's lives, sometimes playing out—through the costs of debt burdens and depleted assets—long after the initial problem has been solved. Health problems rapidly become financial problems.

Mahenoor's situation is an example of selling off precious assets to no avail. She headed the poorest rural household in our Bangladesh sample, and she told us how her family fell into such a state. A decade ago, her husband Salil had been a rickshaw owner and driver, and the household viewed itself as only moderately poor. One evening in 1989 he came home complaining of a pain in his throat. He went to a local doctor and paid for treatment, but it was not successful. He first sold one of his rickshaws, for $34, and then his remaining two rickshaws, for further treatment, again to no avail. His health continued to deteriorate quickly, and he was advised to seek admission to a hospital.

During this period, the five-person household—the couple had three small children—went without income. They borrowed from their friends and neighbors to survive, but they had no source of a loan big enough to finance hospitalization and an operation. No one in the family belonged to a microfinance institution. Even if they had, it might have taken time to get the first loan, which would have likely been small. By now Salil was desperate to cure his illness. He persuaded his wife that they should sell the land that she had received from her family at the time of their marriage. With the proceeds he was admitted to a hospital in the capital. But he died a few days later, from throat cancer. His widow and family were left without a breadwinner, without assets, and saddled with debts.

Shikha and Dinesh are couple from our Indian urban sample who went through two health emergencies, and, although they had better luck than Mahenoor, their extensive borrowing continued to be a burden for years after. They came to Delhi from their home village in 1995 in a state of destitution. They hadn't always been poor: they used to own four acres of fertile land. But two years before they left, Dinesh fell desperately sick, coughing up blood. The family was obliged to start selling their land to pay for treatment, and in the end it all went. Dinesh's illness continued, and in less than a year, Shikha accumulated debts of $212 owed to members of a wealthy moneylending clan at a rate of 5 percent per month. Working hard in others' fields with her son, Shikha managed to clear the debts, but they were left with no farm.

Dinesh, cured, found a job in Delhi as a supervisor in a garment factory. The family followed, and Shikha and her daughter got work as housemaids. Then in 1997, the couple's son contracted tuberculosis, and again they borrowed from any possible source to finance his treatment: $85 from the village, a $212 advance from Dinesh's company, a $212 loan from Shikha's employers, a $21 interest-free loan from their absent landlord, a $64 loan from a shopkeeper (at 10 percent per month interest), and a $32 loan from a wealthy neighbor in the lane, also at 10 percent monthly interest. The total debt outstanding was $1,270, of which $106 was still to be repaid three years later when we met them. Although the couple was able to cope far better than some, with higher income and access to more borrowing opportunities from their employers and neighbors, they carried a heavy debt burden for a long time.

These two examples show that the financial tools poor households turn to when in trouble are often loans. Better ways to borrow reliably and at reasonable prices would have helped them.[21] But, in the end, loans are not the best solution to such medical emergencies. These are problems of risk—problems for which insurance is designed. Not having insurance imposes a double burden on families. First, major health-related emergencies create an urgent need for cash. Second, emergencies simultaneously diminish the ability to repay loans. Salil was in no position to work, nor was his family able to earn much after he died. Dinesh's illness led to a sell-off of land, and forced his wife to take on added burdens. Only insurance arrangements (or tax-funded public safety nets) can aggregate these kinds of risks, provide urgently needed resources at the right time, and do so without creating additional obligations.

Two Sides of Moral Hazard

One of the concerns that economists have about insurance is the problem of moral hazard: that being insured for one's health may also change one's behavior. The problem arises if the insured start neglecting themselves, knowing they have insurance to cover health problems in the future, which increases the likelihood that they will need insurance. The theorist's solution—and the one that underpins rich-world insurance—is to avoid insuring the whole of the risk. Rather, "optimal" insurance contracts expose insured populations to part of the risk as a way to induce them to take due caution and thereby align their incentives with those of the insurer. Typically this is done through a system of copayments (so that the insured must pay a fraction of the health bills) and deductibles (so that coverage begins only after a certain amount of expenditure is incurred).[22]

However, the diaries show a clear flip-side: if doctor's fees, diagnostic tests, and treatment must be paid for directly and there is little cash to spare, treatment may be avoided until health deteriorates seriously, possibly beyond recovery. This is often the case for poor people who have many competing demands on tiny incomes, as the following case illustrates.

Feizal is a 40-year-old man from our rural India sample a mobile trader of aluminum pots. For the first few months of our research, his wife, son, and seven daughters survived on a monthly income averaging $36 that came largely from his trade, along with his son's stipend as a tailor's apprentice and *bidi* rolling (making cheap cigarettes) by the women of the household. Midway through our research, in December, Feizal had a bad fall from his bicycle and fractured his thigh bone, abruptly terminating the main source of income and pushing the household into debt to pay for groceries. Through January and February, the family sought treatment from two traditional doctors at a cost of $33, paid for by the son's wage advances and bank savings that had been put aside for the impending wedding of the eldest daughter. Even when Feizal's leg showed no improvement, the family behaved as though things were normal, spending $30 on the Eid festival and resolving to marry their daughter in the coming season.

Nearly three months after the accident, Feizal's father stepped in and took Feizal to a doctor in Allahabad city who uses more modern methods. The trip, of course, incurred new costs on a scale the family was quite unaccustomed to. They managed to find $53 for diagnostic tests from their bank savings and another wage advance from the son, and a further $64 in doctor's fees was taken on credit. At the beginning of April, there was only $10 left of the $60 saved for their daughter's wedding. But Feizal's father had cleared the major hospital charges of $106, and he assured them he would clear the doctor's bill as well.

By early July, Feizal was mending and finally able to ride his bicycle again. He had earned nothing for nearly eight months, including the period when he would normally bring in most of the income for the year. The savings put aside with great difficulty over the years to fund the marriage of the first of seven daughters were greatly depleted, and the family was more than $100 in debt. But Feizal had received high-quality care, which would have been unthinkable had his father not agreed to pay for it.

In the end, the costs of the accident—both the direct cost of treatment and the indirect costs of earnings forgone—were far greater than they would have been had Feizal gone to a good doctor in the first place. But he went first to a traditional doctor because it was affordable. If he'd known how serious the break was, he told us, he would perhaps have approached it differently, but at the time the priority was to keep saving toward the impending wedding. If Feizal could have relied on an insurance product, paying small amounts dispersed over time, he would have had the incentive to seek early advice, from higher-quality doctors, at much lower cost. This brings us back to one of our central premises, offered at the beginning of the book, that unreliability in financial tools reinforces other areas of vulnerability in the lives of the poor.

Toward Better Tools

The poor need to protect themselves against risk, but commercial insurance contracts, the financial instrument that is purpose-built to do this job, were not commonly used by the diary households. That is not because poor households do not appreciate that financial tools can be used as a shelter against risk, nor because they are in principle averse to using them. On the contrary, households use many tools to combat risk. We described one important tradition of "popular" insurance—the burial schemes of South Africa—that is flourishing. Its existence suggests that given a risk that is frequent and pressing enough, poor households will develop specialized mechanisms to anticipate and, at least partially relieve, its consequences. Similar mechanisms exist for major *planned* financial undertakings such as weddings, as we will see in the next chapter. But the fact that the South African burial schemes stood out as unusual suggests that the difficulties of arranging insurance is one of the main weaknesses of the informal sector. To work, informal insurance schemes need to bind users together in associations that endure over long periods of time, a task that gets ever harder as populations become more mobile and occupations individualized.

Some households also used formal schemes, notably pro-poor life insurance in India and Bangladesh, and funeral plans offered by companies in South Africa. The schemes in India and Bangladesh arose from poverty eradication and development projects, promoted by governments or social entrepreneurs deliberately targeting the poor. In South Africa, where traditional burial societies have long served as funeral insurance for the community, insurance companies and banks have begun to offer similar services. Today informal burial societies coexist with formal funeral policies. Each of these approaches to expanded insurance provision can be developed further. In insurance, partial solutions are welcome: no single intervention can solve all the problems, nor does it need to.

Providing insurance poses challenges absent in providing credit. Most important, the insurance company must earn the trust of customers, while for credit the reverse is true: it is customers who must earn the trust of bankers. Providing insurance profitably also entails high-quality actuarial analysis, careful pricing policies, and wise investments: these are complex skills not widely available outside the formal insurance industry, a fact that makes it hard for informal and semiformal providers to compete with formal providers in the way that they have so spectacularly succeeded in doing for microcredit. On the other hand, insurers like those entering the funeral insurance market in South Africa must not only be confident that moral hazard and fraud are kept to a minimum, but, in order to compete successfully with informal schemes, they must bring down the costs and increase the speed of verifying claims and making payouts. They also need better marketing strategies and better ways of spreading risk through market-based tools.

Insurers need help reaching the poorer and more remote groups. One solution is to form partnerships between formal insurance companies (who have the know-how in the sophisticated areas of actuarial analysis and investment) and microfinance institutions (who have the outreach to large numbers of poor households). Such partnerships are already under way around the world. India, for example, had 35 micro health insurance schemes running in 2006, under this partner-agent model, with nearly 900,000 policyholders.[23]

The diaries show us why microfinance institutions are good at the retail end of this partnership. Their regular contact with clients in their own slums and villages allows them to break up the loan repayments into more manageable pieces. The installments then become small and frequent enough to suit the cash flows of poor households (while not driving transaction costs too high). The same principles apply to collecting insurance premiums. Given all of the other elements of designing a workable insurance product, it is easy to overlook the important role of a convenient payment plan. This chapter has demonstrated the importance of payment systems for the poor households we came to know. Translating that understanding into product design is a key to launching new products for the poor. It is not just the total cost of the product that matters: it is also the timing and the size of installments.

Innovative financiers can also build risk-mitigating functions into services already being mass-marketed to the poor: examples include credit-life insurance built into loans and life insurance built into long-term savings products. SEWA Bank, a pioneer among India's microfinance institutions, has even built health insurance into its savings products, when it docks premiums directly from returns on the fixed deposits of women members.[24]

As formal insurance strives to attract poorer clients, it will prove easier to achieve growth in some forms of coverage than in others. When insured events are easy to define, extending coverage, such as in life and credit-life insurance, is cheap because it is less risky and requires less paperwork and less checking in the field. This efficiency may apply as much to informal as to formal insurance, helping to explain why community-based funeral coverage has thrived in South

Africa, whereas we found no equivalent in the field of health. Other risks that are insurable in principle, such as crop or livestock loss, are harder to implement in practice because of moral hazard, outright fraud, and documentation difficulties—it is notoriously difficult to know exactly whose cow it was that died, or indeed whether it died of natural causes.

Because of these limitations, the poor will continue to face many risks that are not easily insurable. The list of common emergencies in table 3.1 includes, for example, violent crime and the failure to receive a payment. Where financial tools are not available, the result can be emergency asset sales; in the worst cases, those sales strip households of the means to earn future income, triggering a downward spiral toward destitution.

These cases provide rationales for basic public health services, social protection, and other redistributive policies. We saw in South Africa, for example, how important government pensions have been in providing stability for poor households. India and Bangladesh, too, provide forms of state aid and support from NGOs. But such aid only goes so far.[25]

With private insurance unavailable and holes in safety nets, the financial tools for dealing with risk will likely continue to be savings and loans, and not just because of the unavailability of formal insurance. A big advantage of loans and savings is that they are general-purpose tools. Money is fungible, so that a loan issued for one use can be diverted to deal with an emergency if necessary. Insurance is not structured in this way: providers need to be certain that money is only paid out against the insured event. In theory this requirement shouldn't bother poor households: if the risk is real and the coverage represents good value, they should buy it. But in practice poor households may feel that, given their very small resources, they are better off using general-purpose tools. After all, the insured risk may never occur, in which case insurance premiums give no return (other than peace of mind), whereas savings become available for other uses. For this reason, schemes where insurance coverage is attached to what are essentially loan and savings products—as in credit-life insurance, and in life-endowment savings—may appeal to poor households more than a fat portfolio of policies against each and every risk.[26]

Emergency loans, which can be used in any exigency, have proved popular where they have been introduced by microlenders, as by SKS in India and BURO in Bangladesh, among many others. They tend to be very standardized: a fixed amount and a relatively short term of, say, three months, and intended to be taken for any purpose rather than crafted for a specific risk. They may not provide just the right sum over just the right period of time, but they help, partly because, as we have seen in this chapter, poor households are used to patching together resources from a number of providers, and a loan from a nearby source that is disbursed quickly with little fuss can be enormously valuable.

This suggests a broader lesson about insurance. The cost of offering commercially viable comprehensive health insurance to poor households—a service that would have relieved Mahenoor from having to sell all the family's land in order to get her husband into hospital for a doomed attempt to save his life—would almost surely entail premium payments that would be beyond the reach of even the best-off households. But there could nevertheless be substantial demand for cheaper—but more limited—partial health coverage, such as prescription drug benefits or catastrophic health coverage. Funeral insurance in South Africa likewise usually covers just part of total funeral expenses—but still provides meaningful funds at critical times. The portfolio approach suggests that it is not necessary to solve an entire problem in order to improve the well-being of poor communities.

Chapter Four

◆ ◆ ◆

BUILDING BLOCKS: CREATING USEFULLY LARGE SUMS

LIFE presents plenty of financial challenges and opportunities for rich and poor alike: getting a job, marrying, setting up and furnishing a home, and educating children. These are human goals that are blind to levels of wealth. Each of us likes to feel that we have the means to pursue dreams and to grasp opportunities when they arise. And as the petty pace of life creeps along, we all worry about how to prepare for old age.

Richer families take advantage of loans, insurance, and savings plans to produce the right sums at the right time: a mortgage, a car loan, an education plan, a pension. Financial planners advise the well-off to hold part of their savings in reserve, ensuring that there are funds available for other opportunities—perhaps buying a property to rent out or a share in a business. A separate pot of long-term savings should be accumulated over time, to be prudently drawn down in retirement.

This is a world away from the financial lives of the poor households that we came to know. Yet the previous chapters show that, even for the poorest among them, life is more than just scraping by, day by day, and fending off emergencies. Chapter 2 showed that none of the diary households live hand to mouth, not even those living on one dollar a day and less. Putting together large sums for big events, though, is at least as big a challenge as managing the day-to-day basics. Yet many of the financial diaries households managed to do both.

The previous chapter painted a discouraging picture. The households are rarely able to build up enough savings or arrange for enough insurance to recover quickly from major crises. Insured or not, households in all three countries coped with emergencies by exhausting meager savings, seeking debt quickly, selling precious assets, and leaning heavily on neighbors and relatives—often with damaging long-term costs. Putting together large sums would thus seem beyond the reach of most poor households.

But this turns out to be too pessimistic a view. Many diary households did create usefully large sums during the year, and used them to buy household goods like pots and pans, or assets like bicycles or fans, or to seize new business opportunities or buy land and buildings. Many households needed large sums for social occasions. In Bangladesh and India, even the poor host elaborate weddings, and in India, a quarter of our diary households had to manage a wedding in their own household during the research year.

Each household acquired the necessary sums in its own way, but all of them assembled the funds piecemeal. Nearly always households drew on their entire portfolios, simultaneously running down savings and assets while running up debt and seeking donations from friends and family. Equating acquisition of a lump sum only with saving misses key elements of the households' strategies and possibilities.

Standard economic surveys that are built to capture "balance sheets" of assets and liabilities at a fixed point in time do not tell us much about how lump sums are put together. They tend to understate households' ability to generate large sums because many of those sums are created quickly and are not held for long periods.

The same would be true of our own data if we looked only at the balance sheets. In the diary households, year-end balances of financial assets and liabilities are indeed small relative to incomes. Of the 42 households in Bangladesh, for example, only one—a relatively wealthy landowning farmer—held monetary savings worth more than the average annual household income for the sample as a whole. Unlike households in rich communities, the diary households tend not to hold large long-term debt such as a home mortgage. Nor are they building up formal retirement funds (especially outside of South Africa). Nor do young households deposit into long-term education plans to see their children through college.[1] In South Africa, far more often than in India or Bangladesh, we did find households that were able to build up long-term financial assets, using, for example, a retirement plan (provident fund) with their employer. For the sample as a whole though, they were exceptional.

But when we turn away from the balance sheets and look at the flows, the diaries show that many of the households in all three countries nevertheless created and spent large lumps *during* the course of the year. Seldom did we observe households converting these sums into a longer-term financial asset: they were built to be spent.

In this chapter we show the strategies used by households to accumulate these sums. In some ways, the strategies work, but they reveal a striking inability to accumulate over the long term. Without long-term accumulation, households have a hard time building toward bigger goals like better schooling for their children, the chance to migrate in search of better jobs, or securing a stable retirement.

Chapter 6 gives reason to believe that major improvements are possible. There, we describe the remarkable success that Grameen Bank has had in helping its customers build up savings over spans of five and 10 years through innovative "pension" products—which are in practice used for many purposes other than retirement. The evidence here suggests that Grameen's successes can be spread more broadly: tiny incomes need not inevitably condemn poor households to trivial savings balances and low-value short-term debt. The instruments households already use, and the way they use them, point to the potential the poor have to save and borrow bigger sums over longer durations.

The financial capacity of the poor is constrained not just by low incomes but also by the characteristics of the instruments available to them today. New financial services may not be able to address low incomes, but they can do a lot by ensuring access to financial tools that provide the right doses of discipline, security, flexibility, and incentives. In this, the age-old strategies employed by the diary households anticipate solutions to the blend of economic, psychological, and social constraints that are explored in the new field of behavioral economics.[2]

The Poor Can Save—Substantially

It's surprising that there is room in the household budgets of those living on small incomes to set aside substantial amounts to save and repay loans. It's hard to imagine that households can maintain the discipline needed to save regularly and to ensure that loans get repaid on time.

Nomsa's story illustrates the mechanics of saving by the very poor. She is a 77-year-old living with her four grandchildren in the rural village of Lugangeni, South Africa. The two youngest grandchildren, aged 7 and 14, whose mother died of AIDS, arrived just before the research year started. Before they came, Nomsa might have been considered reasonably well off, but now the five of them struggle on her government old-age grant of $115 a month. She has repeatedly asked social workers for a foster care grant that would more than double her income, but despite being eligible, she has been turned away. She supplements her income by selling vegetables from her garden, but she often has to take loans to make ends meet. All the same, she manages to keep up with monthly payments of $40 into her informal savings clubs (which we discuss extensively in a later section). Table 4.1 shows what her budget looked like each month.

Nomsa may seem extraordinary, saving a third of her monthly budget, but her savings patterns are not much different from most of her neighbors. Nomsa has a bank account into which she receives her monthly government grant, but she withdraws the entire amount every month. Likewise, she has a place in the house where she keeps spare cash, but this rarely amounts to much by the end of the month.

Table 4.1 Nomsa's Typical Monthly Budget

Source of funds	**$120**
Selling vegetables	6
Government old-age grant	114
Uses of funds	**$120**
Church fees	4
Home maintenance	19
Food	22
Transport to shopping	2
Paraffin	9
Household products (soap, etc)	14
Pay back loan	10
Savings clubs	**$40**
Net savings in bank	**$0**
Net savings in house	**$0**

Note: US$ converted from South African rand at $ = 6.5 rand, market rate.

Like her neighbors, Nomsa was able to save so much of her monthly income thanks to her two informal savings clubs.

We found that, in all three countries, all families, even the poorest, attempted to accumulate lump sums of money over time through building up savings and paying off loans. Take a household like Sultan and Kanon's. This Bangladeshi couple rented a yard where they sorted and sold waste scavenged in their Dhaka slum, but Sultan was in his fifties and ailing, and the income he raised was rarely more than $1.50 a day. Just before the research year their 15-year-old daughter Sweetie had found a job in a garments factory, at $28 a month plus occasional overtime, much of which she saved for her wedding while contributing her bit to the housekeeping: she married and left home just before the end of the year. Kanon was a client of a microcredit provider, and before the year had taken a loan of $110 that they used for a string of needs: drugs for Sultan's health problems, repaying old loans from neighbors, consumption, and paying overdue rent on the waste-sorting yard. In addition, Kanon's older daughter, already married and away from home, gave her microcredit loan to Sultan and Kanon to help fund Sweetie's marriage. Sultan and Kanon gritted their teeth and kept up with the weekly loan payments on both these loans: $3.76 a week, week in, week out. On top of that, they saved another 75 cents each week with the microcredit NGOs. So, for months on end, they managed to squeeze $4.51 out of a weekly income of $20 or less, to repay their loans and save at the microcredit meetings.

Or take Sita, whom we met in chapter 2, a widow from the India rural site with low and very uneven income as a farm laborer. Sita lives with the eldest and youngest of her three sons: Udal, whose new bride came to join him in the research year, and Lalla. The whole household is illiterate but adult and able-bodied, earning the bulk of income through forms of wage labor—on local farms, on construction sites locally and in the regional capital of Allahabad. Lalla was contracted to a local grain trader to work for 43 cents per day (just under half the local market rate) in order to pay off a loan of $64 taken to pay for Udal's wedding. Sita has title to 3.5 acres of land but only one acre is fertile, the rest rocky and unirrigated, and the fertile section was mortgaged two years earlier to raise money for bail for Udal, who had been charged with a robbery in the village, leaving the family shackled by court fees. The farm income, at $10 for the rice paddy season, was less than half of what Sita had expected. All this added up to an annual income of $353, averaging just under $30 per month.

Despite such low and uneven income, the household managed to put money aside from daily needs to go toward longer-term costs and debts. Over the year, they saved and repaid about $63, a little under a fifth of their annual income. Most of this was saved up from wages and kept in the home to repay a private loan secured by a land mortgage; the balance was in the form of deductions from Lalla's wages, which went toward repaying his debt to his employer grain-trader.

It seems, then, that at both ends of the spectrum of households in our sample—from the responsibility-burdened Nomsa, to the fit but precarious Sita, to the frail and elderly Sultan—there was room in the budget to set aside money on a regular basis. Other research suggests that this may be true for poor households worldwide. In a 2007 paper, MIT economists Abhijit Banerjee and Esther Duflo report that surveys from around the globe show that the poor do not spend every available cent on food, leaving room in the budget for financial transactions that lead to larger expenses.[3] The financial diaries data show that most South African households spent no more than 75 percent of income on goods and services: the balance went toward financial intermediation such as insurance, savings, or debt servicing. The next, crucial step is to find ways to protect the money that has been set aside and to transform it into usefully large sums.

FORMING LUMP SUMS . . .

Our focus in the chapter is on how Nomsa, Sita, Sultan, and their neighbors built usefully large lump sums of money. Their strategy, as we have seen, was to patch together resources from multiple points. Sometimes, however, a single instrument contributed a substantial sum, and much is revealed by looking at how that was done. We defined a "larger" sum as any sum formed completely in a single instrument, rather than patched together through different instruments, and equal to or exceeding one month's household income. In Bangladesh and India, this benchmark was averaged for the country sample and set at about $50. In South Africa, where we had more precise income figures, it was set at each household's own average monthly income.[4] Altogether, our households between them acquired and spent 298 such sums during the research year. The total value of these sums, $80,857, is broken down by country in table 4.2, which also shows the average values of the sums for each country.

In India and Bangladesh the typical household extracted usefully large sums from financial tools with an average value of around three months' income. In all three countries, when we compare wealthier households to poorer ones in the same neighborhood, we find that the poor households are able to draw, relative to their incomes, lump sums that are a larger proportion of income than those of a richer neighbor. Joseph, who lives in the shack areas of urban Langa, outside

Table 4.2 Lump Sums from a Single Instrument Spent in the Research Year, by Country

	Bangladesh *42 households*	*India* *48 households*	*South Africa* *152 households*
Number of sums	94	139	65
Average value	$144	$167	$676
Total value	$13,550	$23,358	$43,949

Note: US$ converted from local currencies at market rates.

Table 4.3 Types of Instruments Used to Form Lump Sums

	Bangladesh *% of total*		*India* *% of total*		*South Africa* *% of total*	
Type of instrument	*Number of sums (94)*	*Average value*	*Number of sums (139)*	*Average value*	*Number of sums (65)*	*Average value*
Savings	17%	$119	26%	$183	75%	$654
Loan	83%	$149	73%	$162	15%	$522
Insurance	0%	N/A	1%	$138	9%	$1,039

Note: Percentage of total and average value in US$ converted from local currencies at market rate.

Cape Town, South Africa, has a stop order on his bank account that transfers a set amount of money to a savings account every month. He managed to save $630 this way over the course of one year, about one and a half times his monthly income. His neighbor, Nobunto, who earns half as much, saved $407, about *two* and a half times her monthly income, through a savings club. Many poor households, then, do manage to create substantial sums in their financial instruments.

Table 4.3 puts another lens on the accumulation of large sums. It shows the type of financial tool—saving, borrowing, or insurance—used to create the 298 lump sums on which we're focusing. A clear difference between South Asia and South Africa emerges. The relatively low shares for saving in Bangladesh and India show how hard it is to save up more than a month's income there—in both countries

Table 4.4 Primary Use of 298 Large Sums

	Bangladesh		*India*		*South Africa*	
Use of sum	*Number*	*% of total*	*Number*	*% of total*	*Number*	*% of total*
Life cycle	22	23%	42	30%	17	26%
Emergency	6	7%	6	4%	11	17%
Opportunity	66	70%	91	66%	37	57%
Total	94	100%	139	100%	65	100%

it is far more common to borrow other people's savings than to build your own. In contrast, most of the large sums in South Africa were raised by building up savings, partly in bank accounts but mostly in savings clubs. Insurance features significantly only in South Africa, which we explored at some length in the previous chapter.

. . . AND USING THEM

Table 4.4 outlines three very general categories of the uses of these lump sums. "Emergencies" include all sudden-onset occurrences that threatened life, health, or property. Under "life cycle" uses we include household consumption, as well as expenditure on births, marriages, and deaths. "Opportunity" is the broadest class, broken down further in table 4.5 and discussed below. Of course, many lump sums were put to more than one use. In those cases, we allocated the lump sum to the use class for which the majority of the sum was used. We discuss these three categories in turn below.

Life Cycle Uses. For economists, the simplest theory of why households borrow and save hinges on life-cycle motivations. It asserts that households aim to match income and expenditure patterns over the long swings of a lifetime, from early on as a young worker, to the years of building a family, and, eventually, to retiring. The theory posits that households borrow when young, before income is sufficient to meet major needs like buying a house. As soon as practical, saving starts with an eye to retirement. And those savings are then gradually drawn down once retirement begins.

But the life-cycle theory captures only a part of what we see here. Its application is limited since even elderly people in our sample work late in life, like 77-year-old Nomsa, who was selling vegetables to care for her grandchildren after her daughter died of AIDS. Yet the life-cycle motive is hardly absent, though it can be hard to see at first.

If we turn from the 298 sums that were spent during the year to the subset of larger financial assets still sitting on the year-end balance sheets of our portfolios, we find that little of this money is in instruments designed to safeguard old age. In South Africa, only 15 percent of the diary households would have enough savings and assets to finance more than five years of retirement.[5] Those wealthier households that do have retirement savings tend to do so through employer-provided instruments, such as retirement or pension funds, but poor households tend to hold very little long-term financial wealth. Making provision for old age just isn't done directly by means of financial tools in our diary households. Still, many conversations with diary households suggest that the desire for security in old age is often behind their financial transactions.

Khadeja from Dhaka, whom we found borrowing to buy gold in chapter 1, saw a gold necklace as a valuable hedge against future uncertainty: the very real possibility, in the environment she lived in, that she could be widowed prematurely, or perhaps deserted or divorced. She used a financial tool—a microcredit loan—to buy gold. Her case is a good example of how poor households may use the short-term financial tools that are available to them to create stores of wealth as substitutes for the long-term financial tools, like pension plans, that aren't available.

Vishaka, a diarist in a Delhi slum, would have seen eye to eye with Khadeja. Unlike Khadeja, who used microcredit, Vishaka used a savings club as her short-term saving instrument. When she received her payout from the club, her husband, Om Pal Singh, suggested that they store the money nearby with a moneyguard, Vishaka's mother. Om Pal Singh pointed out that, with their expenses increasing—they had four children by then—they might need to draw on the money at short notice. This was exactly what Vishaka feared could happen, undermining her longer-term savings goals. Instead, she deposited the money with a goldsmith, who would keep the money at further reach. When she's saved a bit more, she'll purchase some gold—her savings for the future.

A very common use for lump sums is buying land, which we've classed as an opportunity (see table 4.5 for a breakdown of opportunity uses). The precise motive for buying land can be influenced by cultural norms: one of the better-off households living in the slums of Langa, Cape Town, in South Africa was clearly thinking about their last days when they told us that they were investing all of their savings in the home they were building back in the Eastern Cape. This was not because they planned to move there soon, but because, if you have a family of your own, "you can't be buried from your parents' home—they must take the coffin from your own home." But in all three countries, land is seen with an eye toward future security. In Bangladesh and India urban households often sent funds, built through loans or through savings, back to the home village for investment in land or buildings.

Weddings, Funerals, and Broader Life-Cycle Uses. While the basic life-cycle theory of saving focuses on retirement, a broader model would account for major life events along the way. In Bangladesh and India weddings were by far the most common expensive "life-cycle" event. In South Africa, as we saw in the previous chapter, most households did hold specialist tools designed to produce large sums for the most common costly life-cycle expenditure there—funerals. Other important South African life-cycle events, such as the paying of *lobola* (bride price) or initiation school for boys, were also key financial events for diaries households. As Abhijit Banerjee and Esther Duflo find across a range of countries,[6] expenses on religious and social events account for a large share of the expenses of poor households, and often require expenditures in large sums.

In India a quarter of our diary households had to manage a wedding in their own household during the research year, and 45 percent contributed to a wedding outside the home. Not surprisingly, then, of the 42 larger sums that were used for life-cycle events in India (table 4.4), almost all were spent on weddings. But they were rarely enough to cover the whole cost. For those rural Indian households where a child married during the research year, the wedding was an astonishing 56 percent of the total spending for the year. More commonly, then, these larger sums were a major element in the patchwork of resources that had to be assembled from a mix of interest-free loans, gifts, savings, and various forms of credit.

The enormity of weddings in the financial lives of rural Indians bears some explanation. The dowry amassed and the lavishness of the ceremony itself not only honor a daughter leaving home and support her well-being in her husband's family, they are also strategies of aspiration whereby the social-economic standing of her whole family can be improved through a "good marriage."

The situation is similar in Bangladesh. Ataur, the head of one of our rural diary households there, married out a daughter and a son during the research year. For the daughter's wedding he sold assets (a cow for $50, a goat for $10, and some bamboo for $40), saved furiously at home (peaking at $240 just before the marriage), borrowed sparingly on the local market ($10, repaid along with another $10 interest, and then $40, repaid after two months with another $14 interest), and used a $200 loan taken earlier from a microcredit lender. For the son's marriage, a few months later, they were on the receiving end of dowry payments—$100 in cash and $13 worth of jewelry—that more than offset their share of the marriage expenses.[7]

Emergencies. Life-cycle events provide a motive for saving, one that Princeton economist Angus Deaton terms "low frequency" saving because the events are generally predictable well in advance and savings strategies can be put in place without requiring substantial revision.[8] "High frequency" saving, in contrast, refers to the sort of everyday consumption smoothing and cash-flow management that we described in chapter 2. Expensive emergencies are another matter and require larger sums. In the diary households, however, emergencies account for a rather small share of the 298 large sums we identified, as table 4.4 shows.

This low share was not for any shortage of crises, as we've shown in chapter 3. Rather, it is because households were unable to respond to emergencies with tailor-made large sums, there being no systematic insurance tools to allow them to do so. Instead, emergencies were met with a mosaic of smaller loans and savings combined with asset sales. In Bangladesh, microcredit loans were seldom available for emergencies, because they were disbursed on an annual cycle, with prepayments (which would lead to the early release of a fresh loan) not allowed. If microcredit loans contributed to emergencies, they did so indirectly: a microcredit client might be able to secure a private loan, for example, by assuring the lender that she was due to get a microcredit loan within the next few months and thus would be positioned to repay the moneylender. Likewise, many savings clubs in all three countries pay out only at pre-specified times, leaving a saver with a sudden emergency unable to access funds.

Opportunities. It turns out that most of the larger sums were spent to seize opportunities of various sorts. Table 4.5 shows that investments in land and buildings were major uses everywhere, though investments in land tended to be perceived differently in diary households in South Africa than in those in India and Bangladesh. In South Africa, the rural land populated by low-income households is rarely seen as a financial investment, but rather one that is made in order to fulfill cultural obligations and desires. Even in urban townships in South Africa, the secondary market is only just beginning to function and provide owners with the opportunity to buy and sell their properties, holding out slim hope for a return on investment. But in both India and Bangladesh, land is a fast-appreciating store of wealth, and the motive behind investing in land in these two countries is most certainly economic. In India, banks were becoming part of the land investment process. Of those sums used for property acquisition in India, about a quarter were formed in banks, through products that included savings as well as farm loans.

For other subcategories there was considerable variation between the three countries, especially between South Africa on the one hand, and South Asia on the other. Inputs into small business inventory in

Table 4.5 Primary Use of 194 Large Sums Used for Opportunities

	Bangladesh		*India*		*South Africa*		*Total*	
	Number	*% of total*	*Number*	*% of total*	*Number*	*% of total*	*Number*	*% of total*
Personal assets								
Land & building	14	21%	14	15%	13	35%	41	21%
Livestock	3	4%	1	1%	0	0%	4	2%
Business/farming								
Capital goods	2	3%	4	4%	2	5%	8	4%
Stocks/inputs	29	44%	48	53%	0	0%	77	40%
Other								
On-lending	9	14%	8	9%	1	3%	18	9%
Emigration	1	2%	0	0%	0	0%	1	1%
Savings	0	0%	4	4%	6	16%	10	5%
Debt repayment	7	11%	7	8%	5	14%	19	10%
Durable goods	1	1%	5	6%	7	19%	13	7%
Education	0	0%	0	0%	3	8%	3	1%
Total	66	100%	91	100%	37	100%	194	100%

trading enterprises were the most common use in the investment category in both Bangladesh and India, but didn't feature at all in South Africa. This does not mean that there were few small businesses among our South African sample, but business income was a much smaller share of household income than in the South Asian samples. As a result, in South Africa the lump sums used to finance working capital did not reach the value of the average monthly income that we used as a benchmark.

In Bangladesh, the microcredit providers, whose self-declared job it was to provide business capital to poor households, contributed to these numbers, but were responsible for only a minority share of them: about three times as many sums went into businesses from informal private sources than from microlenders. In India, where microlenders were thin on the ground in the diary areas, an even larger proportion of lump sums in the opportunities category were used for business. The majority (58 percent) of these were formed in the informal sector, but a substantial proportion were formed in the formal sector and just a handful through microcredit loans. Nearly all "formal" lump sums used for business came from bank or credit cooperative loans to farmers, another demonstration of the banks' commendable outreach to (larger) farmers, and their poor outreach to other occupation groups.

In our sample, South Asians appear more likely than South Africans to use the sums they formed as a basis for lending to others. Where lump sums can be raised cheaply relative to other means, it makes sense to arbitrage: we have recounted stories where microcredit borrowers quickly lend their capital to others who not only repay and service the loan but pay additional interest, perhaps in the form of contributing the savings deposits into the microfinance account, as Hanif, Mumtaz's boarder, did in chapter 2.

We found several sums being used to actually pay down *other* debt. In Bangladesh, microfinance loans are cheaper than private moneylender loans and are often used to pay off the latter. In India, several lump sums were borrowed by rural respondents to repay valuable lenders such as wholesalers and banks with strict deadlines.

CHAPTER FOUR

Saving and Borrowing: Accumulators and Accelerators

When we began to look at the relative shares of saving and borrowing in the strategies used by the diary households to build larger sums, we were struck by an unexpected observation. Saving and borrowing turn out, in practice, to be surprisingly similar. Both involve steady, incremental pay-ins—saving week after week in small amounts, say, or paying back loans week after week in small amounts. The same is true of the way that common informal devices are designed, like the local savings and credit clubs described below—and, indeed, it is similar to the way that many richer people pay for insurance or contribute to pensions. It is one of the features that microcredit pioneers adapted to form new financial innovations.

We pay attention to this and other special features of the devices and strategies used by the diary households. We focus first on the borrowing side (the "accelerators") and then turn to the various savings devices (the "accumulators"). In both their borrowing and their lending, households have discovered ways to deal with the economic, psychological, and social forces that make the job of amassing large sums of money so difficult.

ACCELERATORS

We started this chapter with the idea that large sums are formed by patching together resources—putting luck, skill, and assets together to amass a needed lump. Loans are part of that process everywhere.

Loans are "accelerators" in the lump-sum-building process in more than one way. Obviously, they give households access to cash immediately rather than after a slow process of saving. But loans often have features that speed up the process even further. Price is one of them. In a slum in Vijayawada, a town in southern India, Seema negotiated a loan of $20 from a moneylender, at 15 percent a month, just after leaving a meeting of her local savings cooperative where she had $55 in a liquid savings account. This struck us as an expensive, perhaps even an irrational choice. But asked why she had done it, Seema said, "Because at this interest rate I know I'll pay back the loan money very quickly. If I withdrew my savings it would take me a long time to rebuild the balance."

This logic is used even by wealthier respondents. Delhi-based Satish's $1,232 of cash assets at year end were the third highest in the whole Indian sample, after those of two wealthy farmers. And yet he loved to borrow, and to borrow above all on interest. He ended the year with $575 worth of debts, over half of it interest-bearing. His explanation was that the pressure of interest charges encouraged him to repay quicker, which he liked. Seema and Satish have their equivalents in wealthy countries: the pattern of borrowing at high cost even when adequate savings are in the bank is a regularity noted by economists working with data from low-income credit card holders in the United States.[9]

Seema and Satish used the pressure of price to make sure they put money aside. Khadeja, who took a loan at 36 percent a year and spent much of it on gold jewelry that she saw as a vital store of value for her future, used the pressure that the weekly discipline of her microcredit provider exerted on her. Like Seema, Khadeja saw the truth of an odd-sounding paradox: if you're poor, borrowing can be the quickest way to save. Khadeja knew that without some external force to help her, her chances of saving enough money to buy the gold necklace were small. So when a microfinance NGO offered her the chance to turn a year's worth of small weekly payments into a usefully large sum, she took it.

We watched as another Bangladeshi discovered the same thing. Surjo, an educated but poor young man, headed a large household that included his widowed mother and several siblings. He tried his hand at various ways of assembling money for the many needs of their growing household. When we met him, he told us that he was determined to save, and that he had opened a bank account to do so. That month he duly deposited $10 out of his $55 monthly factory wage into the account. Next month was the Eid festival, so he excused himself from depositing. The next month he made another excuse. We never saw him deposit again.

But his mother joined a microfinance group, and discovered a much more reliable way to get Surjo to save. During the year, she took

Table 4.6 Where Large Sums Were Formed

	Bangladesh		*India*		*South Africa*	
	Number	*% of total*	*Number*	*% of total*	*Number*	*% of total*
Formal	8	9%	29	21%	27	42%
Semiformal	37	39%	10	7%	0	0%
Informal	49	52%	100	72%	38	58%
Total	94	100%	139	100%	65	100%

a loan of $180 that she used to lease land in their home village, which they then sharecropped out to secure a supply of rice. Surjo realized he would be better off repaying this loan than pursuing his failed attempt to save in the bank. We watched as the family regularly made the weekly repayment of just under $4 right through the year.[10]

If Khadeja and Surjo had savings tools that were safe, and as disciplined as the microfinance loans, they would have been better off, since they would not have had to pay interest. But given the options available to them, their "borrowing to save" strategy makes sense.

We noted in table 4.3 that 83 percent of the large sums that the Bangladeshi diary households took and spent in the research year, and 73 percent of those spent by the Indian households, were formed by borrowing rather than saving. And though they also saved in informal clubs and other devices, for many of our South Asian diarists, borrowing proved the most manageable way to turn their capacity to set money aside into useful sums.

One reason for the preponderance of borrowing in Bangladesh is that, spurred by Grameen Bank's success, the country has many microfinance providers, and, as we have seen, many of our diary households held memberships in these organizations. Table 4.6 reveals the differences between the three countries in the roles played by the formal, semiformal, and informal sectors in the creation of usefully large sums.

South Africa's formal sector reached many of the diary households (Nomsa had her own bank account), but it has a poorly developed "semiformal" (or microfinance) sector, so 58 percent of sums were formed in the informal sector—mostly in the various clubs that we referred to earlier in this chapter. Bangladesh's rich set of microfinance institutions reached a majority of our diary households there, with the result that the semiformal sector was involved in the formation of more than a third of large sums—mostly through loans rather than through savings accounts. India has the highest proportion of informal sector formation of sums: so far, it has fewer semiformal providers than Bangladesh, and its banks and insurance companies were less successful than South Africa's in reaching diary households.

ACCUMULATORS

Thus far in this chapter, we've referred several times to households using informal savings clubs, a very common accumulator throughout the developing world. We saw that Nomsa, who featured at the start of this chapter, saved a large portion of her monthly income with her savings clubs, and she was typical of the South African households as a whole. Although she used a bank account to receive her government old-age grant, the financial instruments responsible for the bulk of her savings were her savings clubs: community-based organizations that are tried and tested methods for helping poor people squeeze savings out of their budget month after month. They are informal in the sense of not being legally incorporated and not relying on legal contracts. Instead they build on the trust and mutual obligations that bind neighbors together.

At the time we knew her, Nomsa was in two different sorts of clubs. The simpler was a saving-up club. It consisted of a group of women from the neighborhood who each deposited about $9 a month. The secretary of the club kept the money in her house. At the end of the year, clubs like these pay out the accumulated amount, splitting it among the members. Nomsa expected to receive $99 (11 months at $9) from this savings club in December.

Nomsa's membership in the club poses a puzzle. After all, she has an account at the bank in her own name, and is used to transacting there. Why would Nomsa not bank this money for herself, avoiding the bother of the club (she has to attend its meetings) and its undoubted risks (what if the money is stolen from the secretary's house?)? Many South African diary households belonged to clubs of this sort, and their most common answer to this question was that club membership was the surest way to discipline themselves to save for a particular event. "You feel compelled to contribute your payment. If you don't do that, [it] is like you are letting your friends down. So it is better because you make your payment no matter what."

Savings clubs, then, do the job that automated payments into savings accounts, or "stop orders" do for earners in rich economies: they shift money into a "hands off" account, acting as a guard against the temptation to spend spare money in trivial ways. In this, they play important psychological and social roles, building on commonsense notions that have only been recently recognized by behavioral economists.[11] The basic idea is that many people, both rich and poor, are often caught in a bind. They feel the need to put aside resources for the future, but they are also impatient to spend today (often with good reason, if, say, health and nutrition needs loom). If impatience outruns concern for the future, little will be saved for later needs.

Given this bind, devices that permit households to commit to save steadily in a prescribed pattern (or to commit to pay down debt quickly) can make the households better off. The devices keep impatience in check and help households bring their two competing desires into balance. In essence, they allow users to exercise their self-control at a critical early moment—in the act of entering into a months-long arrangement—rather than having to battle competing desires (consume now? save for later?) several times each day or whenever important purchases are contemplated. A study in the Philippines, for example, shows that bank customers save much more when offered a type of savings account that allows them to commit to making regular deposits at fixed intervals over a given period.[12] As noted above, richer households have many devices that do these jobs—like automatic salary deductions into retirement accounts. Poorer households usually have to rely on informal arrangements of their own making.[13]

It is not always simple impatience for consumption that poses a dilemma for poor households, but the uncertainty about the weight

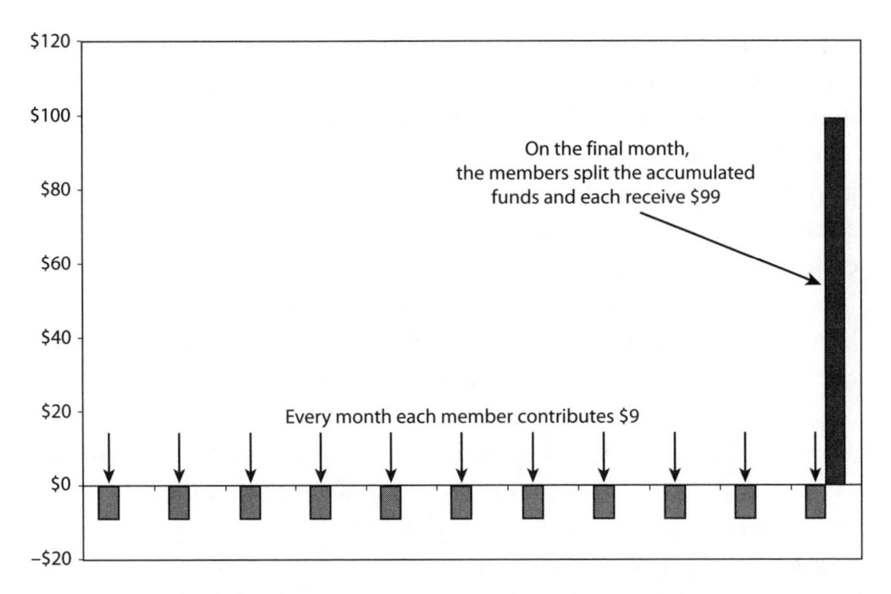

FIGURE 4.1. Cash-flow schematic for Nomsa's saving-up club. US$ converted from South African rand at $ = 6.5 rand, market rate.

of an immediate need compared to that of a more distant one. And it is not always one's own desires and needs that create the conflict. It may be one's spouse who has a different idea of how to allocate funds. Or relatives may unexpectedly arrive with requests for assistance. The requests can accumulate and stretch the limits of generosity. Devices like Nomsa's saving-up club and the other forms of informal savings clubs discussed below provide a common way to set and respect fair and reasonable bounds.[14]

Saving-Up Clubs. Figure 4.1 illustrates the cash flows for the first of Nomsa's clubs—the saving-up club. It reveals the common feature of all such devices: they mobilize small, steady flows—$9 a month for Nomsa—and transform them into one large sum. The relatively small size of the monthly inputs allows them to be made without too much difficulty, but they are large enough to accumulate to a meaningful size over time. The simple idea of the steady schedule underlies these savings devices. Usually, in a saving-up club, the fund builds up in the bank or in a member's home and isn't touched until an agreed term has finished—and very often the term is set to end just before a major expensive festival such as Christmas, Eid, or Dewali.

The "slow and steady" schedule is similar to microfinance loan repayment schedules that so helped Khadeja and Surjo. This is the sense in which saving and borrowing often share a very similar process: small sums are steadily set aside in return for a single large sum received at the appointed date. From this vantage, a key difference between saving and borrowing is *when* the large sum is received: at the very start with a loan, or at the very end through saving.

RoSCAs. Nomsa's second savings club was a "RoSCA," or rotating savings and credit association. In a RoSCA the members save the same amount as each other every period—a month, say—and the total amount saved each period is given in whole to one of the members. This continues until everyone has received the "prize," at which point the RoSCA comes naturally to a close—though of course its members may choose to start another cycle immediately or at any later time. One of the beauties of the RoSCA is that it requires neither storage of group-held funds (there are none) nor complicated bookkeeping (all that is required is a list of who has received the prize and who remains in line).

Nomsa's RoSCA had just three members, close friends, and that made things especially simple. Each of them put in $31 each month, taking turns to come away from the meeting with $93 once every three months. The first time she was paid out, Nomsa used some of the money to repair her *rondavel* (a traditional round building with a grass roof), bought a pot, and paid off one of her debts. The second time she was paid out, she used the money to make further repairs to the *rondavel*, pay someone with a tractor to till the soil of her garden, and, again, to pay off one of her short-term debts.

RoSCAs are flexible enough to accommodate almost any number of members, any interval between payments, and any value of pay-in. They can also change all of their terms from cycle to cycle.[15] On the other hand, they impose strong discipline through their structured regularity.

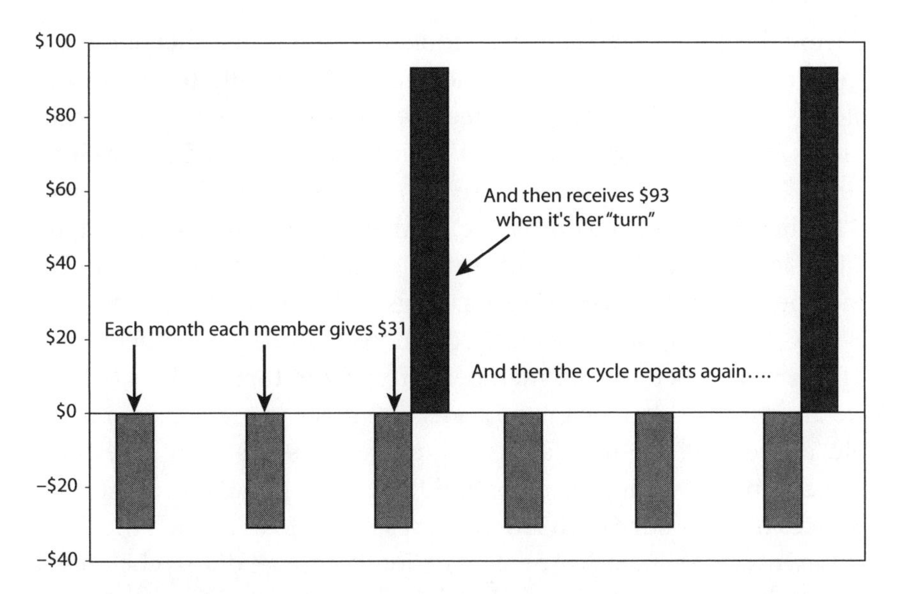

FIGURE 4.2. Cash-flow schematic for Nomsa's RoSCA. US$ converted from South African rand at $ = 6.5 rand, market rate.

ASCAs. A third form of savings club popular among our South African households is the ASCA, or accumulating savings and credit association. Unlike the simpler saving-up club, both RoSCAs and ASCAs make use of the saved money while it is being accumulated, rather than just storing it. In an ASCA, which is a step closer to a credit union or credit cooperative than a RoSCA, members save regularly, but they do not "zero out" the fund each meeting by giving it in whole to one member in the way that a RoSCA does. Instead, the ASCA lends the fund in part to individual members (and in some cases to nonmembers), in varying amounts, charging interest on the loans and agreeing to a repayment schedule with the borrower. It may also accumulate any unlent part of the fund, storing it with the group's treasurer or in the bank.

Nomsa didn't belong to an ASCA, but Sylvia, another of our South African diarists, did. It had 33 members who each paid in $30 per month. As the pooled fund accumulated, members were *obliged* by the club's rules to take part of the fund and lend it to nonmembers during the month. Sylvia usually took quite large amounts of money from the ASCA to lend to her neighbors. From July to November alone, she lent to a total of sixteen people an average of $60 each. They were charged 30 percent per month, the rate stated in the club's rules. The interest earned on these loans was paid into the club, where it further increased the fund's size. At the end of an agreed period the club closed, and savings and profits were distributed back to the members in proportion to their savings and lending record.

ASCAs like Sylvia's obviously do more than help members save. They are designed to help members profit from their savings (which we discuss further in chapter 5), a feature that can make them unstable, as we shall see in a later section. Nevertheless, they take their place alongside saving-up clubs and RoSCAs as popular accumulator devices used by our South African households to overcome the difficulties of saving. In all, 67 percent of South African diarists belonged to at least one saving-up club, RoSCA, or ASCA.

Mutation, Adaptation, and Evolution of Informal Clubs. We have used South African examples to illustrate savings clubs because, as table 4.3 showed, saving was the preferred way of forming "usefully large sums" there, whereas in South Asia borrowing was more common. Nevertheless, India and Bangladesh have rich traditions of savings clubs of their own. Saving-up clubs, RoSCAs, and ASCAs are all found in the South Asian diaries. As in South Africa, they take many forms, since one of the benefits of informal clubs is that the members' requirements can quickly shape the instrument's structure. As needed, the members can simply change the rules by consensus, without the burden of consulting board members or applying to regulators as formalized institutions must do. The result is the evolution of an almost endless number of different formats of savings clubs, as each tries to get ever closer to a perfect match between the lump-sum needs and the cash flows of its members.

Some arrangements are not so much clubs as informally recognized reciprocal bonds. In the previous chapter we saw them at work in South Africa in one variant of the burial society, where no money changes hands until a funeral takes place, when all the households that form the social network of the bereaved contribute to the costs. Such ties are part of a household's "credit rating," just as in wealthy environments credit card accounts are maintained, though perhaps seldom used, in order to maintain options. These obligations are not "drawn down" continuously, but maintained in good standing against the time they will be needed. In this way, they function as risk-sharing devices rather than simply ways to save or borrow. In India, we see the same tradition used to finance weddings—the most expensive festival in the South Asian setting. One of our Indian diarists, Rajesh, told us that he used to give substantial gifts, totaling some $385, to family members to finance weddings when he was running a successful carpet-knotting unit. He then fell on hard times and earned most of his money through off-farm wage labor in the local market town. Just before our research, he arranged the marriage of his own daughter and financed it largely by getting his past gifts reciprocated, even though some of them were given years ago.

In South Asia, as in Asia generally, RoSCAs are common. There are many variants, and they can be distinguished by the method used for determining the order in which members take their "prize." A few do it by consensus, agreeing the order before the cycle begins, a system that works well when the members intend to repeat their RoSCA cycle after cycle, so that after a few cycles it hardly matters what your "order number" is—you just get a prize at a regular fixed interval. Nomsa's three-member RoSCA was of this sort. Nasir and his brothers, tailors for leather export factories in Delhi, joined a consensus RoSCA at the instigation of a colleague who became the manager. There were ten members contributing $21 each month for ten months. All came from the same district of Bihar (six of them from Nasir's own village, including his two brothers, his first cousin, and his wife's brother) and worked in the same company.

Because of close kin relations and high trust between the brothers and the RoSCA manager (who is also a source of interest-free loans), the RoSCA rules were flexible: fines went uncollected and the brothers regularly paid up for each other as well as for other members. When Nasir and one of his brothers lost their jobs following a protest about wage rates, their eldest brother took responsibility for all three payments to the RoSCA ($64 each month) in return for the others covering his living costs. The RoSCA survived because it had a core of close kin who helped each other out. The three brothers were saving toward the same common goals as a joint family, and the RoSCA, like some of South Africa's savings clubs, brought existing reciprocal bonds into a formal structure.

Such RoSCAs can vary the value of the payments, the number of members, and the frequency of meetings, to arrive at a balance between the timing of contributions and prize-taking that suits particular needs. In the slums of Nairobi, Kenya,[16] for example, Mary's RoSCA helped her reconcile her tiny business—buying a basketful of vegetables daily from the market and selling them to her close neighbors—with the demands of being a single mother. She was in a seven-day daily-payment RoSCA, which delivered her a prize each week the value of which matched the value of her vegetable stock-in-trade. Whenever Mary needed to pay for some unexpected event—her son had fallen from a tree and needed a visit to the doctor on the day we interviewed her—she had to take cash from her tiny business capital, but she found that if she was faithful to her RoSCA savings, which she was, then within a week it replenished her capital in full. For this reason she valued the savings club highly, and returned to it after an unsuccessful try at being a borrower from a well-intentioned microfinance institution that had suddenly arrived in her slum. The problem was that the microfinance loan had a one-year term, which didn't match Mary's cash-flow needs.

In the Philippines, Taiwan, Pakistan, and Egypt, to mention just four countries where we have observed it in action, there is a RoSCA tradition that has found another way of matching needs with cash flows. There, we find RoSCAs that are one-cycle affairs, but each starts with the lump sum need of a particular individual, who then devises a schedule to suit the remaining members. A schoolteacher in rural Philippines who wants to buy a suite of furniture for a new home, for example, will "call" the start of a RoSCA of, say $100 (the amount she needs for her furniture). Her colleagues join in as an act of solidarity, but only if she works out a schedule that suits them—say

$20 a month over the next five months, so that the whole thing is over before the expensive Christmas season starts.

Yet another form of RoSCA uses a lottery, so that the prizewinner isn't known until the hour of the meeting, when a name is drawn from a hatful of eligible names (that is, all the members who haven't yet received their prize) and a big smile breaks out on the lucky member's face. This is simple to administer and it helps to make the order in which the prize is given seem fair. The "lottery RoSCA" may be the most common form of RoSCA in South Asia. In the Indian diary research we found prizewinners of lottery RoSCAs who, sometimes for a price, passed the prize on to other members who needed it more at the time, or who even on-lent it to outsiders, rendering the device more responsive to individual cash flows. Members with larger needs may also be allowed to hold more than one share, or "name" in the RoSCA.

A more refined solution, used by two of our Indian diarists, was another type of RoSCA, the "auction" RoSCA, where those members still eligible for a prize bid for it, with the prize going to whoever puts in the biggest bid. The bid money is then distributed among the members equally, so that those willing to refrain from bidding until the later rounds, when bids are smaller (since there are few bidders left), get a bigger than average prize for a smaller than average bid, as well as enjoying "interest" income from their share of the distributed bid money paid by others. Auction RoSCAs, therefore, cleverly attract savers (who bid late and are well rewarded for it) and borrowers (who bid early and pay heavily for it), and the current price of money is determined at each auction, driven by demand for it at that moment among that group of people. All this sophisticated matching of savers with borrowers, and all the associated accounting, is done without conscious analysis and with no need for pencil and paper. Moreover, the money flows directly from savers to borrowers without any down time or middlemen to cream off their percentage.

In this way, auction RoSCAs could be considered the world's most efficient intermediation system. Perhaps not surprisingly, in India auction RoSCAs have developed into a licensed financial industry, known as "chit funds," with tens of thousands of licensed chit fund managers running RoSCAs on behalf of their members, in return for a fee.

Indian RoSCAs, as everywhere, show their vitality through intriguing local variations. For example, we heard of auction RoSCAs in Delhi that draw lots when there are no bidders, but deduct a fixed sum from the prize that is then distributed to members. This creates a disincentive for those who want the money today but might otherwise be inclined to simply sit and wait, hoping no one else will ask for it. Some Indian auction RoSCAs reward the manager (who may be the originator of the RoSCA, as in the Filipino example described above) by allowing him or her to take the whole prize (nothing deducted in the bidding) on the first round, so that bidding actually begins only in the second round.

We found that people we met through the diaries took their RoSCAs and other similar clubs seriously. They were important to them on two fronts simultaneously: the social and the financial. Kenneth, one of our South African diarists, was a well-respected 81-year-old man from the urban area of Langa. He had both a job and a pension from a previous job, and enjoyed an income of $320 a month. Kenneth was one of only two respondents in the study who held unit trusts (mutual funds): he had $2,900 invested in a well-known income fund. But he prized his informal *stokvel*, a local word for various kinds of saving club, even more highly. He had been in the *stokvel* for many years, and rather than miss a payment into it, he would borrow—as we saw him do once during the year. His *stokvel* worked on a rotating basis, though not in the exact same way as a RoSCA. At each meeting, one member received a payment from all the other members. But the amount was not fixed: it depended instead on how much the recipient gave each donor in previous rounds. The rule was to give back a little more than you received. So if he gave $325 to a member when it was his turn, he would expect to receive, say, $355 in his own turn. This type of *stokvel* tends to invite more middle-income and wealthy people in the neighborhood and can generate very high payments: in the latest we saw the receiving member get $14,900 in total!

Kenneth's *stokvel* is not a simple RoSCA or ASCA as we have defined them. It is in fact a very sophisticated way of bringing reciprocal one-on-one lending and borrowing into a structured context to strengthen it. Kenneth has a series of "contracts" with each club member individually—with differing amounts for different people. But this set of reciprocal bilateral deals is played out in public using the machinery of savings clubs—formal set meetings at regular intervals. As a result, the peer pressure, and the trust built from reiterated promises kept, are harnessed to discipline and strengthen the one-to-one deals. Although we did not find this mechanism in Bangladesh and India, we have found it on the other side of the world from South Africa—in the mountain villages in the northern Filipino island of Luzon. There, the *ubbu-tungngul* functions just like Kenneth's *stokvel.*[17] Indeed, the Filipino villagers report that the discipline produced by this device is so strong that *ubbu-tungnguls* can last from generation to generation, with children inheriting membership from their parents. A money-management device strengthens social ties, and the social ties in turn strengthen the money management—a symbiotic relationship that is one of the strongest virtues of informal finance.

RoSCAs and their like blur the distinction between saving and borrowing. In a RoSCA, members are transformed, one by one, from net savers into net borrowers. This happens because the basic mechanism is the intermediation of a series of small pay-ins into a single larger payout, and this mechanism is true for both savers and borrowers.

Not Always Good Enough

The stories we have told in this chapter are evidence of poor households' determination to save or borrow their way to usefully large sums, and of the widespread distribution of powerful and sometimes elegant informal mechanisms to help them do so. We have also seen the emergence in South Asia, and above all in Bangladesh, of new semiformal providers (i.e., microlenders like Grameen Bank, BRAC, and ASA) with equally powerful tools based on loans repaid in small regular installments.

But these are imperfect instruments, and in this section we will review their most common shortcomings: low reliability, inflexible schedules, and terms that can be too short.

UNRELIABLE

Savings clubs, as powerful a savings device as they can be, are not always reliable. They may be unreliable in small ways—a member may not make the expected contribution at the exact time that you need the payout. In Nomsa's saving-up club, for example, not everyone, despite sincerely held intentions and loudly voiced avowals, paid on time every month (including Nomsa), throwing the timing and the amount of the payout in doubt.

Or such clubs may be unreliable in more devastating ways, as Sylvia discovered. Sylvia, as described earlier in this chapter, was in an ASCA whose members lent out a good part of the fund to nonmembers, at a high rate of interest. Unfortunately, Sylvia did not earn as much as she expected from the payout of this ASCA. First, when some of her borrowers failed to repay, she had to do so from her own pocket, seriously eroding her profits. Second, just before the payout, the treasurer of the ASCA was robbed and killed on her way back from the bank. As it happened, she was only carrying part of the ASCA members' money. Sylvia received $246 from the member who was holding the other half of the money, but she had expected to receive twice as much.[18]

It is not just in South Africa that savings clubs can fail. Nearly half the incidences where Delhi households reported being cheated out of money involved ASCAs. In the Bangladesh sample, Surjo, the youngster from Dhaka, tried hard to stop his sister from joining an ASCA at her factory precisely because he himself had just been part of a 10-man club—a RoSCA—that had collapsed when several members failed to pay in. He lost about $14. As it happened, his sister's ASCA, which was run by workers who shared the same floor of a factory and were paid similar amounts, worked well. Surjo told us that through the two experiences he had "learned a lot. . . . Now I know what kind of people you should let into your club, and how to run it." But he didn't hurry to join another one.[19]

The dearth of the "right" kind of people to join a RoSCA was a key issue for Delhi respondents. Nasir, as we saw earlier in the chapter, enjoyed well-run RoSCAs, but two of his neighbors said they didn't have sufficiently trusting relations with anyone in their neighborhood, or even in Delhi, to depend on them to pay their dues. A respondent from another slum said he'd been trying to join a RoSCA for some time and couldn't find one that would have him as a member. Finally, he met a manager of a RoSCA, who told him he could join only if he agreed to take the prize last. Two of his neighbors were excellent RoSCA members, but they had to travel all the way across Delhi to the meetings each month. Neither felt they would find anything suitable closer to home.

Two other RoSCAs used by our Delhi diarists were put under strain, if not broken, by the diary members' own failure to pay their dues. The first instance was that of Sultan, a small businessman, who received his reduced prize after struggling to pay for several months. After deciding that he couldn't continue, he arranged to be replaced by an old client of his who still owed him money. The client was to contribute the balance owed to the RoSCA each month, in lieu of paying Sultan. This move was smartly arranged, but risky if the client hadn't fulfilled his obligations. Another case involved Mohammed Laiq, who failed to pay his two final RoSCA installments. A year later he had still not cleared these obligations. Shortly before we completed our research, he announced he'd found another RoSCA that would have him in spite of his poor track record. Among the members, he explained, were friends who had been required to vouch for him and guarantee his full participation.

MISMATCHED

On the whole, though with some disappointing exceptions, the Bangladesh microcredit loans discussed earlier in the chapter worked reliably. As we noted in an earlier chapter, users greatly appreciated their "contractuality"—the fact that workers came to the meetings on time, gave loans on the date and in the amount they promised, and didn't take bribes. But they did suffer from a second general problem that our diary households encountered: schedules that fit poorly with cash flows.

In part, this is a problem that savings and repayment regimes everywhere battle—the tension between flexibility and discipline. At one level this is a mental battle waged inside the head of the user: we all know we should save regularly, but we also know how difficult it is to carry out our good intentions. We seek external help—automatic payments, accounts with penalties for early withdrawal or missed payments—or we devise mental tricks, keeping the rent money in a special place (the teapot that belonged to grandma) and erecting taboos against dipping into it. These "mental accounts" have been the subject of much recent enquiry.[20]

But at another level this is a practical matter. In Bangladesh, to keep things simple, the microcredit lenders offered only one loan term—a year—and only one repayment schedule—equal invariable weekly installments. Such a tight schedule is wonderful for discipline—but quite tough on borrowers with very small and very variable cash flows. So in Bangladesh, we found that the very poorest have been either unable to join microcredit schemes, or, having joined, soon leave after failing to complete a repayment on time. These "very poorest" are typically landless farm laborers, who have between-harvest "down" months when very little income comes in. They can pay each week *most* months, but not in *every* month of the year. Several of our poorest rural diary households had quit microcredit schemes after such an experience, a few were experiencing them during the research year, and others were reluctant to take a loan for fear of failing.

Sita, the Indian diarist we met earlier in this chapter, had a disappointing time as a microcredit client. She had taken her first microfinance loan the year before we met her, after saving for a few months. The loan of $43, to be repaid over a year, was invested in a grocery store on the advice of the loan officer. Within five months, the store had gone bad and she sold off the stock, purchasing a cow with the

$22 saved from it. She continued to repay the loan from her wages (faltering briefly when her daughter-in-law fell ill), and when the local microfinance operation closed toward the end of her loan term, the last two installments were cleared using her compulsory savings. The microfinance institution left the village because there was inadequate demand for its loans. Although, unlike many, she repaid the loan fully, Sita is now convinced she has no use for such loans.[21]

Sita was unusual in having some bank savings, originating from a three-year-old government handout of $426 that she was given to construct a new house. Of this sum she had spent about $170 on building materials, but most of it was used on the marriage of her eldest son, with a small proportion ($45) put aside in a fixed deposit savings account at a bank (due to mature at $53 after five years). But toward the end of our research she was confronted with two emergencies: the funeral of her daughter-in-law, who had died at her parents' home; and the deteriorating health of her oldest son, who needed treatment for tuberculosis. Unable to raise enough from neighbors, Sita's response was to go to the bank to ask to release her fixed deposit six months before its due date. But the branch manager refused. Instead, she used $43 of savings she had been collecting at home for the purpose of releasing her only fertile land from mortgage. Hopes of using the mortgaged land for the next farming season were dashed. So her fixed deposit at the bank remained intact but at considerable cost. It is because of circumstances like this that we saw large lump sums from single instruments so rarely being used for emergencies.

During the year Sita proved that she was able to save and repay loans. She borrowed and repaid three times from neighbors and relatives. She saved continuously in her home, and her youngest son Lalla consistently serviced a debt to his employer through deductions in his wages. And yet because of the mismatch between the products she used and her needs, her saving efforts were in constant jeopardy.

Saving cash with the formal sector (banks and the Post Office), as Sita had done, is far more common among poorer people in India and South Africa than in Bangladesh. India's contractual and fixed deposit schemes (maturing after five or 10 years) tend to have shorter terms than the 15-year LIC endowments described in the previous chapter but longer terms than RoSCAs (where terms are rarely more than two years). Eleven of our Indian households, or 23 percent, held fixed deposits like Sita, or contractual savings, and only two of these households were from the wealthiest of our three ranked groups. These kinds of long-term saving products (and the savings capacity they mobilize) could provide the foundations for creating secured loans—which use the savings deposits as collateral—with a potential for greater flexibility than the typical nonsecured loans offered by microfinance institutions.

TOO SHORT

A third limitation of the tools that our diary households most successfully used to form usefully large sums was that the terms are too short, so that savings plans or loans that require multiple years to fund—such as home mortgages or pension plans—cannot be achieved. In the informal sector, where, as we saw, most lump sums were formed, there are natural limits to term length.

For very good reasons, most informal saving devices are time-bound, and a general rule is that the shorter their term the better their chances of working well. Saving-up clubs targeted at particular dates, like a major festival, last for a year or less. RoSCAs are by nature time-bound: their life equals the number of members multiplied by the interval between meetings, and most of those that work well are over and done with in a year, and often less, though of course they may chose to start another cycle. In Bangladesh, Surjo's sister's successful RoSCA lasted seven months—14 members times the 15-day interval between payday meetings. In South Africa, Nomsa's lasted three months, and, in Kenya, Mary's just seven days. Most well-performing ASCAs also last a year or two at most.[22]

A short life-span provides a regular test of the health of the device. When the scheme ends and the savings and profits are returned to the members, they either get paid in full or they don't. The payout acts as an "action audit." If all is well, members can start over. If not, they can walk away, as Surjo did from his group, having learned not to be in a club with those members ever again. Clubs that continue for long periods are subject to many risks: members may move away, quarrel, or their circumstances may change so that they can no longer participate. Cash left with treasurers can be embezzled. As cash builds up, members, or worse outsiders, can be tempted to try to capture it. Since these are private clubs, not protected by law, recourse when trouble breaks out is hard to find. Better to cash-up and walk away or start over. For all these reasons, it is much easier for Filipina schoolteachers to get together for a few months to fund housefuls of furniture for each other than to get together for many years to fund their pensions.

Much the same is true—and more obviously—of borrowed sums. Informal lenders, whether lending socially or for profit, limit their loans to sums that they can be reasonably sure to recover within a predictable time span during which they expect to be able to keep tabs on the borrower. The microcredit lenders in Bangladesh worked to create a model in which loans were to be invested in small businesses, with loan values calibrated to the capacity of the business to repay it from business surpluses within a short term so that new capital—of a greater value—could be pumped in via a new loan after about a year. But even if this model hadn't dictated their short loan terms, it is doubtful that they could have risked lending, long-term and uncollateralized, to poor households lacking secure legal identities.[23] It is much more reasonable to expect them to explore how to develop long-term savings plans for their clients—an idea we return to in chapter 6.

Conclusions

Like richer households, poorer households need to finance the big things in life. For this, they need big chunks of money. Putting together large sums is, not surprisingly, far harder for the poor. How do they do it?

The first answer is that they do so piecemeal. Large sums are cobbled together from smaller ones: loans are taken, gifts received, savings depleted. Financial tools capable of producing really big sums—simply and in a single place—are rarely there.

But this isn't a pessimistic story. The second answer is that households use financial instruments to trap and hold the small amounts they can squeeze out of a monthly budget. The poor households whose lives we followed did have room in their budgets to set aside funds for saving or repaying loans, and most used that capacity during the research year. Although balance sheets don't show many large-scale items, our households did form several usefully large sums each year—sums that were multiples of an average month's income.

The instruments that helped them leverage their capacity to save into these larger sums were of two kinds. There were the "accumulators" that allowed them to save regularly at fast rates, and the "accelerators" that encouraged them to pay down large loans quickly. The accumulators were mostly, though not exclusively, in the informal sector, and consisted of several kinds of savings clubs. The accelerators were found in the informal, semiformal (microfinance), and to a lesser extent, the formal sectors.

The underlying mechanism was the same in the two kinds of instrument. Both help poor households maximize their budgeting capacity by exchanging usefully large sums for a series of small regular payments. In this way, the act of saving and borrowing often looks quite similar in practice (except, of course, borrowers get hold of their sum sooner). In both cases, the sums can be used for any purpose. Microloans, for example, are by no means always used for—nor repaid from—microenterprise profits.

The accumulators and accelerators are often only part of a process. By patiently using accumulator or accelerator devices, poor households can sometimes put together funds that they then transform once more, buying value-preserving assets like precious metals and real estate that can provide security, not least in old age. In this way, poor households can use the short-term instruments at hand to substitute for the longer-term instruments they lack. However, the shift from a short-term instrument into an asset brings the lump sum briefly back into the hands of the household, putting it at risk of being whisked into providing for another, more urgent, need rather than saved for the longer term. We more often observed funds being accumulated and used within the short term than saved beyond the study year.

Existing financial devices, then, have many positive features. But this doesn't mean that the poor should be left to make do with these instruments only. Accumulators and accelerators are not always available or reliable. They are not always able to offer schedules that match household cash flows or to be available for sudden emergencies. And their terms are often too short, hindering long-term accumulation.

By building on the established financial habits of poor households, providers interested in serving the poor can begin devising instruments that offer improved, longer-term versions of accumulating and accelerating devices. Chapters 6 and 7 describe ways that this creation of new instruments is already happening.

Chapter Five

◆ ◆ ◆

THE PRICE OF MONEY

IN THE SPRING of 2007, the Mexican microfinance bank Banco Compartamos completed a highly successful public offering of its stock. Inspired by Grameen Bank, Compartamos had grown rapidly while keeping its focus on a customer base of low-income women. By 2008, Compartamos served over one million customers, using its profits to fuel expansion. In some corners, this was cause for celebration, a vindication of the commercial possibilities of banking in poor communities. But for others the success story was marred by the high interest rates that Compartamos charged its customers. A widely read study reported that, on average, Compartamos's interest rates exceeded 100 percent per year. Of that, customers paid 15 percentage points to value-added taxes, 24 percentage points went to profits, and the rest covered the basic costs of making loans.[1]

Muhammad Yunus, the founder of Grameen Bank, was outraged. His concern aligns with the broadly felt sense that programs for the poor should not take advantage of customers' vulnerability and lack of options. Moneylenders may charge 100 percent per year or more, critics like Yunus argue, but microfinance institutions are not moneylenders. Yet Grameen Bank, like its competitors, does not give away its services for free. It aims to charge reasonable prices for reliable services. In South Asia, interest rates tend to vary between 20 and

40 percent per year, well below the rates charged by Compartamos but well above giveaway levels. A study of nearly 350 microfinance institutions worldwide found that, after taking inflation into account, interest rates generally fall between 10 percent and 35 percent per year—again well below the interest rates of Compartamos.

Still, the same study found that those institutions serving the poorest customers face the highest costs of lending. Finance for the poor means dealing with lots of small loans and, when savings services are on offer, many small deposits. For providers, small-sized transactions mean limited scale economies and thus high costs per transaction. Out of necessity, "pro-poor" microfinance institutions tend to charge the highest interest rates of all; microfinance banks serving better-off customers tend to charge the least. Even if Compartamos had earned no profit and paid no taxes, their interest rates would have still had to be 60 percent per year to cover costs of their strategy for small-scale lending in Mexican villages and towns.[2]

Examples from the diaries confirm that interest rates on financial services for the poor can be very high. In South Africa, most moneylender rates run at about 30 percent per *month*. Even the Small Enterprise Foundation (SEF), a microfinance institution in South Africa with a long-term commitment to serving the rural poor in Limpopo Province, charges an effective interest rate of about 75 percent per year on its loans, but barely covers its costs after paying its staff and accounting for its own capital costs. Interest rates this high sound usurious, perhaps, but borrowers report that local moneylenders, who charge much more, will only lend them much smaller amounts of money. If it were forced to charge much less, SEF would have to rely on donors to a greater extent, and it is far from clear whether donors would be willing to support SEF's operation indefinitely.

For good and bad, then, when it comes to finance for the poor, no issue sparks disagreement as quickly as prices. Prices are important but hard to get a handle on, and we devote this chapter to them.

The financial diaries provide new evidence on the prices paid by poor households, and the ways that households make choices about them. In general, we find that households *are* willing to pay prices that are high when compared to those routinely paid by the better off.

Some economists have attempted to explain the poor's capacity to pay high prices by noting the high return on capital found in microbusinesses.[3] However, this does not explain why households also seem willing and able to pay high rates on consumption loans.

Part of the answer lies in the differences in the way that loans and savings are structured for the poor compared to the wealthy. This makes accurate comparisons difficult, and requires we look at prices from a fresh perspective. As a result, some of our findings will sound surprising. For example, there are good reasons why poor people *pay* to save, even though richer households typically expect banks to pay *them* interest on deposits. We also find moneylenders demanding high interest rates but then settling, ultimately, for a different price, often lower but sometimes higher than their stated rate. Moreover, chapter 2 showed that households are as likely to pay no interest at all for loans (usually offered by relatives and neighbors) as they are to pay annualized interest rates equivalent to 100 percent and more to the local loan shark. Nothing about this or other research suggests that poor households are insensitive to price, but then nothing suggests that price is the overriding concern when they seek financial services.[4]

The polarized positions on the debate over microfinance interest rates are based on distinctions and assumptions that are not always borne out in our data. Pricing is not a simple and transparent matter, and prices actually paid often differ from stated prices. On balance, our findings tend to support the view that legislation restricting interest rates would be counterproductive for pro-poor providers. Price caps would undermine the work of institutions like SEF that fill gaps and open opportunities for households with limited financial options.

Pricing's Complex Origins

In the world of the better-off, interest rates, more than anything else, determine where to borrow and where to save. Why pay 5.2 percent for a mortgage when another bank will give it to you at 5 percent? Or save at 4 percent per year, when another institution will give you

6 percent? Economic theory places price at the absolute center of financial decision-making.

The cost of financial services is important for the poor, too, but it is more difficult to understand how these services are priced. Modern rich-country providers have made huge strides in reducing "transaction costs"—the costs of using an instrument other than the financial cost of the funds used. But transaction costs for poor people usually remain high. They may include the time taken to stand in a long queue, the emotional cost of having to deal with unhelpful, stone-faced tellers, the cost of the bus ride to reach the bank, or the sheer number of lenders who must be persuaded to part with their money before a usefully large sum can be amassed. In the case of some informal transactions, there may be obligations to the lender other than repaying the loan along with interest—to work for some days at a low wage, for example. Price, then, can only take the limelight when multiple other conditions are met, not just large numbers of suppliers in competition, but an operating environment that assumes basic infrastructure, public goods, and a market in which customers "shop" equally.

Among the hundreds of loans recorded in the financial diaries, there are many that appear to have been taken for similar uses but at widely differing nominal interest rates, maturities, and default/rescheduling rates. Similar heterogeneity characterizes savings and insurance contracts. Digesting this data suggests several insights that help us to understand pricing of financial services for the poor.

An immediate insight is that interest rates may often be better understood as *fees* for a service than as a *rate* for the use of money for a specific period. Bankers typically express interest rates in annual terms—that is, a given percentage per year—even when the loan is taken for just a few months or for longer than a year. The APR (annual percentage rate) helps customers compare prices against the same yardstick.[5] That can be useful, but the diaries also show that converting a flat fee on a one-week loan for a small amount of money to an APR, and then comparing it to the APR for a two-year business capital loan, misses the essence of the transaction, as we show in detail in the next section. A second set of insights is that prices adjust to many factors: to personal relationships, to prior obligations between borrowers and lenders, and to the relative status of the partners, as well as the loan's value, maturity, purpose, source, and the likelihood of default. By taking into account data on how often loans are rescheduled or forgiven, and how quickly they are repaid, we get a better sense of what prices mean in the financial lives of the poor.

Fees versus Interest Rates

In rich-world finance, the value of time is essential to investment decision-making. Interest rates represent the cost of losing an opportunity to invest money somewhere else for a given period of time. Financial managers of businesses use concepts like "net present value" (NPV) to help them decide whether to make an investment or not. Calculations such as these compare the expected revenues from an investment with what would be earned by simply placing the money in a less risky investment, like a money market account or a fixed deposit. A new machine costing $1,000 that is expected to generate revenues of $1,100 for the next year is only worth buying if the added $100 is more than could be earned by keeping the $1,000 in the bank. In that way, the current interest rate environment strongly influences investment decisions.

Using concepts like NPV is central to first-world savings and lending, since every day that your current investment does not pay you interest, an alternative investment might have. Attention then focuses not only on the interest you earn each day, but also on the interest earned on that interest—the compounding of interest earnings. Bank savings, for example, will often compound on a daily basis, so waiting a day to withdraw your savings will earn you interest on the interest you earned the day before. In our own personal financial dealings, we also behave somewhat as businesses do: if we can borrow at 5 percent to earn a return of 20 percent, then that's a good deal because we've earned a net gain of 15 percent.

However in the financial environment of the poor, money and time are not so closely associated. Interest is rarely compounded;

sometimes it remains the same flat fee until you repay the loan, even if you've paid back some of the principal. For example, in South Africa, the typical interest rate on loans from moneylenders is 30 percent per month, which would translate into an effective APR of 2,230 percent on the full balance, due to interest paid on interest as a result of compounding.[6]

But such a calculation fails to take into account two common features. First, South African moneylenders rarely use compound interest. This makes their interest rates easier to understand and calculate. It can also favor borrowers who pay slowly. A customer who failed to pay anything toward his loan would owe interest of only 30 percent of the principal alone, not 30 percent of the principal plus outstanding interest.

Second and conversely, the moneylenders don't adjust interest to take into account early repayment, in full or in part. This means that customers paying early or on time pay higher rates than those paying late. In "rich-world" banking, late payers are penalized since they incur costs in additional interest. But for many poor borrowers, it may be more accurate to treat financial returns and costs as flat fees rather than rates that accumulate fees over time.

Seeing interest rates as a fee rather than an interest rate goes some way to helping us understand why households are sometimes happy to pay what we might consider to be astronomically high interest rates. We saw that in some examples given in the first chapter: a poor person may sensibly pay 50 cents to borrow $10 for a day or so to tide her over a problem, even if the annualized rate calculates to more than 500 percent. The absolute outlay is just not that great, even if the percentage rate is astronomical. Later in this chapter we show another example when we discuss rates paid for Jyothi's savings-collection service.

Stated Prices versus Actual Prices

Using these insights, we sought a more coherent picture of interest rates of the loans in the financial diaries. We looked at 57 examples of moneylender loans from the South African diaries database. For each loan, we knew the principal that was borrowed and the cash flows that serviced the loans. These loans had a quoted monthly rate, but, unlike formal loans, borrowers did not pay back on a regular monthly basis. They paid back with very irregular cash flows, perhaps paying a bit before the month was up, then a bit more two months later, and then finally paying off the loan after another two weeks, depending on when they themselves would receive cash from other sources. Interest charges would be adjusted or negotiated on an equally irregular basis. So the nominal rate of the loan doesn't tell us what price borrowers actually pay for a loan. To get a better sense of that, we borrow from the financial management concept of net present value (NPV) mentioned above, and use a related tool—the internal rate of return (IRR). The IRR is the interest rate that sets the NPV equal to 0. In the absence of any knowledge about the rate of return that is appropriate in the NPV calculation, financial managers use IRR to estimate the rate from the cash flows.

From our cash-flow data, we can calculate the IRR of each loan in the sample. First, we calculate a daily IRR and then multiply by 30 to get a monthly IRR. The average stated interest rate on these loans was 30 percent per month. But because they were not compounded, the monthly IRR on the cash flows turned out to be quite different from this stated interest rate.

In all three areas of the South African sample, the monthly IRR is above the average stated interest rate of 30 percent per month. So the flatness of the fee structure works against these borrowers rather than for them. In one of the urban areas outside of Johannesburg, the monthly IRR is considerably above the nominal rate. This is because many of these respondents borrowed for only a few days or a week from a moneylender but paid interest for the full month. Proximity to Johannesburg means that a relatively large number of these households have regular jobs with larger incomes and regular cash flows, so they are able to settle debts more quickly.

On average then, interest rates are high. But if we stopped our analysis there, we would be left with the incorrect assumption that interest rates are astronomically high for all loans. What this aggregate assessment conceals is that the IRR drops dramatically as the

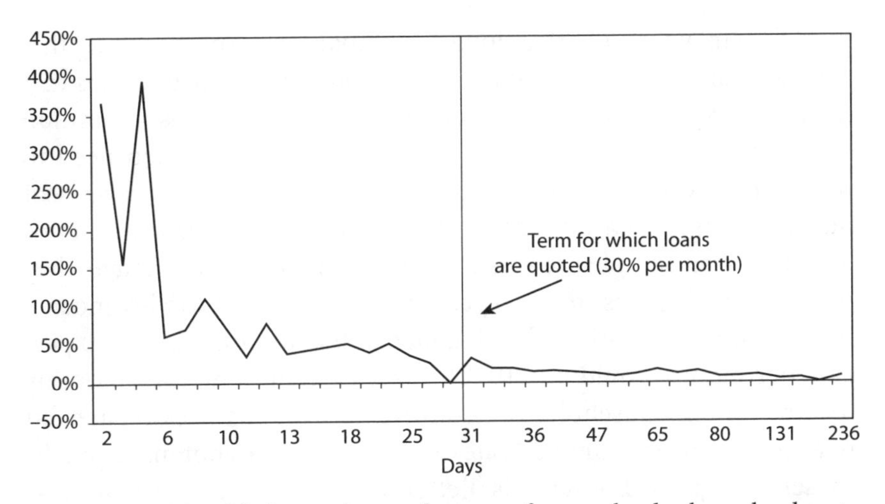

FIGURE 5.1. Monthly internal rate of return of moneylender loans by days to maturity (percent).

term of the loan increases. Figure 5.1 shows this more clearly. All of these loans are implicitly priced as if they are one-month loans. So when a loan is taken for just a few days, the interest rate paid is still 30 percent of the principal, even though the loan was not held for an entire month. So, as we saw, for short loans the monthly IRR is very high indeed (up to almost 90 percent per month!) But because interest is not compounded, the IRR declines steadily with the lengthening of the period over which the loan is held. As soon as the loan has been held for more than a month, the IRR drops dramatically from 30 percent to 17 percent. With a term of three months, the monthly IRR is down to 8.3 percent.

Despite the inherent attractiveness of paying a loan back late under this structure, 33 of the 57 loans considered for this analysis were paid back *before* the month was up. Why would anyone pay money back early when doing so implicitly raises the interest rate? We look to our understanding of portfolio management among the poor for reasons. In chapter 2 we saw that cash-flow timing is at the forefront of most households' considerations when managing their portfolios. Often these loans are taken when money is not readily available but is expected soon. When it comes, the loan is cleared. In this way, we can consider these loans as functioning more as a tool of cash-flow management than long-term financing. Another thing that we know about the financial lives of the poor, from chapter 3, is that lives are risky, and borrowing from a variety of sources is a common way to face emergencies. In order to borrow, though, you need to maintain a good state of creditworthiness. You want to clear debt quickly in case you need another loan. Last, note that the loans in this South African sample are small relative to income. On average, they were for $35 each, less than 10 percent of the average monthly income in these areas. The price of such a loan at the nominal rate of 30 percent per month would be $10. This is 2 percent of average monthly income for the households in South Africa. Holding back repayment to achieve a cheaper implicit rate on their loans does not make practical sense for these households. Better to pay back the loan as soon as the money is available in order to clear the debt and keep the option open to take another loan should the need arise in the future.

As loans get bigger relative to income, repayment gets stretched out over more days. In this process the rate of interest declines, particularly as loans are rescheduled. Our India research team carried out a survey of three moneylenders operating in west Delhi and found evidence of frequent rescheduling.[7] At first glance, the *stated* interest rates charged by moneylenders (ranging between 61 percent and 700 percent when annualized) appear extremely high. However, the *actual* rate of interest comes down dramatically once the repayment period is considered. One branch manager of an informal moneylending business described his clients' behavior. "Half of the poor clients drag the repayments on a one-month term loan up to 90 to 100 days. Most delinquencies occur when the clients are away visiting their villages." Of each 100 poor clients, five are likely to default completely, he told us. "We follow up at the most for three months beyond the scheduled loan period. We try to renegotiate the installment size [making it smaller], but in the end the whole business runs on trust and there's no other means to recover our money."

We saw an example of this behavior when one of our Indian diarists, Mohammed Laiq, borrowed five interest-bearing loans over the research year. In March he took $32 from a professional moneylender to pay for house repairs. For Mohammed Laiq, whose average monthly income is a little over $40 and irregular, this was a significant loan. The stated repayment schedule was 75 cents per day for a period of 50 days, of which 11 cents was interest. This equates to a very high annual interest rate of about 125 percent. However, the repayments didn't happen in the way they were scheduled. By early July he'd paid 27 days, and by early August, a further 8 days. In late September, he still had $8.50 to pay. It was not until mid-February, more than 330 days after he took the loan, that he cleared the debt. However, he still paid interest only on 50 days, not 330 days. This translates into an annual interest rate of about 19 percent, far better than the onerous 125 percent per month he was quoted.[8] He explained to us that he repaid the loan in "batches of days," generally giving $4–$6 at a time, with long gaps in-between. Mohammed Laiq said that the moneylenders don't worry about the gaps—they expect it and it's nothing to them. We might express this in another way: repayment delays are factored into the nominal price, with the effect that the customer who repays on time pays the highest price. This inverted pattern of incentives can be seen as one of the more unsatisfactory aspects of informal loan finance.

Pricing for Profit—or to Minimize Exposure?

It is important to remember that moneylenders are often as much part of the community as their clients, which makes forgiveness and rescheduling even more likely.[9] Moneylenders who feature in the South African diaries are often simply better-off people in the neighborhood. In Bangladesh also, there are very few professional moneylenders who lend for a livelihood. Most so-called *mahajans*, the Bengali word most often translated as "moneylender," are simply "big persons," wealthier people who lend as much out of obligation as out of profit-motivation; this may often be why they are willing to have interest rates negotiated downwards. Indeed because the government-owned commercial banks rarely lend to the poor, *professional* lending to poor people for profit in Bangladesh is done best and most often by microfinance institutions.

In India, professional moneylenders are more prevalent and, like Mohammed Laiq's creditor, are regularly forced to reschedule problem loans. But it is the intermittent lenders, those doing it for a favor or out of a sense of obligation, who show more willingness to forgive the monthly interest rates stated at the outset. In the Bangladesh and Indian diaries, interest stated at the outset was paid in full in less than half of all the private interest-bearing loans reported.[10] In a third or more of all loans, the interest was discounted, forgotten, forgiven, or ignored, and in the remaining cases the position over interest remains unclear. In South Africa, in addition to the 57 moneylender loans we discuss above, we also tracked a total of 45 loans taken from ASCAs (accumulating savings and credit association, a kind of saving club described in chapter 4). The South African moneylender loans were frequently rescheduled, although in only five of the 57 cases was the interest forgiven entirely. However, in ASCA loans, where the lenders were better-off members of the community, interest was forgiven much more frequently—in 13 of the 45 loans.

It is difficult to predict when negotiation on a troubled loan will work and when it won't. Ronakul is a very poor older man in our Bangladesh sample, whose seven-member household lives off irregular earnings of about $68 per month from casual factory jobs and selling vegetables. He had poor health and ended up with significant debt from his medical expenses. As long ago as 1997, when he had severe jaundice, he borrowed a very large sum totaling $400 from several creditors at the high price of 20 percent per month. He has never repaid a penny in principal or interest. The creditors, local slum-dwellers like him, press him from time to time, but he tells them, "I'm too ill and poor to pay anything." In 1998 and 1999, he took three more loans, of $40, $40, and $20 respectively, at 10 percent per month, from three local housemaids, and has similarly repaid nothing. The three women regularly gave his long-suffering wife Razia a tongue-lashing. Too poor to pay off these big debts, the couple did attempt to negotiate a deal during the research year, agreeing to repay the principal if the interest were forgiven. But they paid nothing.

In that case negotiation failed, but our research shows that it often succeeds. Salam, one of our urban respondents in Bangladesh, is slightly better off than Ronakul, supporting a family of eight on a monthly income of about $97. He had a three-year-old debt of $160 at 10 percent a month when we met him, on which he had paid nothing, so that the interest debt alone had risen to $180. During the research year he successfully negotiated a deal under which he agreed to pay $120 in interest (which he did) and repay the principal at some later date with no further interest. Sattar, from another urban Dhaka household, had taken a loan of $300 when his son broke his leg in 1997. He had made some payments on it, but in the research year the creditor told him "Okay, that's enough—just repay the $120 principal still outstanding, but you needn't pay any more interest."

Sandeep from Delhi had a three-year-old loan when we met him, taken to build a house in the village. At the start of our research, $85 of the original $340 was still outstanding, charged at a rate of 5 percent per month. Gradually he revealed that he'd paid about $426 for the first 18 months, at which point the lender had said he'd paid enough interest and the balance, of around $277, was now interest-free.

Discounting or forgiving, on the evidence from our study, depends on the relationship between borrower and lender. In Delhi, we came across a community (from southern Maharashtra) whose members frequently played the role of intermittent lenders to other members of their own community, on the same standard terms of 40 percent annual interest. As long as the interest was paid annually, the principal, we learned, was often carried over for several years. When some members lent to poorer neighbors outside of their own community, they did so at the higher rate of 10 percent per month.

So for sizable loans with longer terms, it is common to see a high stated cost that is later negotiated down. From a lender's point of view, this has two benefits. First, it acts as a deterrent—if I state a high price, maybe the would-be borrower (whom I know to be poor and likely to have difficulties repaying) won't take the loan, or will take less. Second, it assures me that I will get some early return on the loan: if I manage to get 10 percent a month for the first three months but then earn nothing more, my overall rate for the term of the loan as a whole may still be positive. Many microfinance institutions charge up-front fees on their loans for similar—and good—reasons. It is an obvious way of reducing risk.

Microfinance Lending

Within this environment, how have the microcredit institutions adapted? In Bangladesh, where they collect loan interest along with repayments at weekly intervals, they and the formal banks are the only providers that earn interest on a consistent basis. Following Grameen, most microlenders in Bangladesh and many others worldwide charge interest on a "flat" rate, in which principal and interest payments are included in weekly installments of a fixed unvarying size. This is not quite the same as the method used in formal banking to keep the monthly installments on home mortgages the same every month. In a mortgage repayment schedule, the share of the installment represented by principal and interest varies each month, with the interest share dropping and the principal share rising as the loan is progressively paid off. The microlenders' system starts with the assumption that borrowers are going to stick to the schedule, so they "simplify" matters by making the share of principal and of interest in the installment each week consistent. For example, a 1,000-taka loan is repaid in 50 installments of 22 takas, in which 20 are principal and two are interest. If the borrower departs from the schedule, Grameen and some other microlenders scrupulously recalculate the interest on a declining balance basis at the end of the loan—a task that keeps Grameen workers, armed with calculators rather than computers, sitting late into the night at the branches—and then return overpayments to, or collect underpayments from, their borrowers. Other microlenders are more cavalier, and, like the South African moneylenders, do not precisely calculate interest on the number of days before the loan is repaid, leaving those who repay ahead of schedule at a disadvantage. But Bangladeshi borrowers are beginning to notice these discrepancies, and increased competition is driving the microlending industry toward fairer and more consistent practices.[11]

Because they collect weekly, the Bangladesh microlenders' share of reported interest earnings is high: all in all they earned about $436 from our sample households in the year, a 39 percent share of all such interest reported earned on a mere 15 percent share of total transaction values. Private interest-bearing loans in Bangladesh took interest erratically, but because they charge higher rates, they nevertheless took slightly more than the microlenders—$446—and they did it on a smaller share—10 percent—of total transaction values. Although moneylender interest rates were clearly higher than those of the microlenders, we cannot easily use these numbers to make a precise comparison, because of variations in loan term lengths. Microlender loans had longer stated terms, but a bigger proportion of moneylender loans were overdue and not collecting interest, effectively reducing the rate charged. On balance, their effective private interest rate may have been about twice that of the microlenders', a far cry from popular claims that moneylender rates are out of proportion to those in the formal banking sector.

From the Saver's Point of View

Even after adjustments for late or nonpayment, interest rates on loans to poor people are undoubtedly high relative to average interest rates in developed financial markets. But surely that tells us something about the investment opportunities in these slums and townships. If returns are so high, surely someone must be making a killing.

We thought we may have figured who, halfway through the South African study. We realized that when some diarists spoke about taking a moneylender loan, they were in fact referring to loans taken from members of ASCAs, like those described in chapter 4. Suddenly our instinctive mental picture of the lender shifted from that of the "evil moneylender" to that of a group of conservative neighborhood ladies trying to pool their savings together and earn the highest interest rate possible. When we learned that ASCAs and moneylenders charged similar interest rates, we had to think through

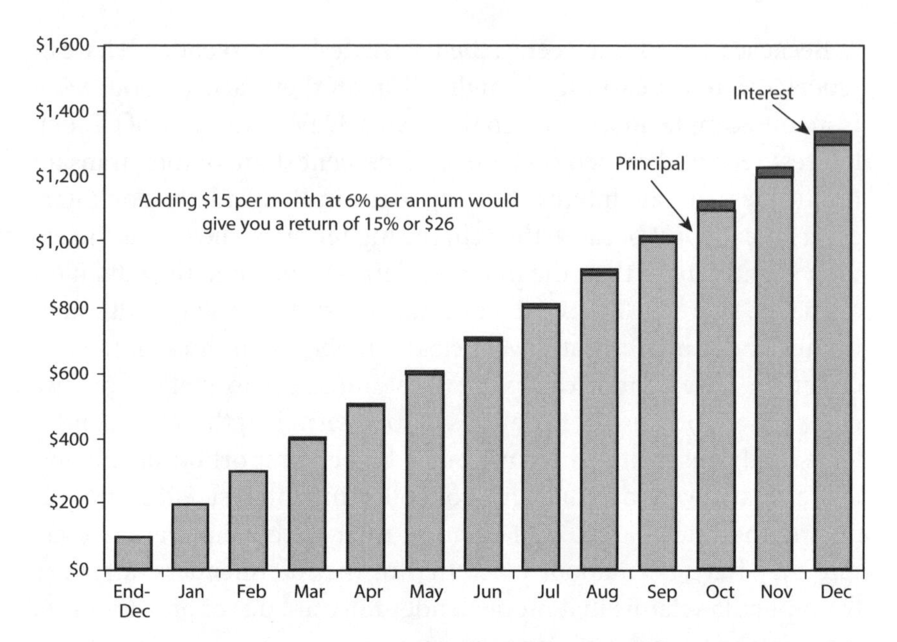

FIGURE 5.2. Accumulating savings with bank interest rate, assuming monthly savings of $15. US$ converted from South African rand at $ = 6.5 rand, market rate.

the possibilities of this from the saver's point of view. Usually members would put a relatively small amount, such as $15, into their ASCAs each month. Then, during the same monthly meeting, they would be required to withdraw an amount of money that they would lend on to their neighbors, friends or family. They would charge interest of 30 percent per month. We had visions of hedge-fund-like rapid appreciation.

Let's say you decided that you were going to put aside money every month in a bank account. You put $15 in a savings account that gives you a generous interest rate of 6 percent per annum, and you continue to save $15 each month in the same account. Figure 5.2 shows the accumulation of your savings. By the end of the year, your balance is $26, or 15 percent, more than the net value of your combined deposits to date.

Now let's say that you save with an ASCA that is charging borrowers a much larger 30 percent per *month*. With the same monthly

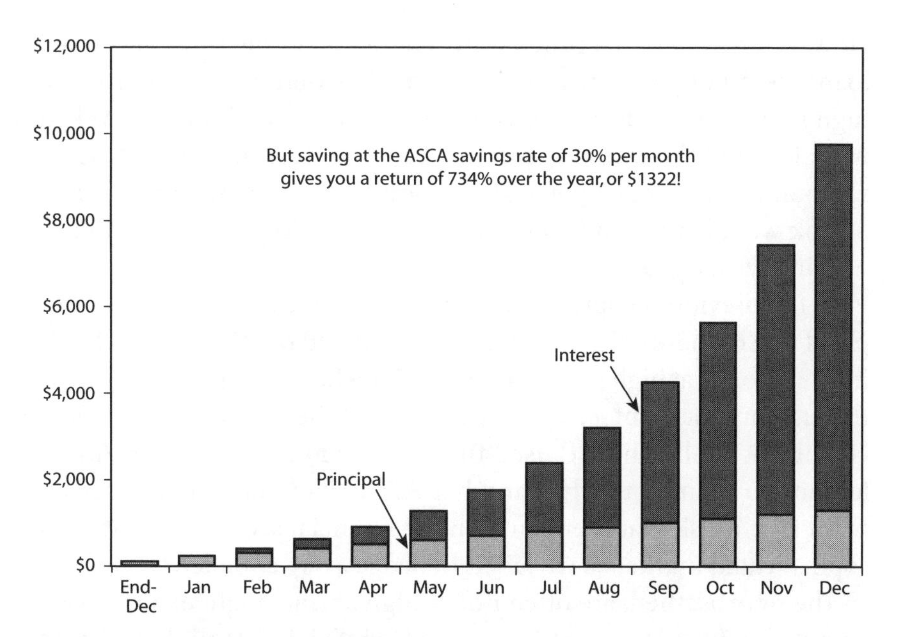

FIGURE 5.3. Accumulating savings with ASCA interest rate, assuming monthly savings of $15. US$ converted from South African rand at $ = 6.5 rand, market rate.

payment of $15, and provided that all the borrowers pay you back on time and with the full interest, your balance at the end of the year will be a hefty 734 percent more than your combined net deposits over the course of the year, generating an extra $1,322 you didn't have before! Figure 5.3 (whose vertical scale is very different from that of figure 5.2) shows this.

However, to achieve this rate of return on savings requires that each loan be paid back within a month, which is rarely the case. First, many borrowers take more than a month to repay, and interest charges are not compounded over time, as the calculations in the bank example are. Second, some borrowers may not pay back at all, forcing the ASCA members to dip into their own pockets to pay principal and interest, reducing the net return.

In the South African financial diaries, we counted 21 ASCAs that had one or more of our respondents as members, and which lent out money in this way. Most charged interest of 30 percent per month.

However, not all of the funds were lent out all of the time, and some loans were not paid back. In the loans that were given, there was a high rate of loss or forgiveness of both principal and interest. When we calculated the monthly internal rate of return for these ASCAs, we found it was only 1 percent per month. This is a higher rate than a bank would give, but it was far less than the 30 percent per month nominally charged to borrowers.

In the previous chapter we recounted in some detail a good example of one of these ASCAs. Sylvia's ASCA relied on its members lending out money at high rates of interest. But when we tracked the ASCA through our diary interviews, we found that the borrowers often paid late or not at all, which caused the effective rate of return on ASCA lending to plummet. Sylvia and her ASCA had fallen foul of repayment risk, a risk that is endemic in the financial sector and that even sophisticated markets have failed to hedge away completely.

The returns, then, are often not as high as one might expect based on a stated interest rate, and as we see from Sylvia's story, the risks are high. This might explain why households are willing to tolerate zero interest rates on their savings, such as we see in most RoSCAs (other than auction RoSCAs). More important than the return being generated is reliability, security, and an appropriate structure that works with the particular cash-flow timing of the household.

An example from India shows us just how important these elements are to the poor saver. Jyothi works in the southern city of Vijaywada and was described in an earlier book by one of our authors.[12] Jyothi is a middle-aged woman living in the slums she served, and her service consisted simply of walking round the slum each day collecting small deposits from her customers, most of them housewives. She gave them a crude passbook, just a card divided into 220 cells made up of 20 columns and 11 rows, so that savers could keep track of their progress. When all 220 cells were ticked off, Jyothi returned the savings to the value of 200 of the 220 cells, holding back the remaining 20 cells' worth as her fee for her service. Thus someone depositing a total of $44 with her, at 20 cents a day, would get back $40. If we consider this 20-cell fee as interest, and we assume a growing balance as 220 deposits are made over 220 days, then Jyothi is effectively paying her customers a negative rate on the savings—*minus* 30 percent a year.[13] Put this fact to the savers and they will tell you to forget your fancy calculations: the fact is that they needed their $40 to ensure that they could pay school fees to keep their children in class for another year. With husbands earning irregularly, the only sure way to build up this sum was to take pennies from the housekeeping money each day and hand it over to Jyothi. It costs them only $4 to form the $40, and Jyothi did all the work. Taken within this context, this is a reasonable price to pay to build badly needed savings.

It would be easy to assume that Jyothi is earning monopoly profits: if she had more competition from (better) suppliers, she'd surely have to bring her rate down. Who, then, might these competitors be? Probably, organized brand-name deposit collectors, such as Sahara and Peerless, that are widespread in India. Such service providers pay, rather than charge, interest (4–6 percent in 2001) for an otherwise very similar service, though for longer terms.

But, counterintuitively, residents' degree of comfort and control with Jyothi may be higher than with regulated brands such as these. Brands like Sahara and even the state-run LIC rely heavily on agents paid commission to reach out to and take full responsibility for customers. This model, with its incentive structure, is highly efficient but leaves the brand and its reputation vulnerable to the behavior of agents. Indian diarists recounted stories of loss and cheating. Two of our respondents had personally lost money to Sahara agents, and at least one to an LIC agent in the recent past.

These cases were over and above a major loss that befell our Indian rural site two years before we arrived. A company that had registered under new legislation simply disappeared from the area after accumulating large sums through a variety of savings products. Four of the Indian rural respondents had lost money this way.

But there is another risk too, the risk that customers bear when their savings are invested in markets that are distant and about which they have very little information. Feizal, whom we met in chapter 3, had a son who, despite his family's financial difficulties, managed to make payments to a contractual savings scheme offered by a new company in the area. When we went to meet the company's managers, they told us that the savings collected were invested in debentures issued by small companies based in the state capital. We watched nervously as the company changed its name twice and rumors circulated that it was about to close shop. Unlike these companies or, rather, their agents, Jyothi is local, visible, and has social ties with her clients. Thus she has an incentive to treat her customers well and a disincentive to make off with the principal.

Jyothi's customers were not victims of a local money illusion. Around the world we find similar systems that have been going for generations. Perhaps best known are the West African examples, which have become known collectively, if rather loosely, as *susus*, after the name used for them in Ghana.[14] They take many forms, but a common one is used by market traders, who hand a fixed amount each day to a "*susu* collector," and take the money back at the end of each month less one day's worth. Again, this means that customers earn a negative interest rate, but again this is a small fee to pay for a service that efficiently bundles a month's worth of daily savings into a usefully large lump sum, servicing the traders' constant requirements for capital to buy inventory.

Notice something else about savings collectors that sheds further light on the pricing of informal products, even on how we should define them. Most of Jyothi's customers, and virtually all *susu* customers, repeat their savings regimes cycle after cycle. They get into a rhythm in which during each cycle they pay in a series of small amounts and take out one big amount. If that series of cycles began, years back, with the lump sum, we would call each cycle, technically, a loan: but if it began with the small sums we would call it savings. But five years later, the distinction is meaningless. Those of us not familiar with this fact of life fall into a conceptual trap: $4 on $40 over 220 days doesn't sound too bad as a loan interest rate, but minus $4 on $40 sounds unbelievable as a savings rate. In Vijaywada, there are customers who simply didn't distinguish between deposit collectors and moneylenders, so similar is the service provided. Both offered repeated money-accumulation cycles for a fee.

Conclusions

The chapters thus far have uncovered a diversity of financial relations and devices used by the poor. Sylvia, one of the South African respondents, for example, holds in her portfolio not only her ASCA but several non-interest-paying RoSCAs, a low-interest bank account and a savings plan for her daughter. The lending ASCA is the high-risk, high-return part of her portfolio, but one that is hedged by other less risky instruments that fulfill different cash-flow planning needs. In this, Sylvia was behaving like many of our diarists. In South Asia, diarists held an average of nine different kinds of instruments, of varying levels of risk. It seems that, just as we wouldn't want to invest our entire retirement portfolio in hedge funds, the poor use different instruments that serve different needs in an attempt—not always successful—to balance their portfolios.

Such diversification means that households hold both interest-bearing and interest-free borrowings in their portfolios, simultaneously. Why don't households try to borrow as much as possible interest-free and save as much as possible with interest? One reason, which we discussed in chapter 2, is timing. While one might have several helpful friends and relatives willing to lend interest-free, they might not have the cash available when one needs it. Or one might already have borrowed from them.

But another reason hinges on what price really means to customers. In this chapter, we've explained the reason why context matters when considering the price of money in poor areas. It is easy to assume that the main reason behind high interest rates is the risk of doing business with low-income people.[15] But there are several other reasons why the price of money is high: the short-term nature of lending, the relatively small size of the principal, the lack of compounding interest, and the flexibility of arrangements. Not only is price only part of the picture, but price itself adjusts to many other factors.

The diversity of poor people's portfolios, then, comes about partly because the right kinds of providers are thin on the ground, and this helps to explain the astonishing demand for those services that approximate the needs of the poor. Because formal service providers have been wary of the potential markets in slums, townships, and villages (perceiving high default risk and the need for high interest rates to compensate), the scarcity of reliable providers continues. Such service providers deny an opportunity to themselves as well as to these poor communities. If they were to aim for larger scale, with better systems and technology, they could surely drive down their costs: microfinance providers have amply demonstrated that.

But would they also drive down prices generally, giving the moneylenders a run for their money? In Bangladesh, the arrival of widespread microfinance has driven down prices, but not quite in the way that was anticipated. Advocates of microfinance hoped that moneylenders would be forced to reduce their rates. They haven't, but an increasing share of a growing total of lending is being done by microfinance institutions, so the average price of borrowing has declined.

Moreover, throughout these chapters we have shown that informal financial services, though extremely valuable, are not always reliable. Formal service providers, which are more often set up with an eye toward sustainability, are arguably more reliable than informal service providers. And reliability is a key characteristic of the types of financial services that the poor need.

What is the nature of this unreliability with respect to price? First, informal service providers lack transparency because of the differences between stated and renegotiated contracts. While this provides some flexibility—an attribute highly valued by poor users, as we have shown—it also requires and invites special efforts by clients to secure more lenient terms, so such flexibility itself comes at some cost. Those paying late, for example, nonetheless withstand threat and anxiety. And, of course, not everyone can negotiate effectively, so customers are rarely treated on equal terms. Second, informal provision has built-in incentives to drag out repayments, punishing good clients and rewarding bad. While this structure can perhaps be viewed as a kind of distributive justice (profits are made from those with, rather than those without, the money available), it is one of the reasons why moneylenders remain restricted in scale and limited to poor and high-risk markets: since they do not reward "good" clients who have capital, they are likely to attract "bad" and cash-strapped clients disproportionately. Third, most informal interest-bearing loans are troublesome to arrange, in spite of their price. So there is an additional transaction cost that is not reliably priced for every borrower or perhaps even for the same borrower over time.

Poor households care about price, but they also care about convenience and flexibility and are willing to pay for those features. They are also happy to pay for reliability of the sort that Jyothi provides, and they are agreeably surprised when they find reliability combined with a relatively low price, as they do, increasingly, at microfinance institutions. Convenience, flexibility, and reliability are at the heart of building workable financial tools for the poor, and are a key to understanding the economic lives of poor households more broadly. Just as we found no households truly living hand to mouth—even among the very poor—we found no households so absolutely limited in their resources that price was the overriding determinant of financial choices.

Chapter Six

◆ ◆ ◆

RETHINKING MICROFINANCE: THE GRAMEEN II DIARIES

THE Grameen Bank of Bangladesh is the best-known and most widely imitated microfinance pioneer. But Grameen found itself in trouble in the late 1990s. Loans were no longer being repaid at the on-time rate of 98 percent that the bank had long advertised: in some areas it had fallen below 75 percent. In 1998 a devastating flood, one of the worst in the country's history, damaged many millions of households and exacerbated Grameen's problems by a further dramatic erosion of loan repayment. The bank had a crisis on its hands.

It responded with a major rethink; old premises were discarded, new approaches—some of them adapted from the work of local competitors, others entirely new—were brought on board. In 2001—just after we completed our original Bangladesh diaries—Grameen's management was ready to roll out a series of new and modified products, which it called "Grameen II." The rollout proved successful, in ways that sometimes surprised even the bank's leadership. The process shows the possibilities for building on the perspectives that we've developed in the previous chapters.

Grameen has since enjoyed a spell of renewed rapid growth in its clients and its portfolio, a growth paralleled in other microfinance institutions in Bangladesh, including Grameen's two biggest competitors, BRAC (now a name rather than an acronym) and ASA (the Association for Social Advancement). In late 2006 Grameen and its founder, Muhammad Yunus, were awarded the Nobel Peace Prize. A year later *Forbes*, an American business magazine, placed ASA at the top of its first-ever list of the world's 50 best microfinance institutions.[1]

To understand these developments from the point of view of the clients, we ran a special set of financial diaries in Bangladesh in 2002–5.[2] The diaries show that several of the insights generated by the original diaries (and set out in the preceding chapters) are—quite independently—being used to develop workable new products by Bangladeshi institutions as their understanding of the market improves. As there are now approximately 20 million microfinance customers in Bangladesh, this is no trivial development.

Organized Finance for the Poor

There have been many attempts to bring organized financial services to the poor, stretching back at least as far as the rural credit cooperatives of nineteenth-century Europe. But in the 1970s in Asia and the 1980s in Latin America, new pioneers deliberately set out to provide retail financial services *en masse* to poor and very poor populations while charging prices high enough to cover the costs. These advances, it is generally agreed, marked the start of a distinctly new tradition of "modern" financial services for the poor.

Grameen was started, in 1976, not by a banker but by an economics professor, Muhammad Yunus. He was not inspired by the prospect of making profits from banking with poor people, but by the idea of alleviating poverty in his war-torn and desperately poor country. His work was first recognized as important by development aid officers who began to fund it, and by humanitarian nongovernmental organizations (NGOs) that began to imitate it. Indeed, it looked as if he had developed an antipoverty device as much as a new form of banking.

The device was attractively simple. Grameen focused on the poorest rural households—those owning less than half an acre of cultivable land.[3] Representatives from households that met this criterion were invited to form groups of five, each from a different household. The groups were of a single sex, and at first there were as many male as female groups, though by the 1990s nearly all were women. A number of such groups met weekly in their village with a Grameen worker. The main purpose of the meetings, at which members also made a small compulsory savings deposit into a jointly owned fund, was to facilitate the repayment of the loans that each member took from Grameen and which she promised to use in a new or existing small business. As a group, members undertook to monitor each other's loan use and to ensure that all loans were repaid on time. The repayment schedule was a fixed amount each week for a year, covering both principal and interest. Successful on-time repayment guaranteed the rapid release of another, bigger loan. Providing such microenterprise credit was viewed as the most effective way to unleash the productive capacity of villagers trapped by cycles of low incomes and low skills. All of this was achieved while charging customers interest rates on loans of about 20 percent per year, a rate similar to the US bank charges for unsecured loans, such as on credit cards.[4]

When Grameen Bank reached its millionth client in 1991, the community of activists, donors, and policymakers working on international development took special notice. By the time of the first Bangladesh diaries (1999–2000) there were more than two million active Grameen "members," as the clients were called. In the meantime, dozens of NGOs in Bangladesh had set up similar schemes, and BRAC and ASA had grown to be almost as big as Grameen. The first set of Bangladesh diaries showed that no fewer than 30 of the 42 randomly chosen households we studied held accounts with one or more microfinance institutions. On the whole, as we showed in chapter 4, they liked what they got—financial services with relative reliability, conveniently small and frequent repayment installments, and the chance to bank without having to leave the village.

The key messages came to be recognized around the world: success, measured by the economic and social progress of borrowers, depended on women, on group solidarity, on microenterprises, and on loans. Grameen II, however, would contribute to a different set of messages, based around the provision of broad banking services, including savings, increasingly tailored to individuals and their multiple needs.

Grameen II

Grameen's new "Generalized System," or "Grameen II," came about in response to a decline in the quality of the bank's loan portfolio. The decline was intensified by the 1998 flood, but the bank realized that there were underlying problems that would not go away once the flood had been mopped up. In a frank public discussion of these problems, Muhammad Yunus wrote of "internal weaknesses in the system. The system consisted of a set of well-defined standardized rules. No departure from these rules was allowed. Once a borrower fell off the track, she found it very difficult to move back on."[5] In response, Grameen II made two sets of changes. The first tackled the rigidity and inflexibility in the lending system that Yunus referred to. It recognized that a single loan term (of one year) and a single repayment schedule (of equal invariable weekly installments that cannot be prepaid but have to be paid each and every week for the full year) simply did not match the cash flows of many poor households. Chapter 2, where we study cash flow in detail, confirms that insight. Grameen II accordingly brought in a wide range of loan terms from three months to three years.[6] To help if and when cash flow starts to dry up part way through a loan, or if some new investment opportunity arises, loans could be topped up to their full value before they were fully repaid. In cases of serious repayment difficulties, borrowers could reschedule their loans by extending the term, thus reducing the installment value. This is done within a system that contains incentives to "get back on the track" in the form of a promise of renewed borrowing rights once the problem has mended. Lending became more flexible by removing the requirement to borrow continuously. Grameen II also stepped back from group solidarity, outlawing any arrangement that makes borrowers responsible for repaying each other's loans.

The second set of changes comprises new or modified products that extend the range of transaction possibilities open to the clients. In so doing, Grameen II no longer assumes that its clients are exclusively interested in borrowing: most of these changes concern saving. Here again our own conclusions, drawn from the financial diaries, support this insight. In the original version of Grameen, copied by all the other Bangladesh microfinance institutions, members were required to save a small amount each week, deposited into a group-owned account. These deposits could not be withdrawn until the members had held their accounts for 10 years, or relinquished their membership of Grameen Bank. Under Grameen II, this compulsory saving was abandoned, and two new savings products were introduced in its place. A personal passbook savings account allowed individuals to deposit and withdraw savings at any time in any value. A commitment (or "contractual") savings plan, known as the Grameen Pension Savings, or GPS, was also introduced that offered a good rate of interest in return for regular monthly deposits over a five- or 10-year term. Here, Grameen was following pioneering work done earlier by ASA, by moving away from compulsory nonwithdrawable savings, and the midsize competitor BURO,[7] by introducing commitment savings.

These changes hold out the promise of making it easier for cash-strapped poor households to manage cash day to day and to accumulate large sums in a secure savings device, two of the core financial service needs we identified in earlier chapters. Note, however, that achieving this outcome was not Grameen's main objective in making these changes. Rather, Grameen wanted to create a source of loan capital by mobilizing more savings. When the flood occurred in the late 1990s Grameen found it harder than it had anticipated to obtain fresh capital. With Grameen II, not only was Grameen able to raise more savings from its poor borrowers, but the bank intensified its mobilization of deposits from the ordinary public. This was dramatically successful: by the end of 2004 the bank's deposit portfolio exceeded its loan portfolio for the first time ever, and savings have continued to grow ever since at a faster rate than the loan portfolio.

By the end of 2007 Grameen clients collectively owned $1.40 of savings in the bank for each $1 they had in loans.

In effect, Grameen turned itself from a microenterprise lender into a true retail bank, but one that continued to focus on poor households.

The Grameen II Diaries

From 2002 to 2005, the NGO MicroSave, who wished to learn more about the Grameen II innovations, supported a fresh set of financial diaries in Bangladesh. These "Grameen II diaries," as we shall call them here to distinguish them from the original Bangladesh diaries, ran for three years rather than 12 months, and diary households were visited once a month (at least) rather than every second week. As a result of these changes we got less detail than in the original, fortnightly, diaries, but we were able to watch changes unroll over a longer time-span.

Our selection procedure for households was also different. Rather than choosing households on the basis of their level of poverty, we did so on the basis of their relationship with microfinance providers. Most held accounts with microfinance institutions (many of them with Grameen, on whom the Grameen II diaries were focused, but several with other providers), but we also chose a few households that had no microfinance member at all, or had former microfinance members. This enabled us to study and compare a broad range of portfolios of households from the same villages but with varying, or no, microfinance partners.

In general terms, the portfolios from the Grameen II diaries are similar to those of the original Bangladesh set, and thus to the portfolios researched in India and South Africa. Once again it was clear that these households, though poor, are active financially. They work with many financial partners, principally but not exclusively in the informal sector. Flows of cash through the instruments they use are large relative to the balances. The mix of instruments—interest-free and private for-interest lending and borrowing, home savings, moneyguards, savings clubs, and semiformal providers, among others—is similar to the first Bangladesh set. Conversations with the diary householders once again showed that they took their financial life seriously, worried about it, and were on the lookout for ways to extend and improve it.

But there were some striking differences, too. Notably, microfinance providers loomed larger in the later diary set. Comparing households in the original 1999–2000 diary set who had access to microfinance providers, with microfinance-using households in the later Grameen II set, we found that a bigger proportion of the financial transactions of the latter group passed through microfinance providers. In part, this reflects the rapid growth of the microfinance sector in Bangladesh, with the three big players—Grameen, BRAC, and ASA—together adding nine million accounts between 2000 and 2005. As a result, diarists in the Grameen II set were much more likely to have accounts with more than one microfinance provider. They also transacted with their microfinance institutions more often and in larger amounts, taking advantage of the new products.

In the sections that follow we look at the impact of Grameen II's innovations on what we have identified as the key financial needs that millions of poor families find difficulty in meeting: managing cash flow, and building lump sums through long-term saving and through borrowing.

Managing Cash Flow with Passbook Savings

At the time of the original diaries, Grameen Bank customers were required to deposit funds weekly into a saving account, but their access to the funds was severely limited. Grameen II followed a shift in Bangladesh toward open-access, individually owned savings. By the time of the Grameen II diaries (2002–5) most microfinance customers, including those of Grameen, allowed members to save and withdraw as they liked at each weekly meeting (though they generally had to travel to the branch office to pick up the withdrawals). The shift met early resistance from bank workers, who worried that unlimited withdrawals would push balances too low for comfort, but the customers were pleased. Many used their new savings accounts to help solve the cash-flow management problems that, as we identified in chapter 2, absorbed so much time and gave so much trouble to the original diary households. For most of these users, this was the first time they had had access to a flexible but reliable account of this kind. Typically, they saved a little each week, and withdrew between two and three times a quarter.

Kapila Barua was one of our Grameen II diarists. She did some craftwork at home to supplement her husband's farm-laboring income of about $1.50 a day, earned on those days when he could find work. In our first interview with her she told us how much she liked Grameen's new personal savings, where she had a balance of a little under $18, explaining that withdrawing at will enabled her to manage many small expenses. Her diary shows that she used the weekly meeting to deposit about $4 to $10 each quarter.[8] She made at least one withdrawal each quarter. In the first quarter it was $1 for a food shortfall; in quarter 2 she took out $13 for school costs for her son, and then in the third quarter $4 to help a fellow member make loan repayments, and in the fourth quarter $2 to top up her own loan repayments. In quarter 5 she withdrew $1 to pay her Grameen loan insurance contribution, and in quarter 6 took out $11 and put it toward the purchase of gold earrings. After this she took a breather, making no withdrawals in quarter 7, but in quarter 8 she took out $11 to buy handicraft inputs, and in quarter 9 $4 to buy into Grameen's newly introduced life insurance scheme (insuring her husband's life). Then for six months she made no withdrawals as she saved hard for medical treatment for her son, and in the last quarter that we tracked, she took out $15 to pay doctor's fees and buy drugs for him.

Kapila's final large withdrawal brought her balance down to little more than a dollar. Her modest average balance in her passbook account was typical for the Grameen II diarists, though the combined personal savings of 37 Grameen II diary households with these kinds of accounts did rise somewhat over the three years, by 21 percent from $248 to $299 (about $8 per saver). But aggregate flows were very large relative to opening and closing balances: these 37 households deposited $4,228 between them in the three years (including interest earned), and withdrew $4,176. Thus, as in chapter 2, we saw large flows and small average balances, but the flows were notably bigger than for the microfinance savings in the original 1999–2000 diary set, when deposits into microfinance savings were standardized at a low rate, and withdrawals much harder to make. What these households were getting was more than simply a chance to withdraw savings: they got a wholly new and valuable money-management device of a sort none of them had experienced before. Because the institutions sent a worker to the village, it was easy to save a little each week into a resource that could be tapped at will for any purpose. This finding reinforces those from chapter 2: that poor households welcome safe, local, convenient open-access savings and use them intensively.

It also shows the perils of inferring that poor households don't *want* to save based only on the fact that they may not *currently* save much. Grameen II demonstrates that introducing better products can dramatically change an equation: with the introduction of the easy-to-use passbook savings account, saving activity rose dramatically.

Managing Cash Flow and Forming Large Sums with More Flexible Loans

Readers will have noticed that among the uses to which Kapila put her Grameen II savings withdrawals was making repayments on her Grameen II loans. This had previously been frowned on by Grameen, but in practice it made loans much easier to manage—when you were short of cash to make a repayment you could fund it in the short-term out of savings. Using savings for this purpose might often be less stressful than relying on help from neighbors, if that's even an option.

A Grameen II novelty that has proved convenient, and was welcomed by many borrowers, is the "loan top-up" facility, under which loans can be refreshed to the amount that had originally been disbursed. This could happen part way through the repayment cycle, so that if you started with a $200 loan and had already paid off $100, you could borrow that $100 again to get back up to $200 and continue with weekly repayments for an extended term. This works to make loans a better fit with poor-household cash flows.

The "top-ups" were especially appreciated by very poor households like Ramna's, who was another of our Grameen II diarists. She and her husband were completely landless, sheltering on her brother's land and trying to bring up two school-age sons. The husband had few skills and was in poor health, and though he tried day laboring, working in a tea stall, and fishing for crabs, he was never able to maintain steady income during the three years we knew them.

Ramna had joined Grameen II a year before we met her, and had taken a loan of $83 used to buy food stocks in a lean period. She was repaying weekly from a variety of sources including her husband's income, interest-free loans from family and neighbors, and her own Grameen II personal savings. In April 2003 she "topped up" her Grameen loan and used it to buy grain to keep in reserve for the coming monsoon period. This and her subsequent top-ups didn't mean that Ramna was falling into deeper and deeper debt: the top-up merely allowed her to refresh her loan to its original disbursed value, not more. Then in October her father-in-law died and they financed the funeral with another top-up, worth $67. They managed to make repayments during the winter dry season, so that in May 2004, when she was eligible for another top-up, she took it and stored it with a moneyguard, from whom it was later recovered and used to pay down a private loan that had been hanging over them for some time. She topped up with another $75 once more in December, the month of the main rice harvest, and it was spent on stocks of grain and on medical treatment for her husband, with a portion held back to make weekly repayments. They struggled to repay in early 2005 because her own father was ill and they had to find money to pay for his treatment, but in early July she was able to top up again ($65), this time paying school fees as well as restocking with food. When we saw her last at the end of 2005 she had a loan balance of $70 to pay and was looking forward to another top-up.

Her loans cost her 20 percent a year, and were not invested directly to produce income, but Ramna was sure that the facility was helpful. Without it, she asked us, how could she stock up with food, keep the boys in school, and buy her husband drugs when he needed them? All these maintenance tasks would have been much harder and much more expensive without access to the flow of usefully large lump sums from Grameen loans. Ramna's story highlights two lessons from earlier chapters: that loans can be successfully used both to smooth consumption across seasons and to manage risk, and that reliability matters. Ramna was able to get and use her loans as she wished within a rule-bound reliable framework that she could count on and plan on.

Just as with Kapila's savings account, so with Ramna's loans, we see large flows and small balances. Ramna started with $35 outstanding in her loan account, and ended with $70: in the intervening three years she took loans worth $337, repaid $302, and paid interest of $44.[9] The frequency and reliability of the Grameen loan service makes it both attractive and manageable for households like Ramna's. Indeed, of three households that we selected because we thought they were so poor that no microfinance institution would ever take them, two did in fact open accounts during the three years of the research, drawn in by the observation that the microfinance institutions were now offering a service that suited them, as opposed to being suitable only for "those who can invest."

This echoes another of our themes: the focus on microcredit for microenterprise has contributed enormously to the attraction, success, and spread of microfinance, but has had the unfortunate side effect of diverting attention from a much wider set of households who seek, value, and reliably repay loans for many other purposes. Happily, Ramna was in practice able to use her loans as she wished, notwithstanding Grameen Bank's traditional injunction to spend them only on a "productive investment."

THE USE OF MICROFINANCE LOANS

Because they dealt with the intimate details of customers' financial transactions over three years, the Grameen II diaries provided one of the best opportunities that researchers have ever enjoyed to understand how microfinance loans are actually used.[10] During the course of the diaries, 43 of the households took at least one microfinance

Table 6.1 Grameen II Diaries: Total Disbursed Value of Loans, by Source

	Value of loan	*Percentage of total loans taken*
Interest-free loans from family & neighbors	15,989	23%
Credit advanced by shop-keepers	1,692	2%
Loans on interest from family, neighbors & moneylenders	9,033	13%
Loans from savings-and-loan clubs	2,468	3%
Loans from formal banks	2,167	3%
Loans from microfinance institutions	39,668	56%
Total	$71,017	100%

Note: US$ converted from Bangladesh takas at $ = 60 takas, market rate. The table includes all loans, not just microfinance loans, both outstanding at start of period and taken during period for all 43 Grameen II diarists.

loan—from Grameen or from other institutions. Between them they used 239 microfinance loans with a total disbursed value of about $39,000 at the average exchange rate for the period. The average disbursed value of the individual loans was $165 (with a median of $120).

Impressive though these numbers are, they represent only a part of all their borrowing, since households were also borrowing from their families and from savings clubs, neighbors, moneylenders, and even a little from banks. Our diary technique allows us to compare these sources, as shown in table 6.1.

Microfinance institutions, then, supplied comfortably more than half (almost 56 percent) of the disbursed value of all loans taken by these households, though all of them also borrowed from one or more other sources. This is a considerably bigger proportion than the 38 percent in the original 1999–2000 Bangladesh diaries.

What were these loans used for? As shown in table 6.2, we sorted 237 of these loans into six main categories.

We were able to allocate most loans to a single broad category of use, but the 55 in the "mixed" category were split between various

Table 6.2 Grameen II Diaries: Number and Disbursed Value of Microfinance Loans, by Use Category

	Number	*%*	*Value (US$)*	*%*
Stock for retail or trading businesses and crafts	75	32%	15,231	39%
Asset acquisition and/or maintenance	37	16%	5,583	14%
On-lending to others outside the household	27	11%	5,764	14%
Paying down other debt	25	11%	3,413	9%
Consumption	18	8%	1,425	4%
Mixed uses	55	23%	7,535	19%
Total	237	100%	38,951	100%

Note: US$ converted from Bangladesh takas at $ = 60 takas, market rate. A total of 239 microfinance loans were used by 43 borrowers. The two loans unaccounted for were placed into savings instruments.

uses. Of these, 35 (almost two-thirds) included a large share for "consumption"; 30 (a little over half) included a large share for paying down other debt; and 26 (just under half) included some kind of investment (in assets or in business stock) as an important use. So a typical "mixed use" loan might be $150, of which $30 used for food, $70 for repairing the house, and $50 for repaying other debt.

Our "asset" category is broad, and includes buying, mortgaging-in or leasing-in of land, house construction and repair, and buying or repairing a wide range of vehicles and boats, farm or business equipment, and tools for trades like carpentry.

If we regard the first two categories—business stocks and all kinds of assets—as "productive" loan uses of the sort that microfinance loan officers prefer, we see that roughly half are used in those ways (a little fewer than half of all loans, and a little more than half of the loan value).

This does not, mean, though, that half of all *users* used their loans for "productive" purposes. This is because productive uses tend to be strongly associated with particular borrowers. Out of the 43 borrowers in the sample, a handful—just six—were responsible for $11,810—three-quarters—of the value of loans in the biggest category, "business," and between them took two-thirds of all loans issued in that category. So though business was the most common use of loans measured by the number of loans and their value, it was not the most common when measured by the number of borrowers involved.

The six households who dominate the business category all have well-established retail or trading businesses and borrow to buy stock as often as they are allowed. Several of them are Grameen members, and for them the introduction of the loan top-up system is a boon. Most take capital from several microfinance institutions. One cattle trader, for example, has a Grameen basic loan that he (or rather his wife) tops up every six months, taking around $100 each time, and has concurrent loans of up to twice that value from two other institutions. The user who has taken more loans, of a higher total value, than anyone else in the sample runs a well-stocked grocery store: during the three years of the research he borrowed $4,580 in 15 loans from three providers (Grameen, ASA, and *Safe*Save), the biggest being a $1,670 "special investment loan" from Grameen. Altogether this one borrower alone took 12 percent of the total value of all loans in the sample.

The most striking finding of this brief review is the diversity of uses on display, set against the concentration of some uses among distinct types of users. On the one hand, it is clear that an early hope of microfinance lending—that virtually every loan would be invested in a microenterprise—has not come about. On the other hand, businesses and asset-investment uses are responsible for more than half the value of loans disbursed, though concentrated among the minority of borrowers well placed to use them in this way.

Accumulating Large Sums in Commitment Savings Accounts

One of the big changes made to poor-owned portfolios by new products at microfinance institutions, then, was to shift some day-to-day money management into microfinance savings and loan accounts. The other was to open up the scope for building longer-term financial assets that produce usefully large sums. We have just seen how Ramna, who used loan top-ups for her father's funeral, for her son's school fees, and for her husband's medicines, was able to access useful sums quickly through a reliable and flexible loan facility. A slower but ultimately more powerful way to create large sums is to accumulate them in a reliable savings account.

Commercial banks in Bangladesh long offered "Deposit Pension Schemes" to their non-poor clients, and the schemes had proved very popular as ways to commit to saving over the long term. A few microfinance pioneers, notably BURO, had experimented with a pro-poor version in the 1990s, but the idea did not really take off until Grameen II made it available to its several million members.[11] The Grameen version, called Grameen Pension Savings (GPS), offers a good rate of interest to members who agree to save a regular sum of at least one dollar per month for a term of five or 10 years. It is a "pension" in name only. Use is not restricted for retirement needs; indeed, many younger families see the "pensions" as ways to build resources for expenses that loom in the medium term—like the eventual need to pay for children's schooling or weddings.

Like the informal devices such as a RoSCA (see chapter 4 for definitions and descriptions of RoSCAs and other savings clubs), commitment plans like the GPS offer a structure of regular deposit periods. The structure helps its users to discipline themselves to deposit regularly and to maintain the savings for future use.[12] Unlike savings clubs, however, the term does not have to be short enough to eliminate the risks that come from the accumulation of capital owned by multiple people in an informal environment: commitment plans can be long term if the provider is a trustworthy regulated entity such as Grameen. The GPS has a maximum term of 10 years, but on maturity the savings can be transferred into a fixed deposit account and another GPS begun. In future, Grameen could offer a GPS with an even longer term.

When the GPS was first offered to Grameen clients, there were some who were already familiar with the idea of commitment savings—perhaps they knew of people who held one with BURO or with a bank—and others for whom it was new. The first group, often among the less poor, tended to welcome and use it immediately. Jharimon is typical. She and her husband have a well-established home, and, relative to the neighbors, he makes a good income of around $3.50 a day from operating a small laundry in a rented shop. This puts them near the top of the income ladder for microfinance members, and until Grameen II came along the couple hadn't bothered with microfinance membership. But Jharimon was one of several of our diary households who joined Grameen specifically to access the GPS.

The couple assumed at first that they could take advantage of the GPS without joining the bank as a full borrowing member, but the bank did not allow it. So in 2002 Jharimon joined a local Grameen Bank group and immediately opened a GPS worth $3.50 a month with a 10-year term. She wanted to save for the future marriages of her two daughters, one 12 years old and the other still a baby. She also took a small loan "because they offered me one," paid it off quickly, and didn't renew it (despite some gentle pressure from the Grameen worker who preferred to have his members borrowing). In April 2004, satisfied that the GPS was well managed, she opened another 10-year GPS, this time of $2 a month, to fund advanced schooling or a business for her eight-year-old only son when he grows up. Then toward the end of 2004 Grameen, which correctly assessed her as a good client, offered her a big "special investment" loan of $416 to expand the laundry. She took it, and at the same time opened yet another GPS, again of $2 a month. By the end of 2005, Jharimon had saved $262 in her three GPS accounts, net of interest. She had $225 still to pay on her "special" loan. She had become bored with the weekly meetings and now usually just sent her weekly loan repayments and savings through another, poorer member. But she was a satisfied customer.

Jharimon was well-off relative to most diary households, and valued commitment savings before she joined Grameen. But how popular was the GPS with poorer households who had no previous experience of such devices? Answering this question isn't straightforward, because Grameen II officially requires a GPS of $1 a month as a qualification for borrowing any sum more than $133: so some GPS users hold them only because of this condition. But client Sankar's story helped us understand what was going on in the minds of some of the poorer household heads when faced with this requirement.

Sankar was a landless, illiterate rickshaw driver, whose wife had Grameen membership. They had borrowed from Grameen Bank a few times—in fact one loan had helped him buy his rickshaw. Suddenly his wife told him they would have to open a GPS in order to get the next loan. He was suspicious, he told us. "And now?" we asked. He chuckled. "Now, we try to avoid loans and just use the GPS." Pressed to explain, he said that his income was small but sufficient for their daily needs and they had nothing to invest an expensive loan in. Their priorities now were for their children, and the GPS seemed, compared to borrowing, a cheaper, more relaxed, longer-term way of providing for their future (marriage for the girl, a business for the boy). Like Jharimon, Sankar borrowed sometimes and saved always. "Grameen should have done this years ago," he said, echoing what many others had told us.

Of the millions of GPS holders, we don't know how many appreciate the account in the way that Sankar does, and how many are holding them just because members are required to do so in order to access a loan. But in our diary households we can get some indication. Of the 27 households in our sample who held a GPS, 20 held more than the minimum required to take a loan, and 11 of these held more than one GPS. In most of these cases, presumably, the GPS was held for its own sake, and not just as part of the price of borrowing. Of the remaining seven, some may be like Sankar—that is, savers who began reluctantly but have become enthusiastic as time has gone by. Altogether, it looks as if an understanding of the virtues of "commitment saving" devices is well established and growing.

The 27 Grameen II GPS holders have portfolios that are somewhat different from those of the original 1999–2000 diary set. Not only is the microfinance institutions' share of total savings balances twice as big (31 percent as against 14 percent), but part of that savings is now held in secure, individually owned and consistently growing long-term instruments.

The GPS helped transform clients' portfolios, but it also helped transform the financial health of Grameen Bank itself. When we started our research late in 2002, the bank's total savings portfolio, at 8,284 million takas (about $142 million at that time), was 68 percent of its loan portfolio of 12,149 million takas. When we finished at the end of 2005, the loans had grown rapidly to 27,970 million takas. But the savings had increased even faster, to 31,659 million takas, 13 percent bigger than the loan portfolio. Looked at from the viewpoint of chapter 4, where we saw the difficulties faced by poor households in accumulating usefully large sums of capital, and at the mechanisms they turned to in order to achieve this end, the evidence suggests that accounts such as the GPS—provided they remain well managed—would represent a major step forward in financial services for the poor if they could be emulated or bettered worldwide.[13]

Grameen III?

Bangladesh's microfinance industry, one of the world's oldest and biggest, continues to develop at a rapid pace. The combination we have described in this chapter—open passbook savings, more flexible ways of lending, and commitment savings accounts—shows how much has been achieved in Bangladesh to improve financial services for the poor. Muhammad Yunus's original vision for Grameen Bank helped the world see the power that access to simple loans can have in helping villagers build small businesses. The innovations brought by Grameen II address a broader set of critical needs that we discovered in the financial diaries: managing cash flows, coping with risk, and accumulating usefully large sums over time.

Still, not every microfinance customer is a Kapila, a Ramna, a Jharimon, or a Sankar. Even those four, like most customers, continue to transact largely in the informal sector, and it is not hard to see why. The interface with the microfinance institutions remains the weekly village meeting, a breakthrough of the 1970s that is now looking somewhat stale: meetings consume too much precious time, there is no privacy, individual needs go unrecognized, the male workers tend to patronize the women members, and more and more members skip the meeting if they can, preferring just to show up and pay their dues as quickly as possible. Working almost exclusively with women may well have started as a commendable attempt to right a gender imbalance, but, as time goes by, more and more critics point to the failure to find ways to serve men. Many microfinance institutions say that they have abandoned joint liability, but field staff, fearful of loan arrears, continue to impose some forms of it. Similarly, despite attempts to make repayment terms and schedules more flexible, most loans are still for one year with equal invariable weekly payments that cannot be prepaid: the flexibility offered by Grameen's top-up system and competitors' short-term emergency loans remains an exception rather than a rule in the industry. Most clients are still routinely pressured into taking out a fresh loan as soon they have repaid an earlier one.[14] High rates of account closures suggest that many members find these conditions difficult.[15]

Moreover, Bangladesh's regulatory regime is now falling behind that of other countries: unlike other Asian states such as Cambodia or Pakistan, there is no legal identity designed expressly for microfinance providers. Thanks to special legislation, only Grameen Bank is allowed to mobilize savings freely, even though many of its microfinance competitors have shown themselves able to look after deposits safely; and a lack of clarity about what NGOs can and can't do is holding back microfinance NGOs that want to move into leasing, insurance, or small-business lending. Conversely, clients have little recourse in cases of abuse by microfinance institutions, and this is made worse by the failure to provide basic written terms and conditions for microfinance products: ironic at a time when Bangladesh's NGOs are beginning to work in the arena of "rights to information."

Today's shortcomings can be overcome. Given time, legislators will enact an improved microfinance law. Drawing on what we have learned from our diary households, our vision for what microfinance in Bangladesh could then become—perhaps some future

"Grameen III"—is of microfinance institutions positioning themselves as providers of integrated money-management systems for poor households. As such, they would no longer insist that their clients borrow continually, nor borrow exclusively for microenterprise investment. Rather, they would continue to improve the flexibility of the three core products—the passbook savings, the loans, and the commitment savings—to make them less of a "one-size-fits-all" service and more capable of achieving ever closer matches with the expressed demands and actual cash flows of poor households. Once that set of flexible "core services" is in place, improved specialist savings, loan, and insurance services can be developed. They would respond to demands for products for home improvement, medical and educational expenses, and pensions, for example, as well as for microenterprises.

In Bangladesh the purpose of microfinance has always been seen as the eradication of poverty, and its microfinance providers remain focused on the poor. They have shown an astonishing capacity to develop products and take them quickly to scale. That combination—a focus on poverty plus the capacity to scale up quickly—should enable them to exploit new ideas and technologies that can improve quality and build on the foundations laid by Grameen II, again providing a model of financial innovation from which the rest of the world can learn.

Chapter Seven

◆ ◆ ◆

BETTER PORTFOLIOS

Not having enough money is only one part of what it is to be poor. Households like those who feature in our diaries face many challenges of poverty that go beyond the lack of money. They may face discrimination because of their ethnicity or class, find that their legal rights are poorly enforced, or have to struggle with low-quality public services and low skill levels. Measures of well-being such as the UN's Human Development Index track health and literacy as well as income, broadening the domain of poverty reduction.

Yet the financial diaries made us think afresh about poverty in terms of money—and, more specifically, money management. We saw that without access to basic forms of financial intermediation, poor households found their health emergencies triggered broader economic crises; they were prevented from seizing opportunities to increase income; and they were pushed into relying on neighbors and relatives in ways that often brought shame, anxiety, and dependence.

When incomes are small, tools to *manage* income well become vitally important. The money that the poor earn too often arrives at the wrong times, can be hard to hold onto, and is difficult to build into something larger through borrowing and saving. This is the fundamental tragedy of poverty as seen through a financial lens: the triple whammy of incomes that are both low and uncertain, within contexts where the financial opportunities to leverage and smooth income to fit expenditure are extremely limited.

A focus on money management does not shut out more ambitious aspirations such as improving health, education, and farming practices. On the contrary, it can help to realize them. A striking example was found in a study of fertilizer adoption in western Kenya.[1] The biggest difficulty farmers adopting new technologies faced was not in understanding the methods and their benefits, but in timing savings in order to purchase the fertilizer when they needed it. When financial tools were provided that solved this problem, fertilizer use and production increased. By getting the fundamentals right—by making it easier for poor people to get a grip on time and money so that income earned in the past and income anticipated in the future can be tapped in the amounts required at the time most needed—basic money management tools are the very foundation for aspirations of a broader nature. At an aggregate level, studies of economic growth also point to the fundamental contribution of improved financial access.[2]

Striving for Universal Service

Financial services for poor people—that is, microfinance, as provision of these services has become known—is enjoying unprecedented growth. New resources of all sorts are pouring in from every side. More and more providers are setting up shop in more and more countries around the world, some of them fired up by the vision of improving the lives of the poor, others lured by the prospects of profits, and many—the so-called double bottom line institutions—attracted by both. In the last few years, the level of private financial investment has increased sharply, so that microfinance is no longer so dependent on the public purse.[3] New technologies, especially mobile devices in the hands of field staff and clients, and smart computer programs in the back offices of providers, promise huge boosts to productivity, lower costs, and greater convenience.[4] Ideas for new financial products for the poor are being launched almost daily, and clever ways of testing their efficiency and their impact are being devised. New research, such as we have described in this book, is shedding fresh light on what poor people seek when they look for financial partners.[5]

The poor-owned portfolios that are revealed by the financial diaries suggest that the surge of interest in supplying financial services to poor people is likely to be matched by real, ongoing, and substantial demand. The diaries have shown that it is because of, not in spite of, their low and uncertain incomes that poor people are extremely active in financial intermediation, through whatever means are available to them.

As providers get better at responding to this demand over the next decade or so, financial services will enter a race that was unimaginable before now—the race to become the first high-quality basic service available to the poor on a near-universal basis. Poor people in most countries today remain more likely to have a school or a health clinic in their village than a branch of a microfinance bank. But many of those schools and clinics continue to deliver poor services, and it will require large doses of public money and considerable political will to get them working reliably. Microfinance's advantage in this race is that it can pursue the task of delivering reliable and affordable services to the poor independent of public resources. It can also operate with less dependence on political will once there is a suitable legal framework in place for microbanking, something that many governments are already offering.[6]

Financial services for the poor are a good in themselves, but as they become widespread they will also help to push forward improvements in other services. Many of our diarists place a high value on getting their children into school and keeping them there, but with poor quality money-management tools they find it hard to ensure that they have the school fees or money for uniforms and books on hand when needed. In the previous chapter, we saw how Kapila Barua and Ramna used savings and loans offered by a microfinance provider to manage medical expenses as well as school costs; they were able to do so because the provider's financial tools were reliable and convenient. As poor people are enabled, through better money-management, to back their demands for health, education and other services with more resources, they will exert more pressure for improvement.

Opportunities and Principles

This book has been full of detail. We have traced out the thousands of small transactions made by poor households and delved into intimate questions about why they occurred. Example after example revealed that poor people do indeed *manage* their money. But they also showed that the portfolios which result from their efforts are often fragile and incomplete.

What, then, are the most promising ways of improving the portfolios? By distilling the detail from our diaries we have identified three big opportunities that providers can seize, and we offer a set of principles that should help guide them as they do so.

OPPORTUNITIES

Each of the 250 or so poor-owned portfolios that we examined for this book is unique. Each reflects the characteristics of the household members who own it: their ages, their professions and incomes, and their aspirations and expectations. Such characteristics shape financial preferences. Pumza and Zanele are two 74-year-old women from South Africa, each heading a multigenerational household that depends heavily on an old-age government grant. But the two women take very different approaches to managing their grants. Pumza is an optimist, and leverages her grant through debt, only to go through lean times when the loans have to be repaid. Zanele, by contrast, avoids debt, even at the cost of going hungry, and saves wherever she can. Two brothers-in-law from India, Sandeep and Prakash, are another contrasting pair: Sandeep is outgoing and uses his huge acquaintanceship to develop a host of informal financial partnerships, whereas the more retiring Prakash nurtures his savings privately and cautiously.

Despite their differences, all of them, as the diaries show, seek financial intermediation services to further their ends. Sometimes the devices they use succeed for them, sometimes not. Taking the broadest view of their portfolios, we distinguish three key services that are greatly in demand but often inadequately provided. Offering solutions to these key services give microfinance providers three big opportunities:

1. Helping poor households manage money on a day-to-day basis
2. Helping poor households build savings over the long term
3. Helping poor households borrow for all uses

In some places, providing insurance will also provide a big opportunity, but the diaries remind us that from a household's perspective what matters is being able to manage risk, not being insured per se. As chapter 3 described, having a chunk of savings to fall back on and being able to borrow when needed are often the most critical ways to manage risk.

Cash-Flow Management. By cash-flow management we mean day-to-day money management: manipulating small and irregular or unreliable incomes to ensure that cash is available when needed, so that there is food on the table every day, small but unpredictable needs like a visit to the doctor are met, and low-value but recurrent outlays, say for school fees or books, can be provided for. We saw in chapter 2 that managing money in this way absorbs a very large share of the time that poor households give to financial affairs. This is true for a big majority of households, irrespective of preferences or of circumstances.

The first of our three big opportunities, then, is to offer poor households access to a cash-flow management facility that combines convenience with capacity. It would provide the chance to make small-scale savings of any value at any time with the right to withdraw on demand; and at the same time it would offer loans of a modest value that can be taken quickly, on demand, at any time, and repaid in small (and, if necessary, irregular) installments.

Building Savings. The diaries show that poor households have room in their budgets for savings and understand the need to save. Their use of savings clubs shows how they welcome the chance to save regularly over time. But because most savings clubs have limited lifespans, poor people have very few opportunities to build up savings into large sums over the long term. This is a serious limitation, since building long-term cushions of savings is a vitally important way of dealing with expensive life-cycle events, with purchases of big assets, and with emergencies.

Our second big opportunity, therefore, is to offer long-term contractual savings products. These mimic savings clubs by making it possible to save small sums on a regular basis, but add the opportunity of doing so safely over the long term. As chapter 6 has shown, an account of this kind that is already common in the villages of Bangladesh has met with resounding demand, and there are similar schemes working well elsewhere. But this revolution in long-term "microsaving" is only just starting, and is yet to begin in countries where legislation to allow reliable microbankers to mobilize savings is not yet in place. The diaries show why it is important to overcome these obstacles.

Loans for All Uses. Even if poor households are provided with ways to build savings over the long term, they will still need to finance a wide range of larger expenditures through borrowing. There are so many demands for large sums that they cannot be met by saving alone. But the diaries show that poor households lack dependable access to credit, especially for larger sums that are needed to deal with major life-cycle events, big purchases, and emergencies.

Our third big opportunity, then, is lending for a wide range of uses. The basic mechanisms are already available, because the development of uncollateralized lending has been the single biggest and most widespread achievement of the microfinance movement. But many microfinance providers still prefer their borrowers to use their loans for just one purpose—microenterprise. Where this is enforced, clients cannot borrow for other vital uses even when they have the cash flow to service the loans. Our own research in Bangladesh, as revealed in the previous chapter, shows that many loans ostensibly taken for microenterprises are used for other purposes. It is time for microfinance not merely to face up to this reality, but to embrace the opportunity that it presents. By offering *general-purpose* loans, matched in value and structure to the cash flows of poor households, microfinance would open up to the biggest single market it is likely to find among the poor (especially the urban poor who tend to be waged rather than self-employed), and one that would be greatly appreciated by most of our diary households.

Many of these loans will be used to deal with emergencies. This will be so even though, ideally, risk should be addressed through insurance. True insurance—the pooling of contributions that are paid out unequally to those who suffer the insured event—works only when the insured risks are well defined so that false claims can be rejected. This requires each risk to be separately insured. Low-income households are unlikely to want to spend money on multiple policies for a range of risks, knowing that only some of them will bring returns. If there were such a thing as "general purpose insurance"—an insurance policy that paid out for a wide range of events—poor households would be more likely to embrace it. In its absence, the next best way of dealing with risk is through savings, backed up by access to loans, as the stories in chapter 3 vividly show.

PRINCIPLES

The words *reliability*, *convenience*, *flexibility*, and *structure* occur often in this book. They are the key principles for policymakers and microfinanciers to bear in mind as they develop regulations and products for pro-poor financial services.

Reliability. Reliability—the delivery of products and services at the promised time, in the promised amount, and at the promised price—is the single biggest improvement that microfinance can bring to the financial lives of the poor. The accounts we give in earlier chapters, of what poor households must go through to achieve their financial goals, show why this is so. Reliability is uncommon in the lives of the poor: most services they deal with are unreliable, from the school and the clinic, to the electricity supply, to the police and the courts. Their own incomes are unreliable: always small but often irregular and unpredictable as well. One of the biggest challenges of living on two dollars a day is that it doesn't always come. Were you to have two dollars coming in reliably every day, you could plan expenditure, and calculate your capacity to save or repay, with a precision that would magnify the purchasing power of your income. The next best thing to having reliable income is to have reliable financial partners.

Convenience. By convenience we mean the chance to take and repay loans, and make and withdraw deposits, frequently, close to home or work, quickly, privately, and unobtrusively. As the level of convenience rises, the volume of intermediation possible for a poor household multiplies. Deposit collectors and moneylenders in India and Africa show that a daily visit by a friendly collector to a client's home or place of work is rewarded with a level of transactions far in excess of what that client would be capable of under other circumstances. Microfinance providers around the world have shown that establishing a convenient local venue for frequent meetings with their clients usually leads to excellent loan performance based on very high on-time rates of repayment. An older financial system, pawnbroking, has always offered a speedy and private way to turn assets temporarily into cash and has been valued for its convenience.

Flexibility. Flexibility refers to the ease with which transactions can be reconciled with cash flows. The level and type of flexibility will vary with the service. For day-to-day money management, flexibility in the value and frequency of transactions is needed, so that poor households can maximize their intermediation by being able to transact in any sum, no matter how small, at any time. For building savings, poor households will need some flexibility in the payment schedules, so that short-term difficulties do not prevent savers from benefiting from the account's long-term advantages.

For loans, flexible adaptation to client cash flows can take many forms. Clients can be offered a range of loan terms to choose from so that they can avoid having to make repayments in "hungry months." They may be allowed to prepay loans when larger sums become available to them, or to refresh loans when liquidity becomes constrained part way through a payment regime. Repayment schedules can be made flexible without abandoning discipline by allowing grace periods, by rewarding on-time payment with increases in credit limits, by allowing borrowers to draw down savings to make repayments when things are difficult, or by granting short-term supplementary loans. In Dhaka, *Safe*Save, a microfinance provider founded by one of the authors, allows borrowers to repay what they like when they like, but multiplies their chances of repaying quickly by visiting them each day.[7] In India the "Kishan Card" has had some success by allowing farm-loan repayments to be made as flexibly as conventional credit-card debt. Although uncollateralized lending has been one of the proudest boasts of the microfinance movement, the judicious use of financial collateral can make loans more usable for the poor: the diaries show that many poor people do not object to "borrowing back their own savings" partly because they value the savings so highly that they would rather borrow against them than draw them down, and partly because having the savings reassures them that should difficulties arise they can set their loan off against their savings.

Structure. Regularities—such as scheduled visits by bank workers, or planned savings or loan repayment schedules—that promote self-discipline are what we mean by structure. Structure becomes important as values rise and term lengths grow, above all in commitment savings plans and longer-term or higher-value loans. As we have seen, for short-term day-to-day money management, structure in this sense is not important, and may shut out some transactions, but for long-term savings regimes and repayment schedules, it is helpful, especially where its harshness is softened by appropriate kinds of flexibility. Structure reinforces reliability.[8]

The Supply-side Challenge

As recently as a decade ago, we might have been accused of wishing for the impossible. But recent developments in microfinance, coupled with evidence that poor people are willing to pay for such services, have changed the outlook entirely.

In chapter 6 we reviewed the rapid strides made by microfinance providers in Bangladesh that have brought convenient money-management accounts, structured savings, and more flexible loans to most of the nation's poor households. They have done so profitably at loan interest rates similar to credit-card rates in the United States. Also in Bangladesh, *Safe*Save, offers its clients exceptionally high levels of convenience. Clients are visited every day at their home or workplace, and may take loans without fixed terms that can be paid down day-by-day as the client likes. Yet this service too is delivered profitably.[9]

Bangladesh is densely populated, in the villages as well as in the towns, a characteristic that undoubtedly helped it pioneer mass microfinance. But Kenya, with a much sparser population, also boasts remarkable examples of convenient and flexible services. Equity Bank has had success with "mobile banking," using four-wheel drive vehicles to reach remote villages on a weekly basis to offer a range of low-cost savings and loan products. This allowed Equity to quickly build a big clientele among poor and middle-income Kenyans. Examples of providers exploiting the potential of wireless devices can also be found in Africa: M-Pesa of Kenya was one of the first to roll out services featuring money transfers over mobile phones, though it was beaten to it by providers in the Philippines.

The potential of these advances is now well recognized by the wider financial services industry. Not everything that is new will meet its promise, but microfinance has now entered a period of fast evolution in which, sooner or later, suppliers are likely to figure out how best to serve the real financial needs of poor households eager for good-quality financial services.

Maximizing Money

Not having enough money is bad enough. Not being able to manage whatever money you have is worse. This is the hidden bind of poverty. For lack of a tool to marshal money into the right sums at the right times, a missed doctor's visit tips into a full-blown family health crisis. A lack of ready cash deprives a child of a place at school, or prevents an adult from seizing an opportunity to increase income and gain greater economic stability.

Reducing poverty will take much more than financial sector development. Access to good jobs, a foundation of steady economic growth, and the strengthening of public infrastructure and safety nets, are all essential. But the diaries reveal how central finance is to the lives of the poor; this is shown clearly in the time and energy that they must devote to grappling with financial challenges and opportunities. Far from living hand to mouth, consuming all income as soon as it arrives, they keep savings at home; join savings clubs and savings-and-loan clubs; transact with family, friends, neighbors, and employers; and, where doing so is feasible and attractive, sign on with formal licensed providers. These sets of relationships and transactions constitute the poor-owned portfolios that we have examined in this book.

With added tools, the portfolios can perform better, magnifying the value that households can squeeze out of each dollar. To do this, they need, above all, reliable access to three key services: day-to-day money management, building long-term savings, and general-purpose loans. By combining the insights from the diaries with the experience of the new wave of microfinance organizations, we can ensure that poor households have a chance to better their financial strategies and improve their lives.

Appendix 1

◆ ◆ ◆

THE STORY BEHIND THE PORTFOLIOS

THE MOST IMPORTANT sources for the findings reported in this book are the words and actions of poor people themselves. In particular, we rely on the yearlong "financial diaries" that were written in collaboration with about 300 poor households in Bangladesh, India, and South Africa at various times between 1999 and 2005.

The intensity of getting to know the characters in the financial diaries informed our perspective on financial behavior as much as our scrutiny of the data we collected. We and our field team got to know not only which respondents were using what financial devices, but also gained a deeper and more personal understanding of who these people were: who was often confused about their finances, who had family disagreements that guided their decisions, who was not coping with the circumstances they found themselves in. Money is powerful, particularly when you don't have a lot of it, and it was only by going to the "coal face" of financial interactions between the people themselves that we felt we could understand how and why the poor managed money the way they did.

Mixing Qualitative and Quantitative Research Methods

Very little systematic research has been done into the precise methods that poor people use to manage their money. Qualitative work by anthropologists such as Shirley Ardener and Clifford Geertz described intricate savings clubs as long ago as the 1960s, and gruesome accounts of the predations of moneylenders can be found in the otherwise dry reports of British officers in nineteenth-century colonial India and elsewhere. Other studies have focused on the mechanisms and products of the informal money market, notably Fritz Bouman's *Small, Short, and Unsecured* which deals with informal finance in the Indian state of Maharashtra.[1]

At the other end of the spectrum are quantitative surveys that ask questions about loans and savings, but these mostly ignore or underreport informal devices and services, and offer only a summarized snapshot of the household's financial behavior.[2] Many researchers use data sets provided by the microfinance institution they are studying or whose data set they have, but the narrow focus of these data sets often means that the wide variety of financial management devices are downplayed or neglected. The quality of data is also weakened by the use of the recall method (how well can you recall details of your financial life 12 months ago?) and the limited trust that could be built up between respondent and interviewer in a one-off meeting (how much information would you give an interviewer at a first-time meeting about your private finances?).

While much in these other kinds of studies is insightful, we felt the need for an approach that would tackle the whole range of ways poor people managed their money over time. What was needed was a method that would capture the richness and complexity of poor people's financial lives while being systematic enough in its data collection to prevent it from being dismissed as a set of mere "anecdotes." The concept of creating a set of diaries that would strike this balance belongs to David Hulme, professor of development studies at the University of Manchester, who has written extensively on poverty and on financial services for poor people.[3] Hulme worked closely with Stuart Rutherford, one of the authors, who was deeply involved in microfinance in Bangladesh. Rutherford had noticed that banks and NGOs in Bangladesh often behaved as if they acted in a financial service vacuum—as if the poor households they served had no financial partners other than themselves. His own conversations with poor households in dozens of slums and villages on three continents—research that he was then working up into a book—had convinced him that poor people typically have rather rich financial lives.[4]

There started the quest, moving along several iterations in several countries, of creating a new mixed-research method. With the benefit of hindsight, we can see that over the course of the research in Bangladesh, India, and South Africa, a relatively ethnographic approach based on qualitative data (with supplementary quantitative data) evolved into a more positivist approach based on quantitative data (with supplementary qualitative data). The Bangladesh diaries, led by Rutherford in 1999–2000, posed a very simple question that had never been satisfactorily answered: do poor people have financial lives? It focused on the range of financial instruments they used, trying to tease out the trajectory of every penny that went through financial manipulation, and find out why households made the choices they did. In the 2000 India study, Orlanda Ruthven sought to understand financial lives in the context of the livelihoods of the households that used them, and to do so she collected more detailed income and expenditure data alongside the financial data.[5] In the 2004 South African diaries, Daryl Collins shifted the emphasis to the quantitative, in order to subject our data to a broader range of financial analysis, creating a system that allows an expansion of the sample size to the point where statistical analysis becomes more feasible. Throughout much of the fieldwork of the financial diaries, Jonathan Morduch, an economist with an expertise on microfinance and poverty, advised and commented on the work.

Finance: Where Time and Money Intersect

The basic concept behind the financial diaries is that finance is the relationship between time and money, and to understand it fully, time and money must be observed together. The best description of how we have managed to do this is to call this method a "diary," a term that appropriately conveys the sense that we are tracking intimate details of financial management over time. However, the financial diaries are not diaries in the literal sense, because not only were many of the diarists illiterate, but the detail of information that we collected was far beyond what households would have the patience or time to keep track of themselves. Instead of relying on the householders to write the diaries themselves, we used a team of skilled interviewers to record the transactions and the comments during home visits that took place at 15-day intervals over the span of a year.[6]

The gathering of such intimate information meant that we had to be clear about whom in the household our interviewers would talk to. Establishing the most appropriate "unit of research" is a common problem in social research. We decided to follow a well-trodden convention and treat the household as our unit. While many one-off surveys would only interview the household head, we asked our team to talk to each of its adult members as often as possible if not at each and every visit.[7] Because of the likelihood of situations that not all members of the households were aware of, or of members concealing information from each other, our interviewers had to be very sensitive. This was part of the considerable effort made to establish a friendly relationship with everyone in the household and to allow a comfortable environment that would encourage respondents to be open. To help enable this environment, we relied upon researchers who spoke the local dialect and were not too distant, in class and background, from the people they were interviewing.

We had, after all, no especial right to demand answers to our very personal and often intrusive questions, or to take so much time out of the busy lives of people, some of whom were struggling at the edge of survival. What was in it for them, we asked ourselves, and were sometimes asked by the diarists. We answered this question as simply and truthfully as we could: the information they gave us was unlikely to help them directly, though it might help to improve financial services for some people somewhere; but the time they gave us would be rewarded by a gift at the close of the research year.[8] We were ever mindful that this was a very sensitive relationship—with householders revealing their most intimate financial details to us, we did not take our role as "confessor" lightly. This meant playing down the role of the interviews as "work" for which respondents would be paid, and presenting them as conversations that would help both parties understand how people were managing their money. We took care not to overwhelm those respondents who felt they needed to offer us traditional hospitality in the form of tea and biscuits, for example, by taking along our own fruit, biscuits, and money for tea from the local stall. We listened empathetically to respondents who were distraught with events in their lives. But we tried to maintain our role as observers. We took care not to offer advice or judgment, and we tried not to interfere or burden the households. Interviews often took place while the interviewees got on with their everyday work, cooking lunch or feeding the cow, and were often interrupted by other visitors.

Choosing the Households

Before we faced up to these difficulties, though, we had to decide how many households we would talk to and how we would select them. It was clear that we didn't have the resources to tackle a sample size that statisticians would regard as big enough to represent poor households in the entire country, or even to typify an area or particular community. When we started experimenting with this new method, we wanted to focus on getting a depth of information on a single household rather than a breadth across many. In Bangladesh and India, this sample was 42 and 48 respectively. Even in South Africa, where a new data collection mechanism allowed us to efficiently track more households, the sample size increased only to 152, nowhere close to being statistically representative of certain groups or areas, let alone nationally representative.[9] In all three countries we worked with both urban and rural households, in order to capture any variations in financial behavior caused by the differences in economy and environment of the two kinds of location. The choice of communities was guided by those shown to be poor by a national survey, but it was also largely dictated by the practicalities of places where fieldworkers could reliably travel on a fortnightly basis. Table A1.1 summarizes the numbers and locations of our diary households, along with general notes about their communities, livelihoods, and poverty indicators.

Poverty is a dynamic condition, and there are people who at any one time are moving up or down the poverty ladder. Poverty is also relative. For both these reasons we needed to distinguish between degrees of poverty and include a mixed range of households with different social-economic profiles. We took advantage of the reality that, in poor communities, people knew their neighbors well, so we were able to use "wealth ranking" to determine our selection of households.[10] This technique relies on comparing key informants' estimates of the relative wealth of their neighbors to compile a ranked list of households from the most to the least wealthy.[11] This process not only allowed us to select households at the bottom, middle, and top of the list, but it also helped us to develop a relationship with the community and gave them some sense of "ownership" of the study. The wealth rankings were the first step in establishing a relationship with the community as a whole, and we continued to make sure that we maintained that trust through regular report-backs and meetings with community leaders. The general presence we secured helped us immensely when we approached the households themselves to participate.

Once we had our wealth rankings for each area, we drew the sample from the poorest, middle, and the wealthiest in each area.[12] Conditions varied from location to location and country to country, but we defined these different levels of wealth: poor, upper poor, and nonpoor.

- *Poor households*. These are households that display evidence of deprivation of basic human needs that had existed over a long period of time (many months and often years). Examples include going hungry during the "bad season," poor-quality housing, unemployment, lack of access to basic health services, children not attending school, and being socially outcast. Almost

Table A1.1 Areas in Which Financial Diaries Households Resided

Location	Notes
Bangladesh: Rural	
21 households in three almost-adjacent hamlets in rural north-central Bangladesh. Two households quickly proved uncooperative and were replaced, after which we were able to work with the revised 21 for the year	These households were mostly income-poor (per capita levels of less than $2 PPP per capita per day, several of less than $1 PPP per capita per day), but the sample included three farmers with 2 to 3 acres of good land, and four households with active businesses in retail or timber trading. Most other households were landless or land-poor, with men working as farm laborers, coolies, or rickshaw drivers, who eked out a living with some fishing, seasonal work in a brickfield, and gleaning. The poorest was an elderly widow who lived with a partly employed disabled son.[1] Literacy levels were low, though most children were in school. Homes were mainly single-roomed, of mud walls and floors with thatched or corrugated-tin roofs. Most household heads were born on and own their own homestead land and the trees that stand on them.[2]
Bangladesh: Urban	
21 households in three slums at varying distances from the center of Dhaka, the capital city. One uncooperative household was replaced early on, after which we worked with 21 for the year	Every household (we later learned) had migrated from the villages to Dhaka during the lifetime of the household head. Almost all were income-poor, though a few households had regular waged jobs, for example as drivers at $80 per month (equivalent to about $2 PPP per person per day) or as garment factory workers on somewhat lower wages. Most livelihoods were in casual work or self-employment, such as rickshaw drivers, porters, construction laborers, scrap collectors, or tea-stall or food-stand proprietors. Most were wholly landless (though a few still held land in their home villages) and rented bamboo-sided tin-roofed huts in cramped slums with poor

Table A1.1 (*Continued*)

Location	*Notes*
	sanitation. Some owned their own huts and a few rented cement-block one-room homes. Many were illiterate. Most children were enrolled in school but did not always attend. The poorest were the elderly.
India: Rural 28 households in two villages in eastern Uttar Pradesh state, north-central India. One uncooperative household was quickly replaced.	Based across two villages in one of the least-developed corners of eastern Uttar Pradesh state, 15 of our 28 respondent households derived at least a third of their income from farming, either from their own farms, from leasing the land of others, or from wage labor on others' farms. Only three of 28 households were completely landless, while a further 13 (just under half) had only 2 acres of land or less. Those less dependent on farm income undertook either self-employed trading activities, or labored for wages off the farm, as rickshaw pullers or construction workers in regional cities, or locally at irrigation sites and a stone quarry, or by building and repairing houses. The majority (61 percent) of respondent households were living well below the internationally recognized poverty line, earning less than $1 dollar per person per day PPP. A third of households had some or all of their children out of school (either withdrawn or never attended).
India: Urban 30 households in three slums in Delhi. We lost 12 early on when they either left the slum or proved uncooperative.	All 20 households, spread across three of Delhi's squatter settlements, had migrated from rural areas during the life of the household head (averaging 7.5 years in the city). Half of them still had strong links with the village, operating as joint

Table A1.1 *(Continued)*

Location	*Notes*
We replaced 3 but lost another after several months, so the results are based on 20 households.	families with parents and brothers there (with or without farmland), and in some cases, living in Delhi away from their own wives and children who stayed back in the village. Partly due to smaller numbers of dependents, per capita incomes among urban respondents averaged much higher than among rural ones. Eighty-five percent of the households were living on between $2 and $5 PPP per person per day. The wealthiest urban respondents had regular salaried jobs (as helpers, factory workers, security guards, or drivers), while the poorer ones were a mix of domestic workers and casual, piece-rate workers who faced unemployment and/or high expenses with many dependents.
South Africa: Rural 61 households in the rural village of Lugangeni about 1 hour away from the town of Mount Frere in the Eastern Cape; 3 households dropped out during the study year, so the results are based on 58 rural South African households.	The rural population was a mix of the poorest and the best-off in the South African sample. Twenty-five percent were living below $2 PPP per person per day and were mostly dependent on monthly government welfare grants. Another 20 percent, mostly teachers and nurses, were far better off, earning closer to $10 PPP per person per day. Most households owned their own home and enough land to grow corn and some vegetables, but rarely did they sell what they grow. All households had inherited the land they lived on and often the homes they resided in. Homes were a combination of one or several structures, either traditional mud *rondavels* or brick structures with tin roofs. Most children attended school and most of the adults were literate. The poorest were grandparents who were looking after many children who were either orphaned

Table A1.1 (*Continued*)

Location	*Notes*
	or simply not supported by their parents. The village did not have electricity or land telephone lines, although it did have some cell phone coverage.
South Africa: Urban 1 60 households in a township outside Johannesburg; 11 dropped out during the study year, so results are based on 49 households in this area.	Half the urban sample was drawn from the township of Diepsloot, about a 45-minute car ride outside Johannesburg. This sample includes only two households that have PPP income per capita per day less than $2. Fifty-six percent of the able-bodied adults in this sample have regular jobs. The area was originally developed as a relocation area for residents of another flooded and overcrowded township. Diepsloot residents were ultimately promised Reconstruction and Development Programme homes supplied by the governments, but many were still waiting. Three-quarters of the sample lived in tiny one-room shacks. A water tank supplied by the government was the residents' only source of water, and there were a few toilets, also supplied by the government. The other quarter lived in homes that have either been built and given to them by the government or by a home mortgage scheme.
South Africa: Urban 2 60 households in a township outside Cape Town; 15 households dropped out during the study year, so results are based on 45 households from this area.	Another urban sample was drawn from one of the oldest townships in Cape Town, near the city center. About 10 percent of the sample lived on less than $3 PPP per person per day; they were primarily reliant on government grants. The wealthiest 40 percent earned closer to $10 PPP per capita per day, usually households with someone who had a salaried job. The middle-income

Table A1.1 (*Continued*)

Location	*Notes*
	households (between $3 and $10 PPP per capita per day) lived off a combination of casual work, remittances from relatives, and survivalist businesses. Two-thirds of the sample lived in houses that had at one time served as rental stock for the township, but the deeds had been transferred to the residents after the change of government in 1994. Some respondents lived in the backyard shacks of these homes, and paid rent to the owner who lived in the house. Another group of respondents lived in government-owned hostels. An entire family rented one bed and lived in shacks built around the hostel. Lastly, part of the sample was drawn from a neighborhood of shacks, which were largely inhabited by families who had migrated from the rural areas, looking for work in Cape Town.

[1] Full details of this household and an analysis of its livelihood strategy are presented in Hulme 2004.

[2] In Bangladesh, one can own a tree that stands on someone else's land; or tree-owners may "share-raise" a tree, where the owner and the caretaker of the tree share the income from fruit, firewood, timber, etc.

always such households have low and irregular incomes and few assets or negative assets because of indebtedness. The assessments of local key informants confirm that such households are poor or "at the bottom end."

- *Upper-poor households*. These are households that display some features of deprivation, but not as many or not as severely as poor households. Generally they have more regular incomes (low-paid but steady work), higher levels of assets (a tin roof, pots and pans), better access to services (most children attend primary school), and fewer dependents than poor households. Such households only rarely go hungry, but their food consumption is simple and basic. Commonly such households are able to describe how they have "come up" from being poor by hard work, successful enterprises, and inheritance, or how they have "slipped down" through ill health, losing jobs, aging, accidents, and other factors. Local key informants typically describe such households as "in the middle . . . they are not very poor, but they are not comfortable."

- *Nonpoor households.* In all communities we selected a small number of households that local key informants identified as "comfortable," "better-off," and that had incomes, asset levels, and access to services that provided evidence of their economic and social well-being. Such households rarely if ever go hungry, consume a varied set of foods that includes high-cost items, and have good-quality housing and access to schools, health services, and clean water. These households have a high level of security: unless something disastrous happens, they are assured of meeting their basic needs.

During the process of choosing the households, we did not explicitly measure levels of poverty or objectively rank houses, as we believed the resources needed to do this rigorously would have reduced the levels of information acquired about microfinance. For our purposes knowing that households are in one of these three categories, and were moving up, moving down or stable, is sufficient. However, it is useful to outline how our categories relate to international measures of poverty and deprivation. Conveniently, these have been collated into the United Nations' Millennium Development Goals, against which we set the key parameters of our sample. This comparison highlights the following points about our households:

a. All of our poor households are deprived in terms of several key poverty indicators, and some of them, especially in rural India and Bangladesh, are among the world's extreme poor.

b. To varying degrees our upper poor experience deprivations of one or more poverty indicators. Most of them are above the MDG's US$1 per day per person extreme poverty standard but fall below its US$2 per day standard for poverty. Most of these households are, however, vulnerable to extreme poverty. Should their chief breadwinner become sick, a key productive asset be stolen, or a major costly event occur (hospital bill, funeral) then they would fall into desperate conditions.

c. Our nonpoor group generally have incomes above the US$2 per day per person standard and access to essential services. However, within these households, certain members—especially girls, young women, daughters-in-law, and widows—may be experiencing deprivation. Even the most affluent of our nonpoor households would not have achieved the level of economic and social security of a lower-middle-class household in Europe or the United States.

In sum, in international terms our sample is of poor and near-poor people. At the bottom end, especially of our rural Indian and Bangladesh samples, are a significant proportion of extremely poor households. Table A1.2 provides details on the livelihoods of selected households at different levels in all three countries.

A stranger walks into your house and . . .

If a stranger were to walk into your house and start asking nosy questions about your money, would you be honest? Unlikely. We knew we needed a strategy to slowly gain trust and maintain it. Our initial interview let us get to know the household with relatively gentle questions, such as the ages and education of its members. During the next interview we ventured into the slightly more intrusive area of income and livelihoods, and then eventually into financial information.

This preparation helped us to set the basic framework for the financial mechanisms of the household, but it didn't mean that we had perfect information from the start. In all three countries, we had to constantly rework and revisit the data as time went by. One reason for this was that we encountered information that didn't fit the conceptual categories we had trained our interviewers to use. A good example of this was when people began to tell us—as they often did in the rural areas—that they had "placed" a sum of money with a neighbor.

Table A1.2 Average PPP Dollar Per Capita Daily Incomes for Selected Diary Households

Household and household head	*Daily average PPP US$ per capita income*	*Notes*
Bangladesh urban, waged car driver	$1.76	Siraz, 37, earned a dependable wage each month with which he supported his wife and two children. But he frequently borrowed interest-free from colleagues, took wage advances from his employer, used shop credit, and went into rent arrears in order to manage during the month. They also saved at home, belonged to several savings clubs, and gave loans to others. His wife was a member of three microfinance institutions (MFIs) and saved and borrowed at each of them.
Bangladesh urban, construction worker	$1.44	Three people earned income in this three-generation six-person household. Saleem worked casually on building sites, his wife traded chicken scraps, and a 16-year-old son occasionally helped his father. The house had two clay "banks," and they saved in clubs and in three MFIs. They borrowed sparingly, preferring to draw down their meager savings, and go into rent arrears.
Bangladesh rural, illiterate landless farm laborer	$0.75	Helal, 26, had a young wife and one child whom he supported by a mix of farm labor, rickshaw driving, and brickfield labor. They frequently borrowed small amounts interest-free locally to tide them through, but sometimes had to borrow with interest.

Table A1.2 *(Continued)*

Household and household head	*Daily average PPP US$ per capita income*	*Notes*
		They had several informal ways of saving at home and in a club, and late in the year his wife joined an MFI.
Bangladesh rural, elderly widow	$0.73 (includes estimated net value of farm produce)	62-year-old Jasmin lived with her son, 21. They had a third of an acre of land where they grew rice and vegetables, and the son traded fruit when he could get capital, or fished in the public marshes. Jasmin tried to sell eggs. They saved at home in clay banks and through savings clubs, and she also borrowed from her savings club. They gave and took interest-free loans. The son joined an MFI but left when he found the weekly repayments too difficult.
India urban, gas agency worker	$1.56	30-year-old Narendra worked as a fitter for a distributor of natural gas in Delhi. His wife tailored part-time from home, and their three children attended school. Narendra's dependable salary was increasing with promotions, and he could afford to focus on saving toward long-term goals in his Bihar village. After experimenting with group devices, a daily savings scheme and a bank account, Narendra said he no longer needed to borrow with interest since he could manage shortfalls in cash flow through friends and colleagues.

Table A1.2 (*Continued*)

Household and household head	*Daily average PPP US$ per capita income*	*Notes*
India urban, domestic worker	$1.35	Meera, mother of two teenagers now separated from her husband, worked as a maid in four flats supporting her children through school. While her tiny but reliable income permitted regular saving, a savings club (a RoSCA—see chap. 4) helped with the resolve to put money aside every month. As the sole breadwinner, she avoided interest-bearing loans completely, relying on small wage advances and interest-free loans from relatives and neighbors.
India rural, tailor	$1.66	Mohan Ali had a tailor's shop in the local town, his wife Mainum rolled *bidis* (cheap cigarettes), and their only son attended school. The family made little effort to save (other than Mohan Ali's sales on credit) but borrowed actively from an MFI to grow the shop. Mainum's health deteriorated over the year, pushing the family into debt. While high earnings during the marriage season allowed Mohan Ali to keep up repayments, when the dry summer months kicked in, the family slipped into greater debt and default as income fell and Mainum showed no improvement.
India rural, small farmer/ farmworker	$0.98	Sita, a middle-aged widow (whom we met in chaps. 2 and 4) , lived with her two sons, one just married. Most of

Table A1.2 *(Continued)*

Household and household head	*Daily average PPP US$ per capita income*	*Notes*
		their income was from on- and off-farm waged labor, to which all household members contributed. Sita's experiment with a local MFI was not a success. While she managed just to clear her loan, the grocery store she set up failed, and when her daughter-in-law fell sick, she diverted her income to pay for her treatment. The household struggled to save regularly even though Sita had a little-used fixed deposit account at a bank opened to receive a government handout. To finance a marriage and a funeral, as well as daily needs when income was down, the household relied wholly on landlord-employers, neighbors. and relatives.
South Africa urban, self-employed sheep intestine seller	$3.87	Pumza (from chap. 2) was a 54-year-old women living in an overcrowded hostel in a township near Cape Town. Every day Pumza bought sheep intestines, cooked them on an outdoor stand, and sold them to passers-by. Because Pumza's business generated small amounts of income every day, it was difficult to save for longer-term goals like school fees, so she was very active in savings clubs—belonging to eight different clubs. One of these suited the high-frequency/low-value nature of her cash flows perfectly, requiring a small contribution every day.

Table A1.2 *(Continued)*

Household and household head	*Daily average PPP US$ per capita income*	*Notes*
South Africa urban, construction laborer	$8.25	Thabo (one of the sample portfolios) was a 26-year-old man who lived with his wife, Zukiswa, and two children in an urban shack settlement. He was the sole earner as a construction laborer. He was paid via direct deposit into his bank account, and he took advantage of this by setting up a stop order to send 20 percent of his income every week to a fixed deposit account. He had managed to save $1,815 (in 1993 PPP dollars) this way during the previous year.
South Africa rural, grant recipient	$2.82	Sabelo was a 34-year-old man who was physically disabled and partially blind, living with his partner and four-year-old child in a single-roomed mud hut. He usually survived on a state-provided monthly disability grant, but it was discontinued when the grant office said his records were incomplete. While he waited for his grant to resume, he relied on taking credit from two local shops and took numerous small loans from his neighbors.
South Africa rural, laborer	$1.14	Thando, 39, lived with his wife, Maduna, three children, and a niece. They received state-provided child support grants every month for two of the children. They tried to supplement this income: with a shop that quickly failed; by Maduna making mud bricks; by Thando working as a day laborer.

Table A1.2 (*Continued*)

Household and household head	*Daily average PPP US$ per capita income*	*Notes*
		The low value/high irregularity of their income did not allow them to manage the credit needed for large-scale, formal investments. A refrigerator for the shop that they bought on credit was repossessed because they missed payments. But they did manage to keep up with contributions of $29 (in 1993 PPP dollars) every month to an informal savings club.

Note: US$ converted from local currencies at 1993 inflation-adjusted PPP conversion rates.

What does that mean precisely, we would ask our field researchers—did they *lend* the money to the neighbor or *deposit* it with the neighbor for safekeeping?[13] Sometimes we got the answer to our question, and sometimes not. We had to accept that in some cases this "placing" of money was deliberately (if unconsciously) ambiguous: as part of the traditional system of pooling savings and of reciprocal lending and borrowing, neighbors do sometimes hold money that may be perceived as a loan or as a deposit, depending on circumstances that can change as time goes by.

But there were other reasons why it took time for us to puzzle out the actual behavior of households. Financial behavior is complex and personal and often involves relationships with a wide set of partners, both informal and formal, from bank managers to friends and neighbors. There are many reasons for not telling the full story to even the most trusted outsider.

Take, for example, Kalim, the head of one of the better-off households in our rural Bangladesh sample. He told us that he had a considerable sum of money stored in a savings account at the bank.

He chose not to show us the passbook, citing concerns about privacy that we respected. Only much later did he tell us that the money wasn't stored at the bank at all but was held by a friend who ran a shop in the market. The reason he'd dissembled, he told us, is that he has an overdue loan from the bank and that until he was absolutely sure he could trust us, he didn't want to reveal that he had savings elsewhere, lest the bank manager hear of it through us.

We were also puzzled, for many weeks, by the source of some income that Thabo, who lived in rural South Africa, received from time to time from the bank. Was this someone sending him money? No, he would say, it's my money. Eventually, after many conversations, we realized that these were interest payments from a sizable investment in a fixed deposit account. After Thabo had been retrenched from his job several years ago, his ex-boss recommended that he put his retrenchment payout into a fixed deposit account. Most of the time Thabo reinvested the interest for the next month, but every now and then he instead used it for a special purpose, and it would come to our notice. Thabo didn't know how to explain this investment, and we had not imagined that someone like him could have such a large investment. It was only through the persistent efforts of many interviews that we could tease out exactly what was happening.

None of this is peculiar to poor people: in developed economies people may also be unclear about their financial actions and may possibly be even *more* reticent. But the strength of the diaries approach is that it can, over time, break down much of this reticence and confusion. For this reason, most of the focus during the fortnightly interviews was on gaps and imbalances, which were followed up in subsequent interviews. We encouraged our interviewers to persevere until they had traced the full chains of transactions. For example, if they were told that a loan had been used to buy a cow, the interviewer checked whether the loan had covered the full cost of the cow or whether other funds had been tapped. If told that savings had supplemented the purchase, they asked where those savings had been stored, both at the time of the purchase and during the time that the savings fund was being created. Following this time-consuming routine allowed us to reveal and understand behaviors that were underreported by most other researchers. "Moneyguarding"—storing cash with trusted neighbors, relatives, employers, and shopkeepers—for example, showed up in a way that had never been revealed before.

Table A1.3 outlines all of the financial instruments that we found in each country. "Instruments" are the mechanisms that diary households used to manage their money. They include "services" (such as those offered by banks) and "devices" (do-it-yourself mechanisms like savings clubs). We classify them by their level of formality and also include definitions of less well-known instruments below the table.

The Portfolios

The end result of this fieldwork is a unique and well-identified set of "portfolios" for each of the financial diaries households. Like the financial portfolios of the rich, portfolios of the poor are also diversified between different instruments, which suit various needs and timing. Five examples of household portfolios from each country are included in appendix 2. Backgrounds and portfolios for many more households from all three samples, as well as research on a wide variety of topics using the financial diary data, are available at www.portfoliosofthepoor.com. The complete South African Diaries dataset is available on www.datafirst.uct.ac.za.

Strengths and Weakness of the Financial Diaries Method

Carefully working back through the cash flows of each household highlights one of the strengths of the diaries method when compared with questionnaire-based surveys. In the more sophisticated version of the diaries created in South Africa, Daryl Collins was able to formalize how well the diaries questionnaires captured the full set of cash flows. For each questionnaire period (which usually covered two weeks), the sources of funds (income plus financial inflows into the household) were measured against the uses of funds (expenditures

Table A1.3 Microfinancial Instruments, Services, and Devices

Category	*Instruments found*	*Countries found in*
Formal services		
Services offered by banks, insurance companies, and other regulated entities including formal sector employers and retail companies	Bank loans	B I SA
	Bank passbook savings	B I SA
	Bank term savings	B I SA
	Bank current accounts	B I SA
	Bank credit/debit cards	SA
	Formal insurance life coverage	B I SA
	Formal funeral insurance	SA
	Employee pensions / provident fund	I SA
	Private investment funds, unit trusts	I SA
	Store cards	SA
	Retail accounts	SA
	Wage advances	SA
	Debt under administration	SA
	Chit funds	I
	Pro-poor insurance life coverage	B
	Pro-poor insurance loans	B
Semiformal services		
Services offered by specialist pro-poor non-government and some other organisations	NGO loans	B I
	NGO savings	B I
	NGO insurance	B
Informal services and devices		
Group-based devices		
Clubs owned and run by their users	*Saving-up clubs*	B I SA
	RoSCAs	B I SA
	ASCAs	B I SA
	Burial societies	SA
	Stokvels and umgalelos	SA
	Salary timing	SA

Table A1.3 (*Continued*)

Category	*Instruments found*	*Countries found in*
Bilateral services		
Contracts between two parties	*Reciprocal interest-free lending and borrowing*	B I SA
	Lending and borrowing privately on interest	B I SA
	Moneylending (*mahajans* & *mashonisas*)	B I SA
	Moneyguarding	B I SA
	Pawning	B I SA
	Shop credit (casual)	B I SA
	Shop credit (installment plans)	I
	Wage advances	B I SA
	Advance sale of labor or crops	B I SA
	Casual venture capital	B
	Trade credit	B I SA
	Rent arrears	B I SA
Individual devices		
Personal savings devices	Saving at home or on the person	B I SA
	Remitting cash to the village	B I SA

Note: Less familiar instruments are in italics and described below. The absence of any instrument on this list does not mean it cannot be found in the country—merely that it was not encountered in use among our diary households during the research year.

Chit funds are a government regulated form of RoSCA (see below) found only in India.

Pro-poor insurers are found only in Bangladesh: they adapt the methods of NGO microcredit banks to offer endowments (savings plans linked to life insurance) to the poor, and to recycle the premiums as loans to the poor.

Saving-up clubs are clubs where participants save together toward a particular event, such as a religious festival: they do not recycle the fund as loans.

RoSCAs, or rotating savings and credit associations, are a form of savings-and-loan club in which a fixed number of members pay a fixed sum into a pool at a fixed interval, and on each occasion one of the members takes the whole of the pool (there are many variants on this theme).

Table A1.3 (*Continued*)

ASCAs, or accumulating savings and credit associations differ from RoSCAs in that regularly depositing members accumulate their fund and lend it out when required to one or more of their members.

Burial societies, as found in South Africa, are informal clubs where members insure each other against funeral costs.

Stokvels and *umgalelos* are different names for South African RoSCAs and ASCAs.

Salary timing is an agreement with others to share salaries as they arrive.

Reciprocal interest-free lending and borrowing are loans between friends, neighbors or family members that are interest-free but bear the implied obligation to reciprocate at some time in the future.

Mahajan and *mashonisa* are South Asian and South African terms for local moneylenders who lend for profit.

Moneyguarding is having someone look after your money for you, often a relative, neighbor, employer or shopkeeper.

Remitting cash to the village is often practiced by town dwellers as a way of saving and of building up assets in the home village. Note that in the South Africa study, we treated remitting cash to the village as an expense rather than a financial instrument because we knew that the households receiving the remittances were using it for their own needs rather than saving it. In Bangladesh and India, it was more often (but not always) the case that the money was invested in some way: in land or housing or lent out, for example, and we have treated remittances as savings.

plus financial outflows from the household) with an adjustment of cash on hand at the beginning and end of the interview period. The difference is called the "margin of error," which represents the amount by which the household had over- or underreported cash flows. This was used as a means of tracking data quality. Fieldworkers were then provided with immediate feedback to follow up in the next interview. Figure A1.1 shows how the margin of error decreases over the first six interviews, as interviewer and interviewee learn to understand each other better, and as trust develops. We found that it took half a dozen rounds of diary questionnaires, even after the initial questionnaires, before we felt confident that we had full information on the cash flows of a household.[14]

We also encouraged our interviewers to explore the emotions that accompanied the transactions, to elicit comments on the different devices used and to estimate the degree to which the householders

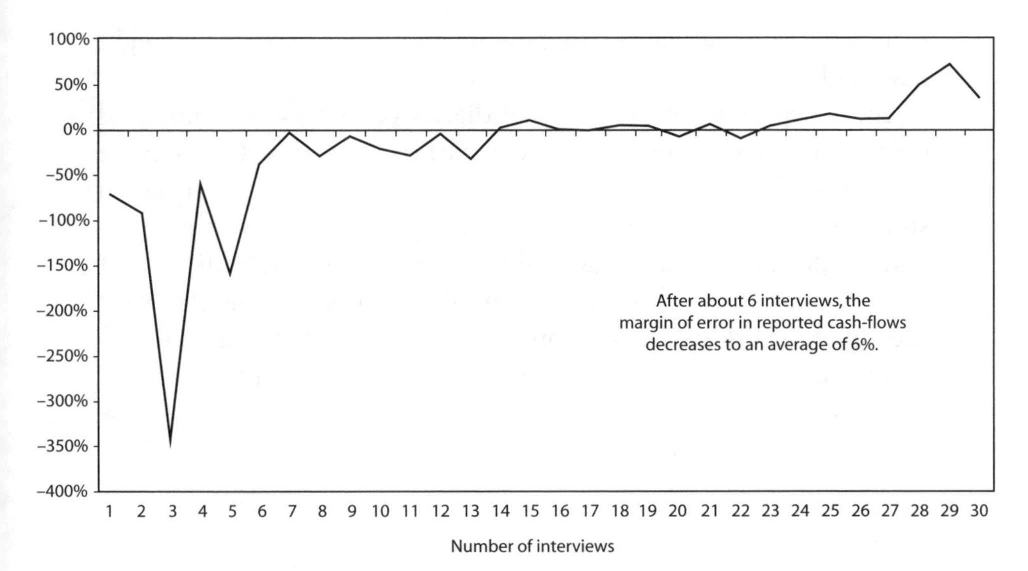

FIGURE A1.1. Margin of error in reported cash flows, South Africa (percent of sources of funds).

saw financial activity as an important or as a trivial part of their lives. We recorded, verbatim, especially striking comments. The result was a simultaneous mixed method—a means of capturing both quantitative and qualitative data in the moment, across time.

The limitations of the diary method are the mirror image of its strengths: above all, as we have said, the number of households we worked with was too small to represent whole populations. There is also a doubt as to whether participating in the diaries changed the behavior of some respondents. In some cases it may have done so. We were tipped off by the thanks we received from some respondents during our final interview, when respondents told us that "we had helped them so much." Wonderful, we said with a sigh. It was difficult to determine if these thanks came from the companionship we provided during the year, or if respondents saw a real benefit to recounting their financial transactions to us. It may have been that, as with Weight Watchers, being constantly asked about financial transactions guided our households into behaving differently than they would have otherwise. However, without a different type of study design, it is difficult to tease out exactly how much of an influence we might have had.

The sharp focus of the financial diaries on the users of financial services and devices also means we have less to say directly about the providers of those services. The diaries do not help us to engage in some of the fierce debates that are raging in the world of microfinance—debates about sustainability and the role of subsidies.[15] But we can bring a fresh perspective to another debate that ought to be at the top of the list for financial providers, an understanding of microfinance services and devices from the clients' viewpoint.[16]

Appendix 2

◆ ◆ ◆

A SELECTION OF PORTFOLIOS

EACH PORTFOLIO in this appendix is a dense collection of qualitative and quantitative information. We begin with a description of the household, where its members may have come from, what livelihoods they pursue, and what physical assets they own. On the page facing this information is a table of the household financial net worth, divided into assets and liabilities and categorized by the formality of each financial instrument. We show the balance in each financial instrument at the start and end of the year. In order to show how important each instrument is in the overall portfolio, the next column shows the percentage of overall end assets or liabilities. As chapter 2 suggested, turnover in some instruments may differ dramatically from the balance, so we next show turnover. Again, we wanted to portray the importance of each instrument by showing the weight in overall turnover in assets or liabilities. We include notes next to each instrument that provide the reader with details about how the instrument is used.

We end each portfolio with a brief description of how the portfolio changed over the course of the year. We highlight which instruments seemed to serve the purposes of cash-flow management, building lump sums and managing risk, as well as noting whether financial net worth increased or decreased, and why.

Two points of caution are needed when interpreting the portfolios. First, the financial diaries allowed us to uncover or reinterpret financial instruments that we did not initially realize that households were using. Although the latter, database-driven version of the diaries in South Africa allowed us to backfill these missing balances and transactions, earlier versions of the diaries in Bangladesh and India were not able to take this into account. This is why readers may note a number of zero starting balances in the portfolios of these two countries. Second, readers must keep in mind that the beginning and ending balances are taken at the beginning and end of each month, but a month's worth of transactions do not begin and end exactly with the calendar month. So, for example, some households in South Africa are paid wages monthly directly into their bank accounts. If our ending balance happened to fall just after the wages were deposited but before they were withdrawn, then we may erroneously conclude that the household had saved substantially over the period. Despite these potential pitfalls, we hope that readers will find these examples and others found on www.portfoliosofthepoor.com useful.

APPENDIX 2

A Driver's Household in Dhaka, Bangladesh

When he was young, Jaded attended school for 10 years in his village, came to Dhaka to look for a job, and managed to learn to drive—not yet a common accomplishment for poor Bangladeshis. He is now in his fifties, and lives in a tin-roofed hut illegally built on a flood embankment, with his second wife and their three children, and an older son from his first marriage. He drove for a middle-class widow for $80 a month, a small sum, but she paid regularly and let him take wage advances. They had few assets besides the hut and its furnishings—a fan, a TV, a timber bedstead, a table, and some chairs, worth altogether about $450. His wife Shirin was a very active personality, and ran her own business selling saris around the neighborhood: often she earned more than he in a month. It was she who was in charge of most of their financial transactions, though by local convention Jaded was regarded by all in the household as its head.

As in many of the Bangladesh portfolios, debt was small relative to cash flow. In this case, assets easily exceeded liabilities although this positive net worth declined through the study year, largely through reductions in their MFI (microfinance institution) savings as Shirin withdrew cash for her sari selling and for household needs. The couple was active in many forms of finance, including the semiformal MFIs (where Shirin and her daughter between them had managed to get accounts at no less than seven MFIs and borrowed from four of them) and the informal sector. They managed their money day to day through loans from her husband's employer, credit from shopkeepers, and a few loans from neighbors, both for interest and interest-free. She was a good saver and was usually able to finance private loans and loans against pawns for others, which she found profitable. The MFIs supplied some finance for her sari-selling business. But she complained about having to spend so much time sorting out her money affairs.

Table A2.1 Financial Net Worth at the Start and End of the Research Year (US$ at market rate)

		Start amount	*End amount*	*Share of portfolio balances*[a]	*Turnover*[b]	*Share of portfolio turnover*	*Notes*
Assets							
Formal	Bank savings	8.00	8.00	2%	0.00	0%	Dormant throughout the year
	Pro-poor life insurance	180.00	190.00	49%	10.00	1%	Didn't make the deposits regularly
Semiformal	MFI savings	216.40	136.70	36%	176.30	20%	Weekly deposits and some withdrawals, several MFIs
Informal	Interest-free loans out	0.00	26.00	7%	72.80	8%	At least 7 small loans to neighbors
	Interest-bearing loan out	0.00	1.60	<1%	1.60	<1%	She charged $1.60 interest on a $1.60 loan.
	Lending against a pawn	0.00	0.00	0%	60.00	7%	2 small loans given against gold jewelry
	Goods supplied on credit	0.00	0.00	0%	258.00	30%	She managed to get all her trade debt repaid.
	Saved at home	100.00	20.00	5%	280.00	32%	She revolved a lot of cash through her steel cupboard.
	Saved in a mud-bank	0.00	0.30	<1%	6.54	<1%	She made feeble attempts to keep a mud-bank.
	Saved on the person	1.00	1.00	<1%	4.00	<1%	Kept by him while working
	Total	505.40	383.60	100%	869.24	100%	
Liabilities							
Semiformal	MFI loan	212.00	98.00	94%	454.00	41%	Loans from several MFIs, used mainly in sari selling
Informal	Interest-free loan taken	0.00	6.00	6%	26.00	2%	2 loans from neighbors, one by the older son
	Interest-bearing loan taken	0.00	0.00	0%	200.00	18%	1 loan, and it was hard to get
	Shop credit	0.00	0.00	0%	80.00	7%	Regular small credit from the grocers
	Wage advance	0.00	0.00	0%	240.00	22%	His employer lent him money every few months against his salary
	Moneyguarding	0.00	0.00	0%	100.00	9%	2 neighbors often stored cash with her.
	Total	212.00	104.00	100%	1100.00	100%	
	Financial net worth	293.40	279.60	Total flows	1969.24		

[a] End-year value of assets or liabilities divided by the total; similarly in the same column in the tables A2.2–A2.15.

[b] Inflows into instruments plus outflows out of them; similarly in the same column in the tables A2.2–A2.15.

APPENDIX 2

A Household of Garment Workers, Dhaka, Bangladesh

We met this household in chapter 4. It consists of Surjo, an eldest son (high-school educated) who, three years before, had brought his mother, a sister, and three brothers to Dhaka from their village home because they couldn't get work there. Once in Dhaka, they set up a joint home in a single rented plastered-brick room. Surjo then set about getting everyone except the youngest brother a job in Dhaka's expanding garments industry, with wages ranging from $20 to $45 a month. The youngest brother, 12, was in school.

They are ambitious and, with the exception of the mother, in good health. They bought goods for the home—a fan and a TV. They were backed up by the security of land they had back in the village, worth around $1,200, and they sustained their links with the village by borrowing from an MFI to mortgage-in more land and have it share-cropped, providing them with some staples each harvest.

They are also shrewd and quickly understood the opportunities offered by MFIs, RoSCAs, and ASCAs, even though the eldest son's RoSCA failed and it looked as if he would loose his investment there. The sister joined a garments-factory-based ASCA that worked well for both saving and borrowing. Despite being new to the slum, they quickly got to know their neighbors (many of whom come from the same rural district), and they were able to get interest-free loans that, though small, often helped with cash-flow problems in their household management.

They quickly involved themselves in a wide range of devices ranging from a formal bank savings account (though the eldest son rarely kept his vow to save a little each month there), through the semiformal MFI, to several informal devices. This helped improve the value of their financial assets. Liabilities increased as well, but that was due to the additional debt financing they achieved through MFI loans to buy more land.

Table A2.2 Financial Net Worth at the Start and End of the Research Year (US$ at market rate)

		Start amount	*End amount*	*Share of portfolio balances*	*Turnover*	*Share of portfolio turnover*	*Notes*
Assets							
Formal	Bank savings	84.00	94.00	50%	10.00	4%	Tried to save a little each month but most often failed
	Pro-poor life insurance	20.00	36.00	19%	16.00	6%	Stopped depositing when agent visited irregularly
Semiformal	MFI savings	12.00	24.50	13%	12.50	5%	The sister had the membership and saved weekly.
Informal	RoSCA savings	20.00	14.00	7%	6.00	2%	This RoSCA collapsed and the son got part of his money back.
	ASCA savings	8.00	4.00	2%	108.00	42%	Sister joined an ASCA run by workers at her factory.
	Interest-free loans out	0.00	0.00	0%	20.00	8%	A loan to a brother-in-law that was very quickly repaid
	Saved at home	14.00	14.00	7%	40.00	16%	The family held some savings in a trunk.
	Saved on the person	1.00	1.00	< 1%	4.00	2%	Kept by the household head
	Remitting cash home	0.00	0.00	0%	40.00	15%	Sent to a brother who stayed in the village to repair the roof of the family house
	Total	159.00	187.50	100%	256.50	100%	
Liabilities							
Semiformal	MFI loan	26.84	50.24	84%	336.60	40%	The mother was the MFI member: two loans, one used for mortgaging land in the village, from which they got some produce.
Informal	Interest-free loan taken	0.00	0.00	0%	156.00	18%	At least 10 small loans quickly repaid
	ASCA loans	0.00	0.00	0%	80.00	9%	2 loans taken by the sister for household use
	Buying goods on credit	10.00	10.00	16%	254.16	30%	Common and frequent, mostly groceries
	Rent arrears	0.00	0.00	0%	24.00	3%	Infrequent
	Total	36.84	60.24	100%	850.76	100%	
	Financial net worth	122.16	127.26	Total flows	1107.26		

APPENDIX 2

A Landless Day Laborer's Household in Rural, North Central Bangladesh

Saiful and Nargis, a young couple with two small children, are landless and illiterate, living in a hut Saiful built himself. He labored on local farms when he could, or else hired and drove a rickshaw. When he did farm labor, he got paid grain worth about 80 cents a day, and another 70 cents or so in cash: with the rickshaw he netted between a $1 and $1.50 a day. On average, he got work about 22 days a month. This household was among the poorest in the Bangladesh sample. The older child was in school, the younger still a baby. The couple were both physically strong, and healthy most of the time.

As with many of our portfolios, the year-end balances of both assets and liabilities were small, both absolutely and in comparison with the amounts of money that flowed through their various instruments. The portfolio was composed of two sorts of transactions—multiple low-value savings and loans on the one hand, used to bridge their cash shortfalls on a day-to-day basis, and a very few larger transactions. The biggest instrument was a loan from an MFI that Nargis joined toward the end of the year because, she said, "I saw other women joining." At first they kept the loan at home, unsure what best to do with it. Then, frightened they would waste it, they lent it, on interest, to family members. This too improved their asset position. Joining the MFI caused her to start saving there.

They had no dealings at all with formal financial providers, even though there are several commercial banks in the nearby market, and insurance companies are active in the area. Their only semiformal partner was the small local MFI that was not well run and subsequently failed. All their other financial life took place in the informal sector, with family and neighbors, and through their own efforts to save at home. They worried about money—she especially.

Table A2.3 Financial Net Worth at the Start and End of the Research Year (US$ at market rate)

		Start amount	*End amount*	*Share of portfolio balances*	*Turnover*	*Share of portfolio turnover*	*Notes*
Assets							
Semiformal	MFI savings	0.00	49.00	70%	49.00	22%	Deposited at weekly meetings
Informal	Interest-free loans out	0.00	0.00	0%	0.60	0%	One short-term loan to a neighbor
	Interest-bearing loan out	0.00	20.00	29%	60.00	27%	Two loans to family, sourced from their MFI loan
	Saved at home	0.08	0.10	0%	103.12	47%	Saved in a cupboard and in a mud-bank, then spent
	Saved on the person	1.00	1.00	1%	2.00	1%	Always kept in his pocket
	Saved with moneyguard	2.00	0.00	0%	4.00	2%	Kept next-door for a while, to avoid temptation
	Total	3.08	70.10	100%	218.72	100%	
Liabilities							
Semiformal	MFI loan	0.00	33.32	63%	46.68	42%	One loan, on-lent, and part repaid by the year's end
Informal	Interest-free loan taken	0.00	4.30	8%	41.70	38%	13 different small loans from neighbors and family
	Interest-bearing loan taken	4.00	10.00	19%	14.00	13%	Two loans, for consumption and for medicine
	Shop credit	1.00	1.00	2%	4.00	4%	Three small episodes, from the local general store
	Labor sold in advance	0.00	4.00	8%	4.00	4%	Money came from his cousin and he planned to repay it through labor at harvest time.
	Total	5.00	52.62	100%	110.38	100%	
	Financial net worth	− 1.92	17.48	Total flows	329.10		

APPENDIX 2

A Timber Trader in Rural, North Central Bangladesh

Both Zaman and Preeti, the husband and wife of this household, had high-school education, and their 18-year-old son is now in school. But education hadn't led to access to capital, and the timber-trading business he ran stumbled for lack of resources: often they were more dependent for everyday income on the small home-based shop that they also ran when they could afford to. Although they are a rural couple, they had no farmland to fall back on, owning just a modest home on a small piece of homestead land.

Zaman's trading took the form of carrying timber between cutters deep in the forest and sawmills based in his local market. He tried to do as much of it as possible on a "no finance" basis—paying the cutters only after he'd been paid by the sawyers. But this was difficult, so that when he did get credit it went into lubricating deals that had got stuck rather than into expanding the business.

To facilitate his timber trading, he sought his credit from as many sources as possible. He had three MFI memberships, and lamented the fact that each of them would only lend to him once per year and that they insisted on weekly repayments, which he found troublesome. Nevertheless, the MFIs were his most reliable lenders, and cheap by comparison with the private interest-bearing loans he took. He used the "reciprocal" local system of interest-free borrowing whenever he could. An old school friend who went into government service agreed to advance him money on a profit-sharing basis under which Zaman would pay interest only if he made a profit. He never told his family of this arrangement, and we were present in the shop the day the lender came to ask for his money back, much to the astonishment of the trader's wife and son.

During the study year, this family's financial status appeared to improve dramatically, moving from a negative net worth position to a very positive one. One reason for this was the savings they accumulated in their MFI account. Another more risky reason was that he advanced timber, cut from his own trees on his homestead in an effort to raise capital, to a sawmill that had yet to pay him. These advances increased his assets on paper, but he took on the risk that the sawmill might not pay him. His liabilities increased as well as a result of increased borrowings from MFIs and several interest-bearing informal loans.

Table A2.4 Financial Net Worth at the Start and End of the Research Year (US$ at market rate)

		Start amount	*End amount*	*Share of portfolio balances*	*Turnover*	*Share of portfolio turnover*	*Notes*
Assets							
Formal	Bank savings	4.00	4.00	< 1%	0.00	0%	Dormant account in her name
Semiformal	MFI savings	82.60	114.30	8%	114.92	8%	They had membership in 3 MFIs.
Informal	Interest-free loans out	0.00	0.00	0%	4.00	< 1%	One small loan to a relative
	Goods given on credit	0.00	1270.00	91%	1330.00	91%	Mainly, an advance of his own timber to a trader and has to wait to be paid.
	Saved at home	3.00	3.00	< 1%	6.00	< 1%	Very small amounts kept in the rafters
	Saving in a mud-bank	0.00	0.00	0%	6.00	< 1%	Used by him to help finance the shop
	Total	89.60	1391.30	100%	1460.92	100%	
Liabilities							
Semiformal	MFI loan	114.50	229.42	52%	1345.08	66%	He was in two MFIs, his wife in one: he borrowed as much as they would let him.
Informal	Interest-free loan taken	0.00	0.00	0%	210.00	10%	We note nine loans but there may have been many more: Zaman was not always willing to tell us every detail.
	Interest-bearing loan taken	98.00	130.00	30%	368.00	18%	We note four loans but there may have been more.
	Buying goods on credit	90.00	20.00	5%	110.00	5%	Shop credit that accumulated over several months
	Borrowing from friend; interest if made profit	58.00	58.00	13%	0.00	0%	A government employee friend invested with him on a profit-sharing basis.
	Total	360.50	437.42	100%	2033.08	100%	
	Financial net worth	– 270.90	953.88	Total flows	3494.00		

APPENDIX 2

A Woman Household Head in Dhaka, Bangladesh

Born and brought up in the Dhaka slums, Amba is illiterate and was about 48 years old when we met her. She was physically very thin and looked in poor health. Her husband abandoned her for another woman some 14 years ago. Since then, she'd shrewdly managed on her own with the help of a teenage son, who occasionally drove a rickshaw, and a nephew who paid for his keep. She also had a young daughter to care for.

Her situation wasn't easy to understand: her one-room home is bigger and better furnished than many of her neighbors, with a fan, a TV, and a big audio set perched on a good timber sideboard. When we first met her the nephew was staying with her, paying rent and paying for food, and we assessed her as being fairly well-off. But the nephew soon left, and her fortunes declined during the rest of the year. She coped by screening off part of her room and taking in paying guests, for whom she would cook. When she could get capital she hawked saris around the slum, where she was well known, or lent the money out against pawns. But during the year her son became addicted to heroin and turned into a drain on the household's resources. She got poorly paid jobs as a housemaid, and had to send her 12-year-old daughter off as a housemaid, too.

Her biggest financial flows were associated with her MFI loans and her lending against pawns: the two are connected because the MFI loans sometimes finance the lending. She borrowed informally, sometimes paying interest, sometimes not.

Because she tried (though with only partial success) to keep up with her premiums paid to the pro-poor insurance scheme, refrained from withdrawing MFI savings (which she persuaded one of her debtors to pay for her), and paid her MFI loans more or less on time, she ended up with an improved financial position, despite financial difficulties with her son. Her biggest liability was a pair of interest-free loans.

Table A2.5 Financial Net Worth at the Start and End of the Research Year (US$ at market rate)

		Start amount	*End amount*	*Share of portfolio balances*	*Turnover*	*Share of portfolio turnover*	*Notes*
Assets							
Formal	Bank savings	8.00	16.00	5%	8.00	3%	We think this balance may have belonged to the nephew.
	Pro-poor life insurance	76.00	100.96	30%	24.96	10%	The policy was in the name of the daughter.
Semiformal	MFI savings	24.00	41.60	13%	17.60	7%	From midyear the savings were deposited by the person to whom she on-lent her MFI loan.
Informal	Interest-free loans out	40.00	40.00	12%	0.00	0%	An old loan, dormant
	Interest-bearing loan out	0.00	135.60	40%	184.40	77%	She lent her MFI loan locally, against pawns, and got some of it back.
	Saved on the person	2.00	2.00	<1%	4.00	2%	Kept it in a purse tucked in her sari
	Total	150.00	336.16	100%	238.96	100%	
Liabilities							
Semiformal	MFI loan	42.40	95.00	43%	267.50	42%	She paid off one loan and took another.
Informal	Interest-free loan taken	0.00	100.00	46%	120.00	19%	She took three loans and repaid the smaller one quickly.
	Interest-bearing loan taken	0.00	0.00	0%	120.00	19%	She took two loans, at 10%, for consumption and debt repayment.
	Borrowing against a pawn	0.00	2.00	1%	40.00	6%	Borrowed to pay for treatment for her addicted son
	Rent arrears	22.00	22.00	10%	88.00	14%	Repeatedly fell behind with the rent
	Total	64.40	219.00	100%	635.50	100%	
	Financial net worth	85.60	117.16	Total flows	874.46		

APPENDIX 2

Two Casual Laborers, Delhi, India

After growing up in Bihar and traveling from east to west for work, two brothers, Somnath and Jainath (whom we met in chapter 2), arrived at the Indira Camp in 1994. They were in their midtwenties with a few years of schooling. Authorized on land made available by Indira Gandhi's government in 1980, the camp accommodates 5,000 households employed in the factories of Delhi's Okhla Industrial Area, in brick and cement "hutments"—rooming houses of two or even three stories, packed along narrow gullies and traversed by a major drain that carries industrial waste and sewage. Both brothers were married, and their families, their parents, and a younger brother lived in the village. With no farmland, these families depended heavily on whatever the two brothers saved from their wages and sent to them. During the research year, the brothers were hardly able to send anything home, which led directly to the family taking high-interest loans to survive. Both men sought work in Okhla's garment and chemical factories. They faced continuous uncertainty, and both had a simultaneous four-month period of total unemployment during our research.

Given the tough circumstances they faced during the year, the brothers slid deeper into negative net worth. They managed to send money to the village just three times, and even then, only paltry sums. They faced a continual deficit of expenses over income, leading to an increase in liabilities. Avoiding borrowing from the few relatives they have in the city, they managed daily needs by small interest-free loans from colleagues and neighbors, and by accumulating debt in rent and groceries over the year. While they borrowed on interest when in the village, they avoided doing so in Delhi because rates were higher. Because wages were low and work was irregular, they were almost completely unable to hold back a portion of their earnings to send home. They felt they would benefit from the discipline of an organized savings scheme (such as daily collections or a RoSCA), but after having been cheated two years ago, the elder brother was reluctant to hand his meager wages to strangers for safekeeping. For these brothers, saving in the bank, even if it had been convenient, was impossible because they had no identity (or "ration") card for their Delhi residence.

Table A2.6 Financial Net Worth at the Start and End of the Research Year (US$ at market rate)

		Start amount	*End amount*	*Share of portfolio balances*	*Turnover*	*Share of portfolio turnover*	*Notes*
Assets							
Informal	Remitting cash home	0.00	48.12	100%	48.12	100%	Only succeeds in sending small sums back to the village three times over the year.
	Total	0.00	48.12	100%	48.12	100%	
Liabilities							
Informal	Interest-free loan taken	31.38	34.52	16%	44.98	8%	Taken four times from friends in Delhi for living costs when out of work and to get home to village
	Interest-bearing loan taken	0.00	71.13	33%	71.13	13%	Two loans taken from moneylenders in the village, for family and living costs in Delhi
	Wage advance	0.00	20.92	10%	20.92	4%	He was barely able to raise wage advance due to work insecurity
	Rent arrears	0.00	41.84	19%	148.54	28%	Unable to pay rent during five months of unemployment
	Shop credit	0.00	46.55	22%	251.57	47%	
	Total	31.38	214.96	100%	537.14	100%	
	Financial net worth	− 31.38	− 166.84	Total Flows	585.26		

A Factory Supervisor, Delhi, India

Originally from Bihar, Satish Pandey had had a base in Delhi since 1988, when he came to find work following a flood that devastated the crops in his family's small farm. The only graduate in our sample, Satish Pandey became a regular employee in a chemical factory in 1991, and, after two promotions, enjoyed a salary of $73 a month in 2001. He owned the hutment he occupied with his brother, as well as the neighboring one from which he earned rent. His wife and children stayed most of the time in the village with his brothers, their wives, and his parents. Since the family could manage basic needs from their farm income, Satish Pandey's remittances were used for life-cycle costs and investments such as the construction of a brick house.

In spite of a (relatively) high, reliable salary and heavy demands for finance (mostly for house construction and weddings in the village, but also for guests and improving his hutment in Delhi), Satish Pandey had almost no links with formal financial service providers. Other than his government pension fund, which was set up through his employer, he had a bank account that he had allowed to fall dormant, explaining that his cash flow was too fast to make use of a bank account. Instead, he supplemented informal "give and take" transactions with more substantial sums raised from interest-charging lenders and group schemes such as RoSCAs and ASCAs. Other than what he sent straight to the village, he preferred to borrow continuously from an expansive network of contacts. Savings that didn't offer leverage to borrow were of little interest to him.

Table A2.7 Financial Net Worth at the Start and End of the Research Year (US$ at market rate)

		Start amount	*End amount*	*Share of portfolio balances*	*Turnover*	*Share of portfolio turnover*	*Notes*
Assets							
Formal	Provident Fund	604.44	733.08	54%	128.67	13%	Government pension deducted from salary (plus equal contribution from employer)
Informal	Interest-free loans given	0.00	0.00	0%	41.84	4%	Three small "give and take" loans, swiftly recovered
	RoSCA savings	– 150.63	4.18	0%	154.81	15%	Auction RoSCA. He took his share before our research started.
	ASCA savings	– 86.82	0.00	0%	86.82	8%	He was the cashier of a work-based ASCA, and had borrowed more than he saved before research started.
	Remitting cash home	0.00	621.34	46%	621.34	60%	Sends large sums home three times toward rebuilding the village home
	Total	366.99	1358.60	100%	1033.48	100%	
Liabilities							
Informal	Interest-free loans taken	83.68	225.94	47%	569.04	43%	He took seven loans for Delhi costs (guests, repair of hutment) and for trips home to village; repaid within three months
	Interest-bearing loans taken	322.18	219.67	46%	102.51	8%	Two old loans on which he paid interest regularly
	Wage advances	0.00	0.00	0%	334.73	26%	Five advances, all for trips to village, taken from salary within two months
	Shop credit	0.00	34.52	7%	296.03	23%	
	Total	405.86	480.13	100%	1302.31	100%	
	Financial net worth	–38.87	878.47	Total flows	2335.79		

A Farmer's Household, Rural Eastern Uttar Pradesh, India

Tulsidas's parents inherited their 10-acre fertile farm from his maternal uncle when Tulsidas was a child, resulting in a dramatic shift in the family's fortunes. They were shepherds by hereditary occupation but, these days, the joint family (Tulsidas, his wife, their two sons, their sons' wives and six grandchildren) focused less on sheep rearing and increasingly on upgrading their farm. The eldest of Tulsidas's two sons, Triveni (40 years old and schooled to 10th grade) had done several stints in Bombay in the past, where he worked as a watchman for periods of several months to supplement income from the farm (which averaged less than $36 a month during our research), returning from each trip with savings of around $105. During our research, Triveni sought a local salaried job (unsuccessfully), reluctant to leave his aging father and growing family.

By local standards, the family's 10-acre farm was large, and it enabled the family to access institutional credit through a variety of channels, notably government-controlled banks and the agricultural cooperative society. While the family relied on an extensive network of friends in and around the village for small loans in cash, goods, and services, they avoided interest-bearing loans completely and were able to sell grain or sheep when in need of quick cash. Because of their assets in farmland and livestock, and the ease with which they could raise cheap bank finance, the household had not (yet) shown interest in the emerging market of cash-based savings products.

During the year, the household's net worth deteriorated significantly. This was largely due to an increase in liabilities. They increased the size of their debt with two large bank loans. The household saved very little and counted on giving interest-free loans as their most significant financial asset. Loans they had given that were outstanding at the beginning of the year were repaid during the study.

Table A2.8 Financial Net Worth at the Start and End of the Research Year (US$ at market rate)

		Start amount	*End amount*	*Share of portfolio balances*	*Turnover*	*Share of portfolio turnover*	*Notes*
Assets							
Formal	Bank savings	5.23	5.23	20%	0.00	0%	He did not use his savings account over the year.
Informal	Interest-free loans given	85.77	20.92	80%	64.85	100%	One large loan to friend outside the village, most repaid within a few months, with balance left outstanding
	Total	91.00	26.15	100%	64.85	100%	
Liabilities							
Formal	Bank loans taken	684.64	1192.47	87%	1960.79	59%	Mostly two large bank loans against land documents, repaid after 12–18 months at 13% per annum
Informal	Interest-free loans taken	0.00	8.37	1%	1215.90	37%	Five small loans and one very large sum from grocer-friend to repay bank loan
	Shop credit	92.05	145.82	11%	103.97	3%	Used regular credit facility for groceries
	Services taken on credit	10.46	18.83	1%	12.55	<1%	Flour mill and doctor
	Stock sold in advance	0.00	6.28	0%	14.64	<1%	Took small amount from poor neighbor seeking to fix a low price for grain
	Total	787.15	1371.77	100%	3307.85	100%	
	Financial net worth	– 696.15	– 1345.62	Total flows	3372.70		

APPENDIX 2

A Pot Salesman's Household, Rural Eastern Uttar Pradesh, India

The illiterate son of a *bidi* (cheap cigarettes) factory manager, Feizal, 40 (from chapter 3), was allotted homestead land in Kushphara, his mother's village, from the village council in 1985. When we met him he was selling aluminum pots to neighboring villagers by bicycle, while his only son was training to be a tailor and his wife and the older ones among his seven daughters rolled *bidis* for piece-rates. At the start of the research year, the family had accumulated significant savings from migrant labor by Feizal and his son, but halfway through, the family's situation took a sharp downturn when Feizal had an accident on his bike, broke his leg, and was unable to work. The family, not wishing to spend money (and busy saving for their daughter's wedding), went to a traditional doctor, but the break got worse, and they were ultimately forced to spend nearly $250 (two-thirds of a year's income of the whole family) on doctors' and hospital fees. In desperation, Feizal was forced into reconciliation with his long-estranged father, who agreed to pay half the bill. For the rest of our research period the family got by without Feizal's earnings.

Despite these unfortunate circumstances, the family's financial net worth deteriorated but did not turn negative. They achieved this result partly by managing to avoid loans on interest completely in spite of the financial crisis following Feizal's accident. Although the microfinance institution operating in the village became popular among their neighbors, the family resisted joining since, argued Feizal, he was able to raise enough capital from local wholesalers to use as stock. Taking other and more expensive loans would mean working harder and faster, a reality that was even less likely after his accident. For the large medical bills following the accident, the family cashed in the son's savings with his employer and drew down their bank savings. But they chose not to break the contractual savings with the private deposit collector. Instead, they borrowed small amounts interest-free from neighbors.

Table A2.9 Financial Net Worth at the Start and End of the Research Year (US$ at market rate)

		Start amount	*End amount*	*Share of portfolio balances*	*Turnover*	*Share of portfolio turnover*	*Notes*
Assets							
Formal	Bank savings	152.72	10.46	11%	167.36	59%	Savings from migrant labor and a matured fixed deposit were put in savings account, then withdrawn following Feizal's cycle accident.
Informal	Saved with a deposit collector	33.47	71.13	73%	37.66	13%	Private company offering contractual savings products invested in regional companies
	Saved with a moneyguard	62.76	0.00	0%	62.76	22%	Son (training as a tailor) kept wages with employer.
	Goods supplied on credit	9.41	16.32	17%	18.41	6%	Aluminum pots sold to surrounding villagers.
	Total	258.36	97.91	100%	286.19	100%	
Liabilities							
Informal	Wage advance	0.00	13.60	26%	97.28	23%	By trainee tailor son from employer
	Shop credit	20.92	39.54	74%	207.95	48%	
	Services taken on credit	0.00	0.00	0%	125.52	29%	Large doctor's bill following Feizal's cycle accident that his father agrees to clear
	Total	20.92	53.14	100%	430.75	100%	
	Financial net worth	237.44	44.77	Total flows	716.94		

APPENDIX 2

A Tailor's Household, Rural Eastern Uttar Pradesh, India

Kushphara is Mohan's father's village, to which Mohan returned after growing up with his mother and her second family. Mohan (35 and barely literate) saw the village as an opportunity to practice his skill as a master tailor and set up shop in the local market town. In the past, Mohan had worked in Bombay earning $55 per month, a little more than he earns today through his shop. He returned to the village because he wanted to be with his wife and son. Early in our research, Mohan's wife, Mainum, became sick and, in continuous pain, was unable to work. Her sickness proved difficult to diagnose (sciatica and bone tuberculosis were mentioned), requiring several trips to Varanasi, Allahabad, and finally Mirzapur, where she stayed with her family until the research's end. Her health became the major drain on the household's resources.

Mainum was a member of the local MFI, and she finished her first loan and took a fresh one of double the size during the year. The couple tried and failed to meet the fast-track repayment schedule (i.e., repaying over 24 weeks instead of 50 weeks, at the same flat level of interest), and were forced to "downshift" to the slower schedule, but even then struggled with repayments as Mainum's failing health ate up income. As her condition worsened, the couple received help from friends and relatives and Mohan delayed rent payment to his shop landlord. While still occasional users of moneylenders, the couple agreed that the MFI provided a new opportunity to borrow for experimental, nonemergency purposes (while borrowing on interest was earlier confined to emergencies). Mohan's regular income meant they could manage repayments even when loans were used for household (rather than business) purposes, but Mainum's deteriorating health changed everything. As table A2.10 shows, their negative net worth deepened over the year, largely because of a sharp increase in liabilities.

Table A2.10 Financial Net Worth at the Start and End of the Research Year (US$ at market rate)

		Start amount	*End amount*	*Share of portfolio balances*	*Turnover*	*Share of portfolio turnover*	*Notes*
Assets							
Semiformal	MFI savings	2.09	0.75	2%	8.03	8%	Small savings collected alongside loan repayments and offset against installments missed toward year-end
Informal	Services supplied on credit	41.84	30.33	98%	95.19	92%	Tailoring services given on credit to friends, who were resistant to repay
	Total	43.93	31.08	100%	103.22	100%	
Liabilities							
Semiformal	MFI loans	19.08	6.28	5%	213.64	36%	The couple struggles with repayment because of wife's failing health
Informal	Interest-free loans taken	3.14	69.67	56%	118.83	20%	Loan taken for wife's failing health, shop rent, and an MFI repayment
	Interest-bearing loans taken	0.00	4.18	3%	10.46	2%	
	Going into rent arrears	29.29	36.61	30%	222.80	37%	Pays his shop rent when he's able according to cash flow. He struggles toward year end as costs rise.
	Services taken on credit	2.09	0.00	0%	2.09	0%	
	Shop credit	0.84	6.80	6%	28.56	5%	
	Total	54.44	123.54	100%	596.38	100%	
	Financial net worth	− 10.51	− 92.46	Total flows	699.60		

APPENDIX 2

A Widow Caring for AIDS Orphans in Rural Lugangeni, South Africa

Nomsa (from chapter 4) was a 77-year-old woman looking after four of her grandchildren, two of whom had come to live with her a year earlier after her daughter died of AIDS. The family lived at the bottom of a track that wound down a steep hill. The homestead was made up of two buildings, both worn and slightly falling down. Before they came, Nomsa might have been considered reasonably well off, but the five of them now found themselves struggling to live off her government old-age grant of $114 per month. She had tried repeatedly to apply for a foster care grant from social workers but was turned away. She was hit doubly hard by her daughter's funeral because she had already gotten into debt with a local store trying to rebuild her *rondaval* (round traditional hut). She managed to pay for the funeral but was unable to service the credit she had taken for it for a year. She got by with the produce from her garden and by taking loans from moneylenders, but she also got very confused about what and to whom she owed.

The portfolio consists largely of debt instruments from various creditors, which explains her year-end negative financial net worth. Notice that she used a combination of interest-bearing and interest-free borrowing, both from moneylenders and savings clubs. She borrowed from the moneylender when she'd already tapped out her other sources. However, she did manage to remain current on her loans, paying back when her grant money came. Her financial position was essentially unchanged from when we met her to when we completed the study. Despite her weak financial position, however, her financial turnover was strikingly high—she pushed and pulled just over $5,300 through her portfolio of financial instruments over a 14-month period.

Table A2.11 Financial Net Worth at the Start and End of the Research Year (US$ at market rate)

		Start amount	*End amount*	*Share of portfolio balances*	*Turnover*	*Share of portfolio turnover*	*Notes*
Assets							
Formal	Bank savings	0.00	23.08	24%	3581.46	73%	Her grant was paid into the bank account and promptly withdrawn.
Informal	Saving-up club savings	0.00	71.54	75%	133.08	3%	She belonged to two saving-up clubs.
	Saved at home	0.00	0.23	<1%	1141.92	23%	She withdrew her grant money from the bank, bought basic goods, then kept the remainder in the house for daily needs.
	Burial society				68.91	1%	She belonged to two burial societies.
	Total	0.00	94.85	100%	4925.37	100%	
Liabilities							
Informal	Interest-free loan taken	0.00	58.46	32%	19.77	5%	Four loans from neighbors and family
	Moneylender loan	20.00	100.00	55%	84.88	20%	Four loans, at between 25% and 30% interest per month
	Shop credit	76.92	23.38	13%	193.35	46%	She consistently took credit from two different shops in the village.
	Loan from savings club	0.00	0.00	0%	124.45	29%	Four loans from a different savings clubs; paid 30% per month
	Total	96.92	181.84	100%	422.45	100%	
	Financial net worth	− 96.92	− 86.99	Total flows	5347.82		

APPENDIX 2

A Woman with Many Burial Societies in Rural Lugangeni, South Africa

Nozitha was a 65-year-old woman who lived with two of her daughters, a nephew, and five grandchildren. They lived along one of the dirt roads that meander through green, breezy Lugangeni. From just outside their home, the land drops down into a steep hill. Across the way are green hills, dotted with round *rondavels* and flat boxlike houses. All the members of the household lived on Nozitha's old-age grant of $114 per month, although in July and October, respectively, two of the youngest grandchildren started to receive government child grants of $26 per month. Sometimes Nozitha's other daughter (who lives outside the household) gave her money or food or net wire for the garden, but Nozitha said it wasn't enough. Her biggest concern was to meet the payments of the seven funeral plans she belonged to. One of the formal plans, for example, was with an undertaker who would cover her funeral—someone came to her house to collect the 75¢ per month. An informal example was a burial society to which she paid $1.53 per month but charged $3.08 if a payment was missed. She worried about missing a payment, so she borrowed to cover the cost of the burial societies and food. During the research year, she had also borrowed from ASCAs and taken credit from the local store. She'd also taken various items—chicks, a wardrobe—on credit from private sellers.

Despite the added benefit of the two child support grants that she began receiving during the year, her financial net worth continued to move deeper into the red. Out of her monthly grant income of $166, she paid $19 toward burial societies alone. Was it worth it? Her portfolio of funeral instruments was certainly within the range of "good value" compared to the portfolios of other households in the village—she would receive $45 in burial services for every dollar that she paid every month. However, even the combined payouts of these seven plans would not cover the funeral expenses for everyone in the house. Each of the four adults would require about $1,500 for their funerals, and the five children would require $750. This means the funeral expense requirements for the family would be $9,750, and the funeral plans that Nozitha was going to such lengths to maintain would only pay for about half that amount.

Table A2.12 Financial Net Worth at the Start and End of the Research Year (US$ at market rate)

		Start amount	*End amount*	*Share of portfolio balances*	*Turnover*	*Share of portfolio turnover*	*Notes*
Assets							
Formal	Funeral plan	—	—	—	30.84	5%	She used two different insurance providers.
Informal	Saved at home	18.46	9.54	100%	527.30	78%	She received her grant in cash, bought the basics, and kept the money in the house for daily needs.
	Burial society	—	—	—	116.89	17%	She belonged to five burial societies.
	Interest-free loan given	0.00	0.00	0%	1.62	< 1%	She gave a small loan to a neighbor during the year.
	Total	18.46	9.54	100%	676.65	100%	
Liabilities							
Informal	Interest-free loan taken	0.00	58.46	32%	11.84	2%	Five loans from neighbors and family
	Moneylender loan	20.00	100.00	55%	77.69	12%	Three loans, at between 25% and 30% interest per month
	Shop credit	76.92	23.38	13%	240.84	39%	She consistently took credit from one of the shops in the village.
	Loan from savings club	0.00	0.00	0%	118.46	19%	Five loans from different savings clubs; she paid 25% to 30% per month.
	Credit from local sellers	0.00	0.00	0%	175.99	28%	She bought items on credit from six different sellers.
	Total	96.92	181.84	100%	624.82	100%	
	Financial net worth	− 78.46	− 172.30	Total flows	1301.47		

APPENDIX 2

An Older Couple in Diepsloot, South Africa

Mary and James were 63 and 56, respectively, when we knew them, a married couple living in urban Diepsloot, South Africa, outside of Johannesburg. Diepsloot is a wide sprawling expanse of different types of houses: a haphazard array of squatter shacks divided by a squalid stream from the stark but orderly rows of government-provided, one-room houses. It is in one of these new houses that the couple lived, at the very end of a row, halfway up the hill. They used to live with their two sons, but both left to go to the rural areas in December 2003. During the year, Mary and James moved from their settlement shack into a house provided by the government. Their uncle was staying in their old shack, but he did not pay rent. James used to have a good job as a delivery man but was laid off in 1995. He received a retrenchment package but spent it on buying a house in the rural areas and fixing it up. Mary was also retrenched from her job as a housecleaner in November 2003, and she did not get a retrenchment package. She started a job in August 2004, receiving $46.15 per month. James did casual work now and then. Otherwise, they lived off money given to them by James's siblings. As if things were not tight enough, their grandchild had died a year earlier. The local undertaker gave them credit for the funeral; they owed him $107.70 when we first met them and paid him back steadily. They had another funeral in August that they needed to contribute to, and they borrowed $61.54 from a friend. They then borrowed small amounts so many times from their neighbors that they were starting to be turned away.

Mary and James had to manage their money very tightly even before their grandchildren died, but the figures above show how badly these two funerals cut into their financial net worth. Most of their transactions were from borrowing from friends and neighbors. This is a classic example of a couple who lived sparsely and close to the edge, and two events knocked them into a serious poverty trap. Although they had a new home provided by the government and could be considered "asset rich," their cash-flow situation was grave.

Table A2.13 Financial Net Worth at the Start and End of the Research Year (US$ at market rate)

		Start amount	*End amount*	*Share of portfolio balances*	*Turnover*	*Share of portfolio turnover*	*Notes*
Assets							
Formal	Bank savings	0.00	0.00	0%	0.00	0%	Two bank accounts were opened to save while they were working; but they lost their jobs, so they closed them.
Informal	Saved at home	20.00	23.00	100%	432.69	99%	They used a hiding place in the house to keep money to manage their daily needs.
	Burial society				5.05	1%	They belonged to one burial society.
	Total	20.00	23.00	100%	437.74	100%	
Liabilities							
Informal	Interest-free loan taken	0.00	50.77	69%	154.41	63%	12 loans from neighbors and family to help them get by
	Shop credit	0.00	23.08	31%	92.31	37%	This was the credit from the funeral parlor that they took and partially paid back.
	Total	0.00	73.85	100%	246.72	100%	
	Financial net worth	20.00	−50.85	Total flows	684.46		

APPENDIX 2

A Superior Money Manager in Diepsloot, South Africa

Sylvia (from chapter 4) was a very disciplined 39-year-old woman living in a shack in Diepsloot, South Africa, outside of Johannesburg. Her neat shack hugs two others in the tightly packed shack area, but one wall has an impressive number of windows, so she could let in the dusty sunlight. She earned about $370 per month as a house cleaner for two separate clients. One of the most interesting financial instruments in her portfolio is an ASCA she had belonged to since June 2003. There were 33 members each of whom paid in $30 per month and lent out the money at an interest rate of 30 percent per month. Members were obliged to take some money to lend out every month. Sylvia kept up a very busy lending schedule. From July 2004 to November 2004 alone, she lent to a total of 16 people an average of $60 each. Unfortunately, Sylvia did not earn as much as she expected from the payout of this ASCA. First, because some of the people who borrowed from her did not pay back, she had to pay back the ASCA from her own pocket, which decreased the net amount she earned. Second, just before the proceeds of the ASCA were paid out, the treasurer was robbed and killed as she was coming with the money from the bank. She was only carrying part of the ASCA money, so Sylvia received a partial payout of $246. She would have received twice as much if the borrowers hadn't defaulted and the robbery hadn't happened.

The ASCA wasn't the only way that Sylvia managed to save money. Every month she had her employers pay her wage into two different bank accounts. One she used for all her expenses and the other she tried not to touch. Keeping two different bank accounts is more expensive in terms of bank fees, but it gave her a mechanism with which to save half her salary every month. She also contributed to a formal savings plan, which will come due when her daughter is 16 and needing money for university. She also tried to keep aside money in the house, a mechanism that requires an extremely disciplined budget. She also concentrated on paying off her two credit cards that she had used the previous Christmas. Sylvia is a good example of a portfolio manager that looks to save across many different financial instruments, and the result paid off in that she more than doubled her financial net worth over the year.

Table A2.14 Financial Net Worth at the Start and End of the Research Year (US$ at market rate)

		Start amount	*End amount*	*Share of portfolio balances*	*Turnover*	*Share of portfolio turnover*	*Notes*
Assets							
Formal	Bank account	1373.38	2086.28	62%	10353.54	54%	She had four different bank accounts, including a long-term deposit account.
	Savings annuity	153.85	369.23	11%	182.71	1%	She had a savings plan for her daughter's education.
	Funeral plan				68.95	<1%	She used one formal funeral plan.
Informal	Saved at home	84.62	483.08	15%	4875.23	25%	She received her grant in cash, bought the basics, and kept the money in the house for daily needs.
	ASCA savings	0.00	246.00	7%	1206.88	6%	She belonged to five different savings clubs with different formats.
	Saving with a moneyguard	0.00	153.85	5%	153.85	1%	She left some money with an aunt in the rural areas.
	Burial society	—	—	—	68.95	<1%	She belonged to five burial societies.
	Interest-bearing loan given	0.00	0.00	0%	2404.38	12%	She lent a total of 42 times during the year.
	Total	1611.85	3338.44	100%	19314.49	100%	
Liabilities							
Formal	Credit card	214.46	0.00	100%	248.17	99%	She had two credit cards, which she steadily paid off over the year.
Informal	Shop credit	0.00	0.00	0%	1.33	1%	She took credit at the local shop once because she didn't have cash and paid back right away.
	Total	214.46	0.00	100%	249.50	100%	
	Financial net worth	1397.39	3338.44	Total flows	19563.99		

APPENDIX 2

A Couple Living in a Shack in Langa, South Africa

Thabo, a 26-year-old man, lived with his wife Zukiswa and two children in a shack in the urban area of Langa, South Africa, outside of Cape Town. Langa itself is made up of many different types of dwellings: blocks of apartments, single-family, two-roomed houses, squalid hostels, and a seemingly endless expanse of tightly packed shacks. When we went to visit Thabo, we had first to find the entrance to the shack area and then pick our way between the shacks, which are pressed tightly together. Thabo's shack was in a sort of a yard, adjoining several of his neighbors. His shack, as they go, was fairly up-market, with two rooms. A nearby bank of removable toilets and a water pipe serviced the area around him.

Thabo earned about $107.69 per week as a construction laborer, and his salary was directly deposited into his savings account. He saved money using a stop order that automatically transferred $23 of his wages into a fixed deposit account every week (this is the same mechanism that Joseph of chapter 4 had). He managed to save $923 this way during the previous year, from which he spent $553.85 and saved $370. By the end of the study year, he had expected to accumulate another $923 or more. He and his friends considered this a savings clubs of sorts. Although each saved individually in his own bank account, they had shared information about how to set it up and encouraged each other. He wanted to put this money toward buying a house. It is interesting that he had spent over $770 on a store credit card last December for clothes for his children, and he planned to spend more the next December. He didn't want to use his savings to pay off this debt. He said that it was more important to have the money in case of any problem.

We noticed an interesting attribute of Thabo's portfolio. He had $931.63 sitting in his bank account from the previous year's saving exercise with his stop order. Yet he accumulated a sizable debt of $686.77 on his credit card paying for Christmas. When we asked him why he didn't settle his credit card with the money in the bank, he said that the money in the bank was for emergencies, and he didn't want to risk not having it. He'd rather continue to pay the debt off little by little. Note as well that where other households would save money in their homes, Thabo didn't. He said that he worried about theft and about fire, both of which are rife in Thabo's area. With his savings, he ultimately hoped to buy a house, but he was concerned that it would take a long time to save enough money. His simple and conservative life-style, and this new way of saving, was helping him accumulate wealth, albeit at a slower rate than Sylvia.

Table A2.15 Financial Net Worth at the Start and End of the Research Year (US$ at market rate)

		Start amount	*End amount*	*Share of portfolio balances*	*Turnover*	*Share of portfolio turnover*	*Notes*
Assets							
Formal	Bank savings	931.63	2165.71	94%	11297.40	99%	He used one bank account to receive his salary, then had a stop order to transfer savings to another account with a different bank.
	Provident fund	106.73	147.84	6%	44.84	< 1%	He had a provident fund provided by his employer.
Informal	Interest-free loan given	61.38	0.00	0%	61.38	1%	He gave one loan to a neighbor and was paid back eventually.
	Total	1099.74	2313.55	100%	11403.62	100%	
Liabilities							
Formal	Credit card	1.54	686.77	100%	14999.00	100%	He had one credit card with a leading retailer.
	Total	1.54	686.77	100%	14999.00	100%	
	Financial net worth	1098.2	1626.78	Total flows	26402.62		

Acknowledgments

◆ ◆ ◆

THE RESEARCH for this book would not have been possible without the participation of many people. We owe a particular debt of gratitude to the respondents in all four financial diaries projects, for their precious time and their generosity with our persistence. They were candid, trusting, and patient enough to open up their lives to us, revealing their financial secrets and exposing both their virtues and weaknesses. We hope that we have done justice to their accounts here.

The Ford Foundation sponsored the writing—we are particularly grateful to Paula Nimpuno, of the Ford Johannesburg office, who embraced the vision for the diaries and bore with us as we spent three years creating a manuscript between four authors spread over three continents. The financial diaries work in Bangladesh (1999–2000) and India (2000–2001) was funded by research grants from the UK's Department for International Development to the Finance and Development Research Programme at the Institute for Development Policy and Management at the University of Manchester. The Grameen II diaries (2002–5) in Bangladesh were commissioned by MicroSave. The South African financial diaries were supported by the Ford Foundation, FinMark Trust, and the Micro Finance Regulatory Council of South Africa. Jonathan Morduch's time was supported by the Bill and Melinda Gates Foundation through a grant to the Financial Access Initiative. The views expressed in this book are our own, and, while we have received much support, the views do not necessarily represent the opinions of the funders or their employees.

We offer our thanks to the field researchers. In Bangladesh for the 1999–2000 diaries, they were S. K. Sinha, Saiful Islam, and Yeakub Azad. The team for the three-year "Grameen II Diaries" (2002–5) was overseen by S. K. Sinha and included area supervisors Mrs. Shamima Sultana, Ms. Kabita Pal, and Mrs. Rabeya Sultana (no relation), and assistants Ms. Parul Akhtar, Mrs. Purnima Barua, Mrs. Provati Akhter, Ms. Jharna Rani Majumder, Mrs. Nilufa Sultana (no relation), and Ms. Shilpi Akhter (no relation). Ms. Nazmun Nahar was employed as a translator. In India, the field researchers were Susheel Kumar and Nilesh Arya. In South Africa, the seven-member team was Tshifhiwa Muravha, Busi Magazi, Lwandle Mgidlana, Zanele Ramuse, Nomthumzi Qubeka, Nobahle Silulwane, and, remembered fondly, the late Abel Mongake. These diligent researchers withstood our persistent questions, and slogged through rain, mud, and intense heat to get to respondents on a daily basis. They managed our relationships with respondents with grace and humanity.

Many colleagues have also helped us with this book. David Hulme, the originator of the financial diaries concept, not only helped us get started and advised on the Bangladesh and Indian research, but also performed a miraculously efficient edit in the final days. Tim Sullivan and Seth Ditchik, editors at Princeton University Press, helped shape the manuscript and provided guidance on the publishing process. Thea Garon proved to be a helpful and careful reader of the final manuscript.

In South Africa, Mark Napier, Christian Chileshe, Darrell Beghin, Jeremy Leach, Rashid Ahmed, Gabriel Davel, Paula Nimpuno, and Murray Leibbrandt all played important roles in guiding the progress of research and dissemination of results from the South African diaries. Particularly warm thanks must go to David Porteous, who championed the initiation of financial diaries in South Africa. We owe great thanks to Christina Scott for witty and pragmatic public relations work within South Africa. Louise Taljaard, a research assistant with a meticulous nose for detail, was invaluable in the cleaning and preparation of the South African data.

In Bangladesh, Imran Matin and Md Maniruzzaman were indispensable members of the supervisory team for the 1999–2000 diaries. For the Grameen diaries Md Maniruzzaman again provided advice and carried out complementary field studies, and we were helped by the Dhaka-based accountancy firm Acnabin and Co., overseen by partner Iftekhar Hossain and led by Mohammad Mia. We are grateful to Grameen Bank, especially its founder and managing director Muhammad Yunus and his deputy Dipal Chandra Barua, for encouragement and assistance, and to the branch managers and field staff of Grameen and many other microfinance institutions for the patient way that they dealt with our constant questions. Graham A. N. Wright and David Cracknell of MicroSave strongly supported the study and contributed many ideas.

In India, we owe thanks to Cashpor Financial and Technical Services for assisting in the selection of our rural sites. The study was greatly assisted by a collaboration with EDA Rural Systems, Gurgaon. Sanjay Sinha and Meenal Patole provided guidance and assistance throughout, from conceptualization to client selection to developing the data set to reviewing drafts and assisting in the write-ups. Also at EDA Rural Systems, Radhika Aghase assisted with a parallel study with invaluable lessons for the financial diaries. Prabhu Ghate, Sukhwinder Arora, Vijay Mahajan, Vikram Akula, Raj Kamal Mukherjee, Kishore Singh, Barbara Harriss-White, Ben Rogaly, and Malcolm Harper all gave comments on papers that came out in the year following the completion of research or helped with getting it started in India.

Lastly, we owe a great deal to the support our families and partners have given us during months of concentrated writing, late nights of conference calls, not to mention the intensity of the lengthy diary fieldwork. Daryl Collins wishes to express a special ode of honor to her husband, Brian Talbot, who ingeniously and meticulously built the database that facilitated the capture of the South African diaries data.

Notes

◆ ◆ ◆

Chapter One

1. To get a sense of the debates, the most sharply worded arguments for aid-fueled strategies are in Sachs 2005, which is countered by Easterly (2006). Wolf (2005) makes the case for globalization, while Stiglitz (2005), for example, points to its limits.

2. If we include the Grameen II diaries (see chapter 6), which covered 43 households, this increases to just under 300 households.

3. The countries we refer to here, as well as the three countries where we collected the diaries—Bangladesh, India, and South Africa—are all fortunate in that they are not at war or in conflict, and have working, recognized governments and functioning economies. Some of what we say in this book may not apply to fragile or "failed" states, or areas where there is no monetized economy. Our broad perspectives have been shaped by research completed by a wide range of individuals and organizations, and we cite representative studies in the text.

4. In important new work, Krislert Samphantharak and Robert Townsend (2008) apply the idea to monthly data from Thailand, providing rigorous methodological foundations for drawing analogues between households and corporate firms.

5. There are eight Millennium Development Goals—which range from halving extreme poverty (defined as living under one dollar per day per person in 1993 PPP dollars) to halting the spread of HIV/AIDS and providing universal primary education, all by the target date of 2015. These have been agreed to by all the world's countries and all the world's leading development institutions. See http://www.un.org/millenniumgoals.

6. An excellent source showing how to calculate dollar-per-day estimates from local currency incomes is Sillers 2004. More on the World Bank International Comparison program and new data can be found at www.worldbank.org. For a related take on the same set of issues see *The Economist*'s "Big Mac" index at http://www.economist.com/markets/bigmac/about.cfm. The 1993 and 2005 figures in table 1.1 are calculated using consumer prices indices from the International Monetary Fund's *International Financial Statistics*. The 2005 comparison using PPP conversion rates are the latest available at the time of writing.

7. A growing literature indicates that income given to women is more likely to be used for investments in education, children's nutrition, and housing than income given to men (see, for example, Thomas 1990, 1994; Hoddinott and Haddad 1995; Khandker 1998; and Duflo 2003). Hossain (1988), Hulme (1991), Gibbons and Kasim (1991), and Khandker, Khalily, and Kahn (1995) also find that microloans given to women are more likely to be repaid than those given to men. For an overview, see Armendáriz de Aghion and Morduch (2005). Nava Ashraf (2008) suggests that some of these differences in preferences may not be based on gender alone but on the structure of control in household financial management.

8. Note that this is not unlike patterns found in developed countries. The 2004 US Survey of Consumer Finances shows that the share of nonfinancial assets in total assets is much higher for the lowest income quintile of households than the highest.

9. The median household showed an increase of 14 percent in their financial net worth over these 10 months. This was not due to a change in value of these assets, the way we think about a wealthy person's stock portfolio. Rather households were *adding* to their financial wealth at the rapid rate of 1.4 percent per month. By tracking households over time, we were able to see that South African households accomplished this rapid rate of financial growth by managing to save, on average, about 20 percent of their income per month. We discuss the instruments that helped them to do this in chapter 4.

10. More details on this analysis can be found in appendix.

11. By "semiformal providers" we mean microfinance organizations and other nonbank providers, such as NGOs, that offer services to poor clients. They are sometimes referred to as "MFIs"—microfinance institutions.

12. See Aleem 1990 on moneylenders and Ardener 1964 on savings clubs. Both literatures and examples are discussed further by Armendáriz de Aghion and Morduch (2005, chapter 2 and 3) and by Rutherford (2000).

13. Smoothing consumption refers to efforts to reduce the ups and downs of consumption in the face of fluctuating income patterns. Consumption can be smoothed by borrowing and saving, for example, and by obtaining insurance through formal or informal means. More on the literature on informal insurance can be found in, for example, Townsend 1994; Deaton 1992; and Morduch 1995, 1999, 2006.

14. In South Africa, we started with a large sample of 181 households. During the year, some households moved away or dropped out, leaving us with 152 full sets of yearlong diaries. Most of the South African data in this book is based on this sample of 152 households.

15. In South Africa, consumer marketing surveys make great use of Living Standard Measures (LSMs) to segment markets on the basis of wealth. The LSM is calculated entirely on observable goods. In local terms, LSM1–5 are considered underserved. We calculated the LSM for every South Africa household in our financial diaries sample and found 90 percent to be in LSM 5 or below.

16. Five examples of household portfolios from each country can be found in appendix 2 of this book. Backgrounds and portfolios for many more households from all three samples, as well as research on a wide variety of topics using the financial diary data, are available at www.financialdiaries.com.

17. While the main problem of poor households is lack of choice, there are local markets in which competition among microfinance providers has grown considerably, including markets in Peru, Nicaragua, the Philippines, and Bangladesh. Real competition will likely increase, but it remains far from the norm.

18. See Aleem 1990 for a survey of moneylenders that helps explain costs from the supply side. A different set of literature tries to understand prices from the demand side, by measuring the return to capital (see Banerjee and Duflo 2004; Udry and Anagol 2006; de Mel, McKenzie, and Woodruff 2008; Morduch 2008).

19. In South Africa, the Small Enterprise Foundation, based in Limpopo Province, has ambitious expansion plans, as do other microfinance groups.

20. Much new work is turning a fresh eye to problems of low quality, unreliability, and corruption in basic services, and some of the work is pointing to new solutions. Bertrand et al. (2007) document corruption in the driver's license system in India. Das, Hammer, and Leonard (2008) describe problems of low quality and unreliability in basic healthcare. Banerjee and Duflo (2006) address possibilities for confronting absenteeism in education and health settings.

Chapter Two

1. Savings programs indicate similar low balances. In the middle of 2003, the average savings balance at *Safe*Save (Bangladesh) was $22, and average savings balance at Bank Rakyat Indonesia (BRI) was $75. See chapter 6 of Armendáriz de Aghion and Morduch 2005.

2. These dollar figures are converted at official exchange rates, which may give too low a sense of the effective value of the assets. When converted using "purchasing power" parity (PPP) rates, the median asset values rise to $293 for Bangladesh, $637 for India, and $1,128 for South Africa. The financial assets of the median South African diary household, in other words, ought to be able to buy goods and services locally that would cost $1,128 if purchased in the United States.

3. Again, this pattern is upheld elsewhere. BURO Tangail in Bangladesh showed that at the end of 2000, the savings accounts of their clients were worth just under 27 million takas, less than 2 million takas more than the year before. But though balances did not grow much in the year, *during* the year the owners of the accounts had deposited more than 62 million takas and withdrawn more than 60 million takas. See Armendáriz de Aghion and Morduch 2005, following Rutherford, Sinha, and Aktar 2001.

4. See Case and Deaton 1998 for a description of the South African transfer system and its benefits for low-income families.

5. Ramadan arrives two weeks earlier each year, because of differences between the Muslim and the Gregorian calendars. During the research year, it happened to fall in November, along with Diwali.

6. More information on the National Credit Act can be found on the website of the National Credit Regulator, http://www.ncr.org.za/.

7. See Collins 2008.

8. David Hulme reports interviewing five rickshaw drivers in Bangladesh in 2006. All five rented their machines. Two had at one time bought their own machine but had them stolen, while a third had borrowed heavily to buy a motorized rickshaw that broke down and was repossessed.

9. The concept of "relationship" banking has real meaning in the financial world of poor people, just as it does for the rich. Microfinance institutions have enjoyed very high repayment rates on uncollateralized loans, suggesting that the value placed on honoring contracts does not diminish, and may even be enhanced, by material poverty.

10. Kishan (farmer) Credit Card, the name of the first product of its kind from the State Bank of India, has become a generic term for similar products offered by other Indian banks, while they carry different names.

11. See Schreiner and Sherraden 2006.

12. The example is from Prahalad 2005, 16–17.

13. All households can have trouble paying back loans when they meet with emergencies, as the next chapter shows. See Johnston and Morduch 2008 for additional evidence from Indonesia on the wide range of uses for loans by low-income households. They find that about half of the loans taken by poor households are used for nonbusiness purposes, including consumption, education, and health.

14. See Sinha et al. 2003.

Chapter Three

1. The data are from World Bank *World Development Indicators*, accessed in July 2008. In 2000 the under-five child mortality rate was 92 per 1,000 children in Bangladesh, 89 per 1,000 in India, and 63 per 1,000 in South Africa. In the United States, by comparison, the child mortality rate was 8 per 1,000 in 2001.

2. On the other hand, the fact of prevalent risk steered the Bangladeshi households away from making investments that could have led to a stronger livelihoods and living standards.

3. The confluence of poverty and vulnerability has become a major theme in the study of poverty, led by a wide range of scholars; for Africa, the work of Oxford economists Stefan Dercon and Marcel Fafchamps is particularly notable. See, for example, the papers included in Dercon 2006. Morduch (1995, 1999) gives a broad frame on the academic work with an eye to policy interventions.

4. The study, by Abhijit Banerjee and Esther Duflo (2007), pools World Bank household surveys from across the world to present a broad view of the economic lives of the poor. The paper reports on detailed survey data, culled largely from World Bank and Rand Corporation surveys conducted between 1988 and 2005, representing the expenditures of tens of thousands of poor households in 13 developing countries.

5. The general problem is framed in Morduch's (1999) essay on the strengths and weaknesses of informal risk sharing. He asks: "does informal insurance patch the safety net?" And answers: "yes, but not very well." The essay also

describes the hidden costs—financial, economic, and emotional—often attached to informal risk sharing. See Townsend 1994 for the seminal paper on formal tests of village-level risk sharing, as well as Deaton 1992, 1997 for similar work in Côte d'Ivoire, Ghana, and Thailand, Morduch 2005 in India, Udry 1994 in Nigeria, Grimard 1997 in Côte d'Ivoire, Lund and Fafchamps 2003 in the Philippines, and Dubois 2000 in Pakistan. Morduch 2005 provides a critical overview of the work on South Asia, and Morduch 2006 provides an accessible introduction to the broader research program. The econometric work on village insurance following Townsend (1994) focuses on coping with income variability *within* villages. It does not focus on what is often a larger problem: income shocks that affect a village or region as a whole.

6. This section draws heavily on Sinha and Patole 2002. The paper reports on a study of financial institutions and products that was carried out alongside the financial diaries in the same India rural site.

7. The LIC agent's manual suggests that the lowest premium product available was about $9.40 per quarter at the time, so this is one of the lowest premium products that Ismael could have taken. See Sinha and Patole 2002.

8. For small and marginal farmers, on the other hand, infrequent and higher premiums may be more manageable, but they need to coincide with seasonal cash flows. All this, of course, would create additional costs for LIC agents and perhaps require a higher commission.

9. See the case study of Delta Life by McCord and Churchill (2005).

10. McCord and Churchill (2005) make the case for developing insurance schemes as a partnership between an insurance company and a microfinance institution. They argue that the risks, administration, and expertise required are such that typical microfinance institutions are ill-placed to provide insurance completely "in-house."

11. For more details on the financial implications of death on households in South Africa, see Collins and Leibbrandt 2007.

12. Dorrington et al. (2006) describe the demographic impacts of AIDS in South Africa. Their estimates suggest the likelihood of death before 60 among adult males jumps from 36 percent in 1990 up to 61 percent in 2008, and among adult females from 21 percent in 1990 to an expected 53 percent in 2008.

13. See, for example, Booysen 2004 on the relationships between AIDS, income, and poverty.

14. The study, by Jim Roth (1999), found evidence that funerals in the Grahamstown township cost approximately 15 times the average monthly household income.

15. A few prominent examples are Avbob, Old Mutual, and Standard Bank.

16. There is evidence that burial societies also exist in a strikingly similar format in other parts of the world. Dercon et al. (2004) survey the informal funeral insurance markets in Ethiopia and in Tanzania. They note that village members tend to know each other well and are often related, which the authors assume would mitigate the informational risks. However, the contracts within burial societies still closely resemble common insurance contracts with constitutions and enforcement rules. Dercon et al. also notice that most groups charge an entrance fee that is inconsistent with most insurance models and indicates that financial stability may prove to be a problem with these groups. As in South Africa, they also find that membership is widespread and that most individuals belong to more than one group.

17. Data are available in *FinScope 2003*; see www.finmark.org.za for more details.

18. South Africa has long used savings accounts through the wide network of Post Offices to increase the number of banked individuals in the country. We found that many of the financial diaries respondents would have both a Post Office bank account and a commercial bank account.

19. For more details on this analysis, see Collins and Leibbrandt 2007.

20. Strictly speaking, the club did not allow such loans. This case shows that such rules are sometimes broken, and this may be one of the reasons why they sometimes run into liquidity problems. Thembi was under pressure to repay quickly, before the loan came to the attention of the general membership of the club.

21. Lim and Townsend (1998) give evidence on the importance of saving in dealing with risk in data from three Indian villages (the specific mechanism is the storage of grain in-kind). In their case, it is self-insurance again that is the main mechanism for coping, not collective insurance per se.

22. The classic moral hazard problem in the health context is described by Pauly (1968), and Morduch (2006) extends the discussion in the context of "microinsurance" in poor communities.

23. The evidence is from International Labour Organisation 2006 cited in Ghate 2006.

24. The SEWA insurance mechanism is described by Ghate (2006).

25. A broader view on safety nets is provided by Barrientos and Hulme (2008).

26. The argument is developed in Roth, Garand, and Rutherford 2006.

Chapter Four

1. In a sign of progress in creating financial products for the poor, six diary households in South Africa bought their homes with a mortgage through a special program. More contribute to pension funds, and, as described in chapter 6, long-term savings plans (called "pensions," though they are more general saving devices) have become a new and popular Grameen Bank product. Grameen Bank has long offered a multiyear housing loan, usually used for home expansion and repairs, and some of the Bangladeshi diary households described in chapter 6 hold them—or have held them in the past.

2. Behavioral economics combines perspectives from psychology and economics. Among the lessons are that assuming the ability to act with perfect foresight and rationality, a staple of twentieth-century economics, ignores the self-discipline problems that challenge rich and poor alike. Another lesson is that the way contracts and financial mechanisms are presented can affect their take-up and usage. See Thaler and Sunstein 2008 for an accessible overview of new thinking in behavioral economics.

3. See Banerjee and Duflo 2007. They find that by households living under one dollar per day per person spend, on average, from 56 to 78 percent of household income on food, with slightly less being spent in urban areas.

4. In South Africa, the average benchmark across households was $425 per month, but an average South African income hides a wide distribution of incomes, even within these poorest of areas. Over all three areas in South Africa, roughly two-thirds of the sample had incomes that are higher (often well higher) than those in India and Bangladesh, but one-third of households had incomes that are as low or lower than $50.

5. Most poor South Africans are dependent on a government-provided monthly old-age grant in their retirement. See Collins 2007.

6. See Banerjee and Duflo 2007.

7. Studies have shown that festivals are major consumer of resources among the poor around the world. See Banerjee and Duflo 2007, which quotes survey results indicating that in several developing countries more than half of all households spend on festivals each year. Fafchamps and Shilpi (2005) found that in Nepal households spend lavishly on festivals as a way of asserting their worth in front of other more economically successful households.

8. See Deaton 1997 for an overview of recent analyses of the economics of saving and risk-sharing in developing economies.

9. See, for example, Laibson, Repetto, and Tobacman 2003.

10. Bauer, Chytilova and Morduch (2008) take a close look at this pattern using data collected in villages in the South Indian state of Karnataka. As a first step, surveys were used to determine households particularly likely to have self-discipline problems that could correlate to difficulties saving (i.e., evidence of "hyperbolic" preferences in the language of behavioral economics). They showed that households with signs of self-discipline problems were more likely than others to borrow through microfinance institutions featuring enforced, regular weekly payments. Though taking the loans was costlier than saving, it provided the households with an effective way to accumulate.

11. For an excellent presentation of these issues, we refer readers to Mullainathan 2005.

12. See Ashraf, Karlan, and Yin 2006. They evaluated the impact of this "commitment" saving product using a randomized controlled trial, where 1,800 customers of a bank were randomized to either receive an offer to open the new type of account or not. (Everyone already had access to a standard account.) Among those offered the new type of accounts, 28 percent opened one. After 12 months, average savings balances increased by 80 percent in the group offered the new type of account compared to the control group. This translates as a 300 percent increase for the impacts among those who actually opened the accounts—a large and meaningful increase in savings.

13. For more on lessons from behavioral economics, see, for example, Laibson, Repetto and Tobacman 1998; Laibson 1997; and O'Donahue and Rabin 1999a, 1999b.

14. Anderson and Baland (2002) argue that informal saving and borrowing clubs in the slums of Nairobi are used by women in part to protect funds from their husbands. Mary Kay Gugerty's (2007) study in western Kenya highlights the use of informal clubs as discipline services.

15. For more on RoSCAs and related devices, see Rutherford 2000. For an introduction to the economics literature on informal devices, see chapter 3 of Armendáriz de Aghion and Morduch 2005.

16. This example and other examples in this section come from non-financial-diaries research by Stuart Rutherford.

17. As researched and reported in Rutherford and Wright 1998 and later described in Rutherford 2000.

18. Compared to saving-up clubs and RoSCAs, ASCAs are in any case more complicated and more difficult to run well because the cash accumulates and has to be tracked through written accounts. Literate people—and so usually the

better off—get picked as treasurers because they can keep accounts, but even the best-intentioned of them can be cavalier with balances that mean much more to their poorer fellow members than they do to themselves. Particularly in recent years since the rise of microfinance, rural Bangladeshis have made less use of ASCAs.

19. For a fascinating account of attitudes toward RoSCAs, see Vander Meer 2009. Vander Meer studied 60 rural RoSCAs in Taiwan over a 21-year period.

20. Studying "mental accounts" has become a central part of behavioral economics; see Thaler 1990. People who use mental accounts may designate a specific savings account or device for a particular purpose (like sending money to relatives) and designate other accounts for other purposes (household needs, say, or school fees). Doing so may add costs, but it can help instill the discipline to keep some pots of money safe for their intended purposes.

21. The microlenders have since improved their products, as chapter 6 will show.

22. Kenneth's RoSCA and the Filipino *ubbu-tungnguls* are unusual in that they orchestrate what is in fact a series of one-on-one contracts into a social event: each individual contract can break down without damaging the device as a whole, allowing them to continue for years together.

23. Grameen Bank's long-term housing loans had poorer repayment rates, and higher write-offs, than its one-year general loans.

Chapter Five

1. The study of Compartamos's interest rates was completed by Richard Rosenberg (2007). Cull, Demirgüç-Kunt, and Morduch (2009) describe the Compartamos public offering and reactions to it.

2. Muhammad Yunus (2007) offers one of the sharpest criticisms. The survey data on interest rates for the 350 institutions is given by Cull, Demirgüç-Kunt, and Morduch (2009). Consistent with their findings, Aleem (1990) found that the high interest rates charged by informal moneylenders in Pakistan reflected the real costs of their lending—costs of screening and pursuing delinquent loans in particular—in these markets. The general pattern of prices is replicated in other sectors: Prahalad (2005), for example, compares the prices paid by slum-dwellers in Mumbai relative to prices paid by the middle class. He finds the poor paying considerably more for basics like water, phone calls,

diarrhea medicine, and rice. In microfinance, interest rates over 40 percent per year and more (after inflation) are certainly part of the landscape, while better-off customers borrow at rates below 10 percent (Cull, Demirgüç-Kunt, and Morduch 2009).

3. Udry and Anagol (2006) estimate returns to capital of small-scale agricultural producers in Ghana to be 50 percent per year for traditional crops and 250 percent per year for nontraditional crops. Banerjee and Duflo (2004) estimate returns to capital for small firms of between 74 and 100 percent per year. De Mel, McKenzie, and Woodruff (2008) estimate for small firms in Sri Lanka of at least 68 percent, though much lower (statistically indistinguishable from zero at the average) for women. See Morduch (2008) for a synthesis of the evidence and issues around measures of returns to capital in microenterprise.

4. Karlan and Zinman (2008) study interest sensitivity for loans provided by a consumer lender in South Africa who charges very high interest rates for installment credit. The interest rates are nearly 12 percent per *month*. Sensitivity to interest rates was gauged by mailing out over 50,000 credit offers to customers. The letters offered interest rates that were selected at random (within bounds), and the question was how much price would affect their interest in taking new loans. Borrowers turned out to react to interest rates, especially to increases, but just modestly. Dehejia, Montgomery, and Morduch (2007) find evidence for substantial short-term interest sensitivity in a study in the Dhaka slums when a microfinance lender increased interest rates from 24 percent to 36 percent per year, but over the longer term, borrowing remained strong.

5. In this calculation, one would take a monthly, weekly, or daily interest rate to the power of the number of months, weeks, or days in a year.

6. The calculation is $((1 + (30/100) \wedge 12) - 1) * 100 = 2{,}230$ percent, rounding to the nearest percent.

7. See Patole and Ruthven 2001.

8. The interest calculations are as follows: His total repayment on the \$32 loan was \$37.50, which means that he paid \$5.50 in interest. If he paid in 50 days, his annual interest rate is $((5.50/32) * (365/50)) * 100 = 125$ percent. If he pays the same interest in 330 days, his annual interest rate is $((5.50/32) * (365/330)) * 100 = 19$ percent. Neither of these rates are compounded.

9. This is not always the case. Sometimes moneylenders are from distant provinces or even from abroad, such as the South Asians who serve mountain villages in northern Philippines. In many states of India and even in Bangladesh itinerant moneylenders are still called *Kabuliwallahs* (people from Kabul, Afghanistan), just as they were during the British colonial period. In this chapter

we quote the case of a Maharashtra-based ethnic group who serve as moneylenders to Delhi slum-dwellers.

10. In the South African sample, we found very few privately arranged interest-bearing loans given or taken. Borrowing either took place with a moneylender or an ASCA.

11. Chuck Waterfield, a long-term microfinance enthusiast, campaigns for greater price transparency in microfinance. See his website www.mftransparency.org.

12. See Rutherford 2000, 13–17.

13. It is important to remember that this calculation is interest charged on an average balance that is growing over 220 days. So the average balance would be about $220/2=110$. Therefore, the calculation would be $((20/110)*(365/220))*100 = 30$ percent.

14. See Aryeetey and Steel 1995, also available on the MicroSave website www.microsave.org.

15. Armendáriz de Aghion and Morduch (2005) trace (and debunk) economists' arguments that moneylender interest rates can be justified by default risk.

Chapter Six

1. Grameen II is vividly described in Dowla and Barua 2006. BRAC was founded in the wake of Bangladesh's 1971 War of Independence, and Martha Chen's 1986 volume remains an excellent guide to BRAC's philosophy and early years. (BRAC's initials originally stood for the Bangladesh Rural Advancement Committee, but, as noted, today the initials stand on their own.) Rutherford (2009) describes ASA's remarkable rise and transformation from its roots as a civil rights NGO. The *Forbes* ranking of the "Top 50 Microfinance Institutions"—with ASA on top—is reported by Swibel (2007).

2. Explanations of how that came about, and of the way we executed the project, can be found in the appendix. We are grateful to Grameen Bank and other microfinance institutions for their cooperation during the execution of the diaries.

3. In practice, the half-acre rule is not followed strictly, but the rule's intention—to focus on the poorest villagers—remains a principle for the bank.

4. Grameen charged a "flat" rate of 10 percent of the loan value. This interest was, at first, collected at the end of the loan term. But soon Grameen decided

that it would be best collected broken into 50 equal weekly installments, like the loan principal repayments. This produces an annual percentage rate (APR) of a little over 20 percent, a figure that rises somewhat if one takes into account the effect of the compulsory savings.

5. See Yunus 2002.

6. Grameen II also provides for repayment schedules tailored to individual borrowers, but (at least in 2005) field staff were rarely implementing this opportunity.

7. BURO, like BRAC, is no longer an acronym, but a name.

8. When she took a loan, she saved more, since Grameen continued to divert a small proportion of each loan into the member's saving account.

9. Between them, the 37 diarists who took Grameen loans of this sort borrowed $13,225 in the three years, repaid $11,347, and ended with $4,455 outstanding. They paid interest of $2,056.

10. See Rutherford 2006, the MicroSave Briefing Notes on Grameen II. Briefing note number 7 is used for these paragraphs with permission from MicroSave. The full set of MicroSave Grameen II Briefing Notes can be found on their website, www.microsave.org.

11. Grameen's advantage over the other pioneers in developing savings products (notably BURO and ASA) is that it has a legal identity that formally licenses it to mobilize deposits from the general public. Most other Bangladesh microfinance institutions are legally NGOs and may take savings only from their group-based borrowers.

12. Evidence on how this kind of structure can help people save can be found in the study of commitment savings in the Philippines described in chapter 4; see Ashraf, Karlan, and Yin 2006.

13. The GPS has been a major source of Grameen's growth in savings, and, with that, has given Grameen Bank an important new funding source. We recognize, though, that the innovations have been launched during relatively favorable economic times, and have yet to be tested by economic slowdown, inflation, or social instability.

14. Critical views on the limits to traditional modes of microfinance, including group lending, are offered by the essayists in Dichter and Harper 2007.

15. In late 2007 there was a period when between 120,000 and 160,000 new members joined ASA each month, but between 100,000 and 125,000 closed their accounts. Interview by Stuart Rutherford with Shafiqual Haque Choudhury, ASA president, November 2007.

Chapter Seven

1. See Duflo, Kremer, and Robinson 2006.

2. See World Bank 2008, chap. 1.

3. Foreign investment in microfinance, for example, more than tripled between 2004 and 2006, to $4 billion. See Reille and Forester 2008.

4. For a review of early experiences with branchless banking, see Ivatury and Mas 2008.

5. New field research adapts methods from medical research, particularly the use of randomized controlled trials, to test the value and logic of financial innovations. Recently, the Financial Access Initiative, a consortium of researchers at New York University, Yale, Harvard, and Innovations for Poverty Action, has been formed to extend field trials in Latin America, Africa, and Asia. Working with microfinance providers, researchers are investigating, for example, how sensitive borrowers are to changes in interest rates, the value of structured savings devices, and the impact of business training alongside credit. For more, see www.financialaccess.org.

6. It is especially important that regulation enables the mobilization of savings. Where reliable microfinance institutions are not allowed to take savings, poor people are driven to riskier places to store their money. Governments must balance the risk of giving free reign to fraudulent savings collectors with the risk of depriving the poor of opportunities to save in an organized way. See Wright and Mutesasira 2001.

7. See www.safesave.org. In the interest of full disclosure, we note that both Rutherford and Morduch are members of the *Safe*Save cooperative, effectively serving as board members.

8. In *Safe*Save, the small microfinance provider established by Stuart Rutherford in the slums of Dhaka, success has been found by providing structure through regular, scheduled visits by bank workers. In some loan products offered by *Safe*Save, borrowers are free to choose when and in what values to repay loans, and to modify these choices as often as they like, but this freedom is provided with structure and reliability by the unfailing daily visit to the client by the field staff. For more, see www.safesave.org as well as www.thepoorandtheirmoney.com.

9. Bangladesh currently lacks a legal identity that would allow *Safe*Save to expand rapidly, so these services have been limited to just 13,000 clients in the capital's slums.

Appendix

1. See, for example, Ardener 1964; Geertz 1962; Bouman 1989; and Hulme and Arun 2009. Rutherford (2000) also describes a wide variety of informal mechanisms.

2. The World Bank has been the leader in developing large household surveys in its Living Standards Measurement Survey program, with some attention to finance. Other important large surveys include the RAND Family Life Surveys and surveys launched by the International Food Policy Research Institute. FinScope provides an example of an annual survey on the use of financial services. It is undertaken across numerous countries in Africa and beyond (see www.finmark.org.za). While extremely useful in documenting the degree to which populations use financial services, including informal services, the survey is a repeat cross-section, a snapshot of household use at any point in time, rather than a survey that tracks the same households over time.

3. Notably Hulme and Mosley 1996.

4. Rutherford 2000.

5. Planning for the Indian diaries had begun even before the Bangladesh ones were under way, and they formed a part of the same Department for International Development (DFID)-funded research project directed by the University of Manchester. Orlanda Ruthven, who had been working with DFID in Delhi, led the research and was valuably supported by Sanjay Sinha and Meenal Patole from EDA Rural Systems, a private consultancy based in Delhi.

6. In Bangladesh, they were led by S. K. Sinha and included Saiful Islam, Rabeya Islam, and Yeakub Azad. In India, they were Susheel Kumar and Nilesh Arya. In South Africa, the seven-member team was Tshifhiwa Muravha, Busi Magazi, Lwandle Mgidlana, Zanele Ramuse, Nomthumzi Qubeka, Abel Mongake and Nobahle Silulwane.

7. We asked field researchers to try to have a private interview with each household member over the year, including children.

8. In Bangladesh, this gift was a sari or a shirt and a box of soaps; in India, a gift of the respondent's choice up to a stated value, and in South Africa, we gave a cash gift that was equivalent to roughly a month of the income. In South Africa, we also gave two very small gift vouchers for a local supermarket twice during the year. In Bangladesh, we also gave modest cash gifts to households who went to great trouble to help us or who were in distress. We did not tell the respondents what the gifts were before we started the interviews. We believed

that it would change the nature of the relationship for participants to feel they were being "paid" for participating.

9. Note that the attrition for the urban samples of both South Africa and India was higher than the rural attrition. One of the reasons for this was that the sample was relatively more wealthy, and we found that wealthier households were more likely to drop out of the sample. In addition, urban households moved around more, and we lost several households when they moved unexpectedly out of the neighborhoods we were working in.

10. In South Africa, we were heavily guided by the Participatory Wealth Ranking (PWR) manual developed by the Small Enterprise Foundation, a local pro-poor microfinance institution. For more details about how the PWR method stacks up against other forms of poverty targeting, see Simanowitz 2000 and Van de Ruit, May, and Roberts 2001. Note that the urban households in Bangladesh were not selected by wealth ranking, because they had moved around so much that they did not know enough about each other. Instead, we selected households randomly according to a set formula.

11. After the study was over, we found that the wealth ranking did indeed give us a good cross-section of some of the poorest, wealthiest, and in-between households in each community, although the wealth ranking was not an exact predictor of either income or wealth.

12. One may ask, how often do these perceptions of wealth turn out to be similar to the levels of wealth that we saw once we had collected diaries information? In South Africa, the wealth rankings were good general predictors of wealth and income, but they were not exact. For example, a household that considered nonpoor might actually turn out to be upper poor, but rarely would someone who was considered nonpoor turn out to be poor. In Bangladesh we revised our ranking of about 15 percent of the sample at the close of the year.

13. The nagging was not to annoy our interviewers but to make them realize that ambiguous answers from respondents would need follow-on questions.

14. For data over 12 months we would recommend 15 months of data collection. The first three months data would be for building trust and background, but not for formal analysis because of its inaccuracy. We also found in South Africa that during times of religious or cultural celebration, the quality of cash-flow information deteriorated. Notice that in figure A1.1, the margin of error ticks up at the end of the period because it was close to the Christmas season, when households were both busy (and not interested in interviews!) and also spending lots of money.

15. For more on these debates, see, for example, Cull, Demirgüç-Kunt, and Morduch 2009.

16. We've been pleased to see independent efforts to replicate the financial diaries approach in other locations, including Mali and Malawi. Samphantharak and Townsend (2008) have simultaneously developed theoretical foundations for developing income statements and balance sheets for households.

Bibliography

◆ ◆ ◆

Aleem, Irfan. 1990. "Imperfect information, screening and the costs of informal lending: A study of a rural credit market in Pakistan." *World Bank Economic Review* 4 (3): 329–49.

Armendáriz de Aghion, Beatriz, and Jonathan Morduch. 2005. *The Economics of Microfinance.* Cambridge: MIT Press.

Anderson, Siwan, and Jean-Marie Baland. 2002. "The economics of ROSCAs and intrahousehold allocation." *Quarterly Journal of Economics* 117 (3): 963–95.

Ardener, Shirley. 1964. "The comparative study of rotating credit associations." *Journal of the Royal Anthropological Institute* 94 (2): 201–29.

Aryeetey, Ernest, and William Steel. 1995. "Savings collectors and financial intermediation in Ghana." *Savings and Development* 19 (1): 191–212.

Ashraf, Nava. 2008. "Spousal control and intra-household decision making: An experimental study in the Philippines." Unpublished manuscript, Harvard University.

Ashraf, Nava, Dean Karlan, and Wesley Yin. 2006. "Tying Odysseus to the mast: Evidence from a commitment savings product in the Philippines." *Quarterly Journal of Economics* 121 (2): 635–72.

Banerjee, Abhijit, and Esther Duflo. 2004. "Do firms want to borrow more? Testing credit constraints using a directed lending program." CEPR Discussion Paper No. 4681.

———. 2006. "Addressing Absence." *Journal of Economic Perspectives* 20 (1): 117–32.

———. 2007. "The economic lives of poor households." *Journal of Economic Perspectives* 21 (1): 141–67.

Barrientos, Armando, and David Hulme. 2008. *Social Protection for the Poor and Poorest*. London: Palgrave.

Bauer, Michal, Julie Chytilova, and Jonathan Morduch. 2008. "Behavioral foundations of microcredit: Experimental and survey evidence from rural India." Unpublished manuscript, Financial Access Initiative. Available at www.financialaccess.org.

Bertrand, Marianne, Simeon Djankov, Rema Hanna, and Sendhil Mullainathan. 2007. "Obtaining a driver's license in India: An experimental approach to studying corruption." *Quarterly Journal of Economics* 122 (4): 1639–76.

Booysen, F. 2004. "Income and poverty dynamics in HIV/AIDS-related households in the Free State province of South Africa." *South African Journal of Economics* 72:22–45.

Bouman, Fritz J. A. 1989. *Small, Short, and Unsecured: Informal Rural Finance in India* New Delhi: Oxford University Press.

Case, Anne, and Angus Deaton. 1998. "Large cash transfers to the elderly in South Africa." *Economic Journal* 108 (450): 1330–61.

Chen, Martha Alter. 1986. *A Quiet Revolution: Women in Transition in Rural Bangladesh*. Dhaka: BRAC Prokashana.

Chen, Shaohua, and Martin Ravallion. 2007. "Absolute poverty measures for the developing world, 1981–2004." World Bank Policy Research Working Paper No. 4211.

Collins, Daryl. 2007. "Social security and retirement: Perspectives from the financial diaries." Unpublished manuscript. Available at www.financialdiaries.com.

———. 2008. "Debt and household finance: Evidence from the financial diaries." *Development Southern Africa* 25 (5): 469–79.

Collins, Daryl, and M. Leibbrandt. 2007. "The financial impact of HIV/AIDS on poor households in South Africa." *AIDS* 21, Supplement 7: S75–S81.

Cull, Robert, Asli Demirgüç-Kunt, and Jonathan Morduch. 2009. "Microfinance meets the market." *Journal of Economic Perspectives*.

Dehejia, Rajeev, Heather Montgomery, and Jonathan Morduch. 2007. "Do Interest Rates Matter? Credit Demand in the Dhaka Slums." Working paper, New York University Wagner Graduate School.

Das, Jishnu, Jeffrey Hammer, and Kenneth Leonard. 2008. "The quality of medical advice in low-income countries." *Journal of Economic Perspectives* 22 (2): 93–114.

Deaton, Angus. 1992. *Understanding Consumption*. Oxford: Oxford University Press.

———. 1997. *The Analysis of Household Surveys: A Microeconometric Approach to Development Policy*. Baltimore: Johns Hopkins University Press for the World Bank.

Dehejia, Rajeev, Heather Montgomery, and Jonathan Morduch. 2007. "Do Interest Rates Matter: Evidence from the Dhaka Slums." New York University, Financial Access Initiative working paper.

de Mel, Suresh, David McKenzie, and Christopher Woodruff. 2008. "Returns to capital in microenterprises: Evidence from a field experiment." *Quarterly Journal of Economics* 123 (4): 1329–72.

Dercon, Stefan, ed. 2006. *Insurance against Poverty*. WIDER Studies in Development Economics. Oxford: Oxford University Press.

Dercon, Stefan, Tessa Bold, Joachim De Weerdt, and Alula Pankhurst. 2004. "Group-based funeral insurance in Ethiopia and Tanzania." Centre for the Study of African Economies Working Paper Series 227, Oxford University.

Dichter, Thomas, and Malcolm Harper. 2007. *What's Wrong with Microfinance?* Rugby, UK: Practical Action.

Dorrington, R. E., L. F. Johnson, D. Bradshaw, and T. Daniel. 2006. "The demographic impact of HIV/AIDS in South Africa: National and provincial indicators for 2006." Centre for Actuarial Research, South African Medical Research Council and Actuarial Society of South Africa, Cape Town.

Dowla, Asif, and Dipal Barua. 2006. *The Poor Always Pay Back: The Grameen II Story*. Sterling, VA: Kumarian Press.

Dubois, Pierre. 2000. "Assurance complete, hétèrogénéité de préférences et métayage du Pakistan." *Annales d'Economie et de Statistique* 59:1–36.

Duflo, Esther. 2003. "Grandmothers and granddaughters: Old age pension and intra-household allocation in South Africa." *World Bank Economic Review* 17 (1): 1–25.

Duflo, Esther, Michael Kremer, and Jonathan Robinson. 2006. "Understanding technology adoption: Fertilizer in western Kenya, evidence from field experiments." Unpublished manuscript, MIT, Harvard University, and Princeton University.

Easterly, William. 2006. *The White Man's Burden: Why the West's Efforts to Aid the Rest Have Done So Much Ill and So Little Good*. New York: Penguin.

Fafchamps, Marcel, and Forhad Shilpi. 2005. "Cities and specialization: Evidence from South Asia." *Economic Journal* 115 (503): 477–504.

FinScope. 2003. "Summary report: Findings of the FinScope study into [*sic*] financial access and behavior of the South African population 2003." Available at www.finscope.co.za./documents/2003/Brochure2003.pdf.

Geertz, Clifford. 1962. "The rotating credit association: A 'middle rung' in development." *Economic Development and Cultural Change* 10 (3): 241–63.

Ghate, Prabhu. 2006. *Microfinance in India: A State of the Sector Report*. Delhi: Care India, SDC, Ford Foundation.

Gibbons, David, and S. Kasim. 1991. *Banking on the Rural Poor*. Center for Policy Research, University Sains, Malaysia.

Grimard, Franque. 1997. "Household consumption smoothing through ethnic ties: Evidence from Cote d'Ivoire." *Journal of Development Economics* 53: 391–422.

Gugerty, Mary Kay. 2007. "You can't save alone: Testing theories of rotating saving and credit associations." *Economic Development and Cultural Change* 55: 251–82.

Hoddinott, John, and Lawrence Haddad. 1995. "Does female income share influence household expenditures? Evidence from Côte d'Ivoire." *Oxford Bulletin of Economics and Statistics* 57 (1): 77–96.

Hossain, Mahabub. 1988. *Credit for Alleviation of Rural Poverty: The Grameen Bank of Bangladesh*. Institute Research Report No. 65. Washington, DC: International Food Policy and Research Institute.

Hulme, David. 1991. "The Malawi Mundii Fund: Daughter of Grameen." *Journal of International Development* 3 (3): 427–31.

———. 2004. "Thinking 'small' and the understanding of poverty: Maymana and Mofizul's story." *Journal of Human Development* 5 (2): 161–76.

Hulme, David, and T. Arun. 2009 *Microfinance: A Reader*. London: Routledge.

Hulme, David, and Paul Mosley. 1996. *Finance against Poverty*. London: Routledge.

International Labour Organisation. 2006. "Answering the health insurance needs of the poor: Building tools for awareness, education and participation." May 29–31. Subregional Office for South Asia, New Delhi.

International Monetary Fund. Various years. *International Financial Statistics*. Available at www.imf.org.

Ivatury, Gautam, and Ignacio Mas. 2008. "The early experience with branchless banking." Consultative Group to Assist the Poor, CGAP Focus Note 46.

Johnston, Donald, Jr., and Jonathan Morduch. 2008. "The unbanked: Evidence from Indonesia." *World Bank Economic Review* 22 (3): 517–37.

Karlan, Dean, and Jonathan Zinman. 2008. "Credit elasticities in less-developed economies: Implications for microfinance." *American Economic Review* 98 (3): 1040–68.

Khandker, Shahidur. 1998. *Fighting Poverty with Microcredit: Experience in Bangladesh.* Washington, DC: World Bank.

Khandker, Shahidur, Baqui Khalily, and Zahed Kahn. 1995. "Grameen Bank: Performance and sustainability." World Bank Discussion Paper 306.

Laibson, David. 1997. "Golden eggs and hyperbolic discounting." *Quarterly Journal of Economics* 112 (2): 443–77.

Laibson, David, Andrea Repetto, and Jeremy Tobacman. 1998. "Self-control and saving for Retirement." *Brookings Papers on Economic Activity* 1:91–196.

———. 2003. "A debt puzzle." In *Knowledge, Information, and Expectations in Modern Economics: In Honor of Edmund S. Phelps*, ed. Philippe Aghion, Roman Frydman, Joseph Stiglitz, and Michael Woodford. Princeton: Princeton University Press.

Lim, Youngjae, and Robert Townsend. 1998. "General equilibrium models of financial systems: Theory and measurement in village economies." *Review of Economic Dynamics* 1 (1): 59–118.

Lund, Susan, and Marcel Fafchamps. 2003. "Risk sharing networks in rural Philippines." *Journal of Development Economics* 71 (2): 261–87.

McCord, Michael, and Craig Churchill. 2005. "Delta life, Bangladesh." Good and Bad Practices Case Study No. 7, CGAP Working Group on Microinsurance, ILO Social Finance Programme, Geneva.

Morduch, Jonathan. 1995. "Income smoothing and consumption smoothing." *Journal of Economic Perspectives* 9 (3): 103–14.

———. 1999. "Between the market and state: Can informal insurance patch the safety net?" *World Bank Research Observer* 14 (2): 187–207.

———. 2005. "Consumption smoothing across space: Tests for village-level responses to risk." In *Insurance against Poverty*, ed. Stefan Dercon. New York: Oxford University Press.

———. 2006. "Microinsurance: The next revolution?" In *Understanding Poverty*, ed. Abhijit Banerjee, Roland Benabou, and Dilip Mookherjee. New York: Oxford University Press.

———. 2008. "How can the poor pay for microcredit?" Financial Access Initiative Framing Note Number 4. Available at: www.financialaccess.org.

Mullainathan, Sendhil. 2005. "Development economics through the lens of psychology." In *Annual World Bank Conference on Development Economics 2005: Lessons from Experience*, ed. François Bourguignon and Boris Pleskovic. New York: World Bank and Oxford University Press.

O'Donahue, Ted, and Matthew Rabin. 1999a. "Doing it now or doing it later." *American Economic Review* 89 (1): 103–21.

O'Donahue, Ted, and Matthew Rabin. 1999b. "Incentives for procrastinators." *Quarterly Journal of Economics* 114 (3): 769–817.

Patole, Meenal, and Orlanda Ruthven. 2001. "Metro moneylenders: Microcredit providers for Delhi's poor." *Small Enterprise Development* 13 (2): 36–45.

Pauly, Mark. 1968. "The economics of moral hazard: Comment." *American Economic Review* 58 (3): 531–37.

Prahalad, C. K. 2005. *The Fortune at the Bottom of the Pyramid.* Upper Saddle River, NJ: Wharton School Publishing.

Reille, Xavier, and Sarah Forester. 2008. "Foreign capital investment in microfinance." Consultative Group to Assist the Poor, CGAP Focus Note 43.

Rosenberg, Richard. 2007. "CGAP reflections on the Compartamos initial public offering: A case study on microfinance interest rates and profits." Consultative Group to Assist the Poor, CGAP Focus Note 42.

Roth, James. 1999. "Informal micro-finance schemes: The case of funeral insurance in South Africa." International Labour Organization Working Paper No. 22.

Roth, James, Denis Garand, and Stuart Rutherford. 2006. "Long-term savings and insurance." In *Protecting the Poor: A Microinsurance Compendium*, ed. Craig Churchill. Geneva: International Labour Organization.

Rutherford, Stuart. 2000. *The Poor and Their Money.* Delhi: Oxford University Press.

———. 2006. "MicroSave Grameen II briefing notes." Available at: www.microsave.org.

———. 2009. *The Pledge: ASA, Peasant Politics, and Microfinance in the Development of Bangladesh.* New York: Oxford University Press.

Rutherford, Stuart, and Graham Wright. 1998. "Mountain money managers." Unpublished report for European Union.

Rutherford, Stuart, S. K. Sinha, and Shyra Aktar. 2001. *BURO Tangail: Product Development Review.* For DFID Dhaka, available from BURO, Dhaka.

Sachs, Jeffrey. 2005. *The End of Poverty: Economic Possibilities for Our Time.* New York: Penguin.

Samphantharak, Krislert, and Robert M. Townsend. 2008. "Households as corporate firms: Constructing financial statements from integrated household surveys." , Unpublished manuscript, University of California, San Diego, and University of Chicago.

Schreiner, Mark, and Michael Sherraden. 2006. *Can the Poor Save? Saving and Asset Accumulation in Individual Development Accounts.* New Brunswick, NJ: Transaction.

Sillers, Donald. 2004. "National and international poverty lines: An overview." Unpublished manuscript, U.S. Agency for International Development. Available at www.microlinks.org.

Simanowitz, Anton. 2000. "A summary of an impact assessment and methodology development process in the Small Enterprise Foundation's Poverty-Targeted Programme, Tšhomisano." Paper for the Third Virtual Meeting of the CGAP Working Group on Impact Assessment Methodologies. Available at http://www2.ids.ac.uk/impact/files/planning/simanowitz_AIMS_paper.doc.

Sinha, Sanjay, Tanmay Chetan, Orlanda Ruthven, and Nilotpal Patak. 2003. "The outreach/viability conundrum: Can India's regional rural banks really serve low-income clients?" ODI Working Paper 229:41.

Sinha, Sanjay, and Meenal Patole. 2002. "Microfinance and the poverty of financial services: How the poor in India could be better served." Working Paper 56, Finance and Development Research Programme, Institute for Development Policy and Management, Manchester University.

Stiglitz, Joseph. 2005. *Globalization and Its Discontents.* New York: Norton.

Swibel, Matthew, and Forbes Staff. 2007. "The world's top 50 microfinance institutions." *Forbes*, December 20. Available at www.forbes.com.

Thaler, Richard H. 1990. "Anomalies: Saving, fungibility and mental accounts." *Journal of Economic Perspectives* 4 (1): 193–205.

Thaler, Richard H., and Cass R. Sunstein. 2008. *Nudge: Improving Decisions about Health, Wealth, and Happiness.* New Haven: Yale University Press.

Thomas, Duncan. 1990. "Intra-household resource allocation: An inferential approach." *Journal of Human Resources* 25 (4): 635–64.

Thomas, Duncan. 1994. "Like father, like son or like mother, like daughter: Parental education and child health." *Journal of Human Resources* 29 (4): 950–89.

Townsend, Robert M. 1994. "Risk and insurance in village India." *Econometrica* 62 (3): 539–91.

Udry, Christopher. 1994. "Risk and insurance in a rural credit market: An empirical investigation in northern Nigeria." *Review of Economic Studies* 61 (3): 495–526.

Udry, Christopher, and Santosh Anagol. 2006. "The return to capital in Ghana." *American Economic Review* 96 (2): 388–93.

Vander Meer, Paul. 2009. "Sustainable financing for economic growth: Roscas in Chulin Village, Taiwan." Unpublished manuscript.

Van de Ruit, C., J. May, and B. Roberts. 2001. "A poverty assessment of the Small Enterprise Foundation on behalf of the Consultative Group to Assist the Poorest." CSDS Research Report, University of Natal.

Wolf, Martin. 2005. *Why Globalization Works*. 2nd ed. New Haven: Yale University Press.

World Bank. Various years. *World Development Indicators*. Washington, DC: World Bank. Available at www.worldbank.org.

World Bank. 2008. *Finance for All? Policies and Pitfalls in Expanding Access*. Washington, DC: World Bank.

Wright, Graham, and Leonard Mutesasira. 2001. "The relative risks to the savings of poor people." MicroSave Briefing Note No. 6, MicroSave, Nairobi, Kampala, and Lucknow. Available at www.microsave.org.

Yunus, Muhammad. 2002. *Grameen Bank II: Designed to Open New Possibilities*. Dhaka: Grameen Bank.

———. 2007. *Banker to the Poor*. New York: Public Affairs.

Index

◆ ◆ ◆